D0330656

The United Nations & the Superpowers

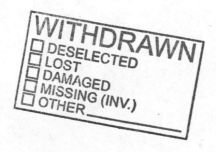

Fourth Edition

The United Nations & the Superpowers
China, Russia, & America

John G. Stoessinger

Hunter College - The City University of New York

RANDOM HOUSE  NEW YORK

Fourth Edition

9 8 7 6 5 4 3 2

Copyright © 1965, 1970, 1973, 1977 by Random House, Inc.

Library of Congress Cataloging in Publication Data

Stoessinger, John George.
    The United Nations & the Superpowers.

    Includes bibliographies and index.
    1. United Nations—United States.   2. United Nations—Russia.
3. United Nations—China.   I. Title.
JX1977.2.U5S8 1977   341.23   76–48733

ISBN 0-394-31269-4

Manufactured in the United States of America

To
Inis L. Claude, Jr.

Preface to
the Fourth Edition

"The crisis of our loyalty to the United Nations is still ahead of us," Adlai Stevenson declared in 1962. The late Ambassador to the United Nations was right in his prediction.

Since the appearance of the Third Edition of this book, the United States has gone into opposition in the United Nations. Who would have guessed that the day would come when the United States would cast more vetoes in the Security Council than the Soviet Union? Or that Americans would one day seriously consider abandoning the United Nations?

If the United Nations today belongs to anyone, it belongs to the new nations that were born in the generation of my students. Many Americans regard this development with considerable suspicion. As one elderly lady asked me recently, not necessarily in jest: "Don't you think there are too many foreigners in the United Nations already?" The younger generation, on the other hand, has greater empathy for the aspirations of the poor and dispossessed for a place in the sun and at the world's table.

In this revision, I have taken into account the dramatic events of the last few years that have made the United Nations once again so deeply controversial: the American discovery of the veto; the rise of Third World power in the General Assembly including the passage of an Orwellian resolution equating Zionism with racism; the deployment of two new peace-keeping missions in the Middle East; fresh initiatives in arms control; the new international economic order; and finally, and perhaps most hopefully, the tentative initiatives—through a network of worldwide conferences—toward global policies for food, resources, environment, population, and the oceans. Perhaps, future historians of the evolution of world government will perceive this new movement toward "planetary management" as a beginning.

"You cannot trust anyone over thirty," some of my students used to say during the days of campus revolutions in the 1960's. In late 1975, on the UN's thirtieth birthday, I attended a ceremony at UN Headquarters. The occasion was the honoring of members of the UN staff who had served for twenty-five years or more in the international civil service. As these aging men and women came forward to receive their commemorative plaques, the realization suddenly dawned upon me that the first generational cycle of the United Nations had run its course. The torch will have to be passed soon to a younger generation. And unless a sense of commitment and even enthusiasm can be kindled in these young people all over the world, the United Nations might indeed be doomed.

Now, a new United Nations is emerging. It has a different agenda and different priorities. These have often made the house on the East River a bitterly contentious arena. North-South tensions have begun to supersede old East-West rivalries. The tug of war between rich and poor and whites and non-whites has begun to overshadow the old cleavages between Communism and the Western world. The struggle for power continues unabated. And yet, there is a new emphasis on the problems that we face as fellow passengers on Planet Earth. At long last, some of us are beginning to see the world the way it really is—a fragile sphere traveling through the infinite darknesses of outer space. When the astronauts first saw the world from afar with neither boundaries nor sovereignties, they began to pray from Genesis. It is this new slow dawning of compassion and of global con-

sciousness that I begin to sense in the United Nations of tomorrow. Hence, despite all the bitterness and all the disappointments
of the last few years, I manage to retain a sense of hope.

J. G. S.
New York City
June 1976

Preface to
the Third Edition

Since the last edition of this book appeared, the international
system has changed before our very eyes. It seems almost as if a
kaleidoscope had been shaken vigorously and the pieces had
formed new patterns. The United States and the Soviet Union no
longer dominate the scene exclusively. China has entered the
arena, and bipolarity has given way to a triangle in which each of
the three has aspired to the role of the lady to be wooed by the
other two. New nations have arisen out of the ashes of former
colonial empires, and old nations in Western Europe are engaged in the process of unification. Old cleavages between East
and West are slowly being superseded by new cleavages between
have and have-not nations. In short, a new generation is in the
process of redefining its international relationships. The United
Nations has reflected these dramatic changes in the global system.

I have done my best to incorporate these developments into
the present edition. The chapter on the Security Council and the
veto power has been updated and now includes an analysis of the
first American vetoes. The China chapter takes the reader
through that crucial vote of October 25, 1971, which seated the
People's Republic, and also offers an analysis of that nation's
impact on the world organization. Recent developments in the
Secretary-Generalship and in peace-keeping operations are taken

into account, and the latest manifestations of the continuing financial crisis are analyzed. The third section of the book includes two entirely new chapters: one on the arms control treaties that were negotiated under UN auspices and the other on the UN's efforts to face the imperatives of the world's deepening ecological crisis on a global scale.

In preparing this revision, I have been confirmed in my conviction that the original conception of the book was sound. I believe that it continues to remain intact today. The United Nations continues to be, for all its members, an instrument for the pursuit of their national interests. The Chinese have recognized this basic truth very quickly and have placed the national interest above purely ideological considerations. The Soviet Union, too, when forced to choose between its ideological commitments on the one hand and its interests as a nuclear member of the Establishment, continues to give priority to the latter. And the United States, largely as a result of its declining influence in the United Nations, is now facing the very crisis of conscience that I predicted in the first edition of this book a decade ago.

Perhaps the most significant single development of the past decade has been the fact that today no single nation or group of nations controls the United Nations. In a sense, this development signals a return to the original conception of the framers of the Charter. No nation today can use the United Nations as a multilateral fig leaf for the attainment of its unilateral objectives. A heavy price, however, has been paid for this process of democratization. The United Nations has become such a large and unpredictable body that most nations have become reluctant to entrust their fate to it. A tendency has developed to bring problems to the United Nations only when nations can no longer cope with them on their own. The United Nations has become a kind of receiver in bankruptcy and, in addition, has often been blamed for being bankrupt. Paradoxically enough, the trend toward universality has been accompanied not by increasing trust but by the opposite. The reason for this development is plain: It is infinitely more difficult to orchestrate over 130 competing national interests into a coherent whole than 60 or even 100.

The key to a rejuvenation of the United Nations will not be found in structural changes such as a revision of the Charter. It must be sought at the political level—in a commitment by the member states, especially the two superpowers and China, to *use* the United Nations rather than to by-pass it and let it atrophy. The instrument is fine. There is nothing wrong with the United Nations except the membership.

When one confronts the Machiavellian truth of the primacy of the national interest, one is struck not by how little the United Nations has done but by how much it has accomplished despite almost insuperable obstacles. The UN's resilience has truly been remarkable. If one of its organs seems temporarily moribund, another grows to take up the burden. Thus, while the Security Council has frequently been paralyzed by Great Power conflict, a promising beginning toward a global environment program has been made at Stockholm. Since pollution does not respect national boundaries, the major powers in this case permitted a larger role for the world organization. Thus, pursuit of the national interest does not always dictate a smaller role for the United Nations; sometimes it permits the Organization to grow. The midget, caught between the giants, continues to steal strength from each.

Over the years I have had a multitude of letters about this book from teachers and students all over the world. Many of these contained suggestions for improvement that have found their way into the present edition. For all of these, I am most sincerely grateful.

J. G. S.
New York City
June 1973

Preface to
the First Edition

This book has a threefold purpose: to study the dynamics of the U.S.-Soviet relationship at the United Nations, to point up the effects of this relationship on the development of the United Nations itself, and to evaluate the significance of this development for the future of superpower relations with the Organization.

Our approach is not general and exhaustive but highly selective. We have chosen nine cases of superpower interaction and divided them into three groups.

Part One is a study of the superpowers' effect on the political and constitutional evolution of the three key UN organs: the Security Council, the General Assembly, and the Office of the Secretary-General. The first case focuses on the superpowers and the Security Council veto. We seek to discover how many of the 105 Soviet vetoes have actually prevented further UN action. How has the Organization circumvented Soviet vetoes, and how have these circumventions affected the distribution of power among the UN organs? We seek to explain the "hidden" American veto and what effect it has had on the United Nations. The second case deals with the changing membership of the General Assembly. Why were only nine states permitted to join the UN during its first ten years, whereas more than sixty joined during the past decade? What were the political effects on the superpowers of the decade of exclusion and the later decade of rapid entry? The problem of Chinese representation is singled out as a good example of the way in which the superpowers, particularly the United States, had to adapt their tactics to the changing General Assembly. The third case, which compares the American attack on the Office of the Secretary-General in the early 1950's with the Soviet assault a decade later, reveals a great deal about the attitudes of the superpowers toward the UN chief executive and the international civil service.

In Part Two we analyze the major UN efforts in peace-keeping. There the Organization has been interposed between the clashing national interests of the superpowers. Our first case study analyzes the superpower confrontations during the Middle East crises of 1956 and 1967 and the birth and death of the UN Emergency Force (UNEF). The second case assesses the shifting U.S.-Soviet attitudes toward the UN Operation in the Congo (ONUC) during the four-year crisis. The third case deals with the financial implications of these two peace forces, which not only threatened to bankrupt the United Nations but created a major political and constitutional crisis. In all three cases, we have traced the UN's quest for common ground between the superpowers' antithetical interests on deeply divisive issues.

Part Three analyzes superpower behavior in three selected problem areas in the economic and social realm. The first case focuses on the superpowers' roles in creating and subsequently undoing the International Refugee Organization; the second analyzes the U.S.-Soviet interaction that created the International Atomic Energy Agency, only to cripple it later; and the final case looks into the superpower struggle over a Special Fund project in Cuba in 1963. These cases reveal clearly that the national-interest considerations that dominated the peace-keeping operations analyzed in Part Two also affected the UN's economic and social activities.

The overall purpose of this book is not to present another review of the development of UN institutions over the past twenty-five years. Our objective is to focus on those trends from the Organization's past which, it appears to us, are going to dominate its future. Such a task led us to concentrate our attention on the interaction of the superpowers at the United Nations.

Briefly, the major points of our position may be summarized as follows. During the past twenty-five years, both superpowers have tried to use the United Nations as a vehicle for the advancement of their individual, antithetical foreign-policy interests. In this quest, the Organization has been a more important vehicle for the United States than for the Soviet Union, because the United States has successfully involved the United Nations in more activities that have served its national interest. The United Nations has often been persuaded to do collectively what the United States might have had to do individually. This has been true for a number of reasons, including the important fact that the objectives of U.S. policy have been more compatible with the UN Charter than those of the Soviet Union. No less important, however, has been the fact that, for most of its history, the United Nations has been controlled politically and financially by the United States and its military allies. On the several occasions when UN action threatened U.S. national interests, the United States reacted vigorously—by casting "hidden" vetoes, infringing on the neutrality of the Secretariat, crippling a UN agency through outside bilateral agreements, and embarking on similar courses of action that are analyzed in detail in the text. Such actions, however, have been relatively infrequent, not because the United States neglected its national interest, but because the UN majority generally cared so well for it.

It is our belief that recent changes in the United Nations, particularly in membership, indicate that the U.S. honeymoon is over. The presence of more than 120 nations in the General Assembly, compared with 60 in 1954 or even 82 in 1959, means —to pick one example—that the United States and its allies have lost the two-thirds majority that is necessary for the passage of important resolutions. In the past, the United States—certain of its automatic majority—could advocate majority diplomacy without fear. Today, U.S. diplomats will have to work harder and make more compromises if they are to continue to build winning coalitions. And these compromises must be struck not with traditional political and cultural allies, as in the past, but with the new Afro-Asian majority, which has different sets of needs and interests. In extreme circumstances, the United States may actually have to use "absolute weapons," such as the veto power, to protect vital national interests. If past performance is any guide, the United States will not adjust easily to its new position. It is possible that, accustomed to having its way for so long, it may precipitate a crisis that will undermine the Organization, or Congress and public opinion may become sufficiently disenchanted to force a sharp cut in American support of the United Nations. We feel that the late Ambassador Adlai E. Stevenson was correct when he stated that "the crisis of our loyalty to the United Nations [was] still ahead of us." It is our hope that our consideration of the background of this forthcoming crisis of conscience will contribute to a discussion that will enable the United States to deal more wisely with it.

The lessons of the past quarter century also show some grounds for optimism. To some, it may appear that because it has been so deeply involved in power politics and the national-interest struggles between the superpowers, the United Nations has been a failure. The most important conclusion of this book is that such a view is wrong. While it is true that many of the UN's difficulties have their origin in the East-West conflict, it is our belief that the Organization has gained in strength by being involved instead of seeking a quieter place on the sidelines. In this role, the United Nations has been bent first one way, then another, as the superpowers attempted to use it, often against each other. But on balance, our study suggests that the UN's strength and influence have grown not only in spite of superpower conflict but also *because* of it. In today's world, the price of relevance for the United Nations is conflict. The struggle toward order finds its nourishment in the same soil as the struggle for power.

Work on this book was begun six years ago, largely in response to the growing disenchantment with the United Nations that I found among governmental officials, colleagues, and students. I acknowledge gratefully the valuable research assistance of Mr. Ralph Hellmold of Columbia University during preparation of the first draft, particularly on Chapters 2, 3, 5, and 9, and of Miss Marcia Rosenfeld, also of Columbia University, for her help on Chapter 1. Both are absolved entirely of any errors or other shortcomings of this book. During work on the final draft, I enjoyed the collaboration of Mr. Robert G. McKelvey of Columbia University, who rendered valuable research assistance on each chapter of the book. He also shared his ideas with the author, particularly on the relationship of the superpowers' national interests to the UN's evolution, and helped to reshape the book along these lines. For this reason he shares partial responsibility with me for the final product. For permission to adapt for this volume passages from some of my previously published works, I am also grateful to the University of Minnesota Press, publishers of *The Refugee and the World Community* (1956); the Brookings Institution, publishers of *Financing the United Nations System* (1964); and New York University Press, publishers of *Organizing Peace in the Nuclear Age* (1953), in which appeared my article "Atoms-for-Peace: The International Atomic Energy Agency."

Finally, it is my privilege to express my appreciation to the man who first aroused my interest in the United Nations as a political institution: Inis L. Claude, Jr.

J. G. S.

Five turbulent years have elapsed since the first edition of this book appeared. These years have not been very productive ones for the United Nations. The world organization has been allowed to play only a marginal role in the Middle East conflict and none at all in the Vietnam War. The fact that the superpowers have pursued opposing policies in both conflicts has made the life of the United Nations very difficult indeed.

On the positive side, some real progress has been made in preventing the further spread of nuclear weapons. Close superpower collaboration in this field has strengthened the hand of the United Nations. And the decline of the UN's role in peace-keeping has been balanced to some extent by the continued growth of the Organization's economic and social activities.

What is significant for the purposes of this study is the fact that the relationship between the superpowers has remained crucial for the evolution of the United Nations. This complex relationship, exhibiting elements of both conflict and cooperation, has continued to define both limits and possibilities of the world organization. In that sense the conception of this book offers a useful perspective on the United Nations as a political institution.

J. G. S.

CONTENTS

INTRODUCTION TO THE FIRST EDITION   xxiii

PART ONE   THE SUPERPOWERS AND THE CONSTITUTIONAL EVOLUTION OF THE UNITED NATIONS   1

     1   The Security Council: The Veto and the Superpowers   3

     2   The General Assembly: China and the Rise of the Third World   26

     3   The Secretary-General: The American and Soviet Attacks on the Secretariat, 1952 and 1960   55

PART TWO   THE SUPERPOWERS AND UNITED NATIONS PEACE-KEEPING OPERATIONS   79

     4   The Middle East Crises of 1956, 1967, and 1973 and United Nations Peace-Keeping Forces   81

     5   The Congo Crisis and the United Nations Operation in the Congo   106

6   The United Nations Financial Crisis and the Superpowers   121

PART THREE   THE SUPERPOWERS AND DEVELOPMENT, ARMS CONTROL, AND ENVIRONMENT OPERATIONS   147

7   A United Nations Dilemma: Cuba and the Special Fund   149

8   The Superpowers and Arms Control   162

9   "Only One Earth": The United Nations Conference on the Human Environment   190

PART FOUR   CONCLUSIONS   209

10   The United Nations and the Superpowers   211

INDEX   239

Introduction to
the First Edition

In this book, Professor John G. Stoessinger depicts with great clarity and accuracy the role of the two superpowers—the United States and the Soviet Union—during the whole of the life of the United Nations. A central feature of the UN Charter, the arrangements for collective measures based upon the presumed unanimity of the Great Powers, soon became a dead letter. The cold war took the place of a united Great Power front in support of peace. A growing malaise, aggravated by profound ideological differences, conditioned the relationships between the United States and the Soviet Union in the United Nations.

It could easily be regarded a matter of astonishment that the United Nations should survive this major rupture between the superpowers, but survive it did and, indeed, on certain critical occasions even blunted the edges of the rivalry. Although the United Nations was the conspicuous and most highly publicized arena of the cold war, through the powerful weaponry of quiet diplomacy, it sometimes nudged the Great Powers out of critical and highly explosive situations.

Professor Stoessinger describes the sweep of this rivalry as it affected the work of principal organs of the United Nations and either forestalled the prospect of agreement on major issues before the Organization or compelled it to resort to special types of improvisation, particularly in the peace-keeping field. He describes the heavy strains placed upon the Organization as a result of these deeply set differences, but also indicates that the Organization derived strength from the rivalry. In a real sense, these continuing storms contributed to the seaworthiness and strength of the Organization. The smaller powers and the Secretary-General found themselves under the almost continuous necessity of filling the serious voids caused by superpower rivalry. The smaller powers often provided both the personnel and the resources necessary for effective action in peace-keeping operations, and the membership depended increasingly upon the Secretary-General to serve both as a catalyst and as an operational executive. If Great Power unity had prevailed, it is certain that the role of the third powers and the Secretary-General would have been less conspicuous and more subordinate.

Although the major theme of the book is an assessment of the rivalries of the superpowers and their impact upon the constitutional and political life of the United Nations, stress is also properly placed upon the separate interests and attitudes of the two superpowers toward the United Nations. In the McCarthy era of the early fifties, the Secretariat was buffeted by heavy attacks from official Washington and from powerful elements in the American public, but with this exception, the United States maintained a scrupulous respect for the role and status of the Secretariat and supported it in its activities. The Soviet Union was never content with its role in the Secretariat nor with the Secretariat's role in the Organization. It believed the Secretariat should confine itself primarily to the servicing of conferences and avoid an executive role in peace-keeping operations. The Soviet government broke with both Trygve Lie and Dag Hammarskjöld for somewhat different reasons, but both men engaged in active roles in major peace-keeping operations, the policies of which ran contrary to the Soviet interest.

Professor Stoessinger's selection of nine case studies is admirable and covers the main spectrum of superpower rivalries and of their separate interests and attitudes toward the United Nations. Although all organs of the United Nations felt the impact of the rivalry, the Security Council, the General Assembly, and the Secretariat provided the main focuses for the tension which cast its shadow on the whole Organization.

The analyses of the Suez crises, of the Congo crisis, and of the ensuing political, constitutional, and financial difficulties in the United Nations cover the major thread in the UN story; the treatment of human rights, atoms for peace, and Cuba and the Special Fund throws much-needed light on superpower attitudes toward these areas of substance and operational activities.

The concluding chapter is a succinct analysis and summary of the major fields and causes of tension between the superpowers.

The book is an invaluable contribution to the literature of the United Nations and should command the interest of many readers.

Andrew W. Cordier
Columbia University

PART ONE

The Superpowers
and the Constitutional
Evolution
of the United Nations

The Security Council: The Veto and the Superpowers

One of the more persistent myths surrounding the United Nations concerns the use of the veto power by the Soviet Union and the United States. It is an established fact that by mid-1976 the Soviet Union had vetoed 110 Security Council resolutions, whereas the United States had cast only 16 vetoes. Hence, it is said that the Soviet

Union's frequent use of the veto has hampered and weakened the United Nations by preventing it from acting, while the United States has exercised remarkable self-discipline by hardly using the veto at all.

This chapter will show that neither part of this myth is accurate. On the one hand, the ultimate effect of the Soviet veto on UN action has been considerably exaggerated. On the other, while it is technically correct to say that the United States has used the veto only sixteen times, we shall see that the United States has, in fact, developed a "hidden veto," which it has used frequently and effectively. In short, it is one thesis of this chapter that the difference in the behavior of the superpowers on the use of the veto is more apparent than real; both have tried to protect their national interests, although by different parliamentary tactics. Moreover, we shall attempt to show that the interaction between the superpowers on the veto has not necessarily had a negative effect on the development of the United Nations. On the contrary, the United Nations has responded to the challenge with imagination and flexibility, and this response has led to important constitutional and political changes within the Organization. One reason why the United Nations today is a different—and possibly stronger—organization from the one established in 1945 has been its ability to rise to the challenge of the superpower veto.

The framers of the Charter gave the Security Council extensive powers to keep the peace. The Council was to consist of eleven members, five of which—the United States, the Soviet Union, Great Britain, France, and China—were to be permanent. In addition, six nonpermanent members were to be elected by the General Assembly for two-year terms. The Charter empowered the Security Council to recommend means of peaceful settlement of disputes; and if a nation committed an act of aggression, the Council was to have the power to apply sanctions against the aggressor. Such sanctions might range from the severance of diplomatic relations all the way to collective military action.

The Big Five were clearly intended to dominate the Council. It was hoped that no aggressor would then be able to challenge such an overwhelming agglomeration of power. The Big Five, in return for their primary responsibility to keep the peace, received commensurate privileges: a permanent seat on the Council and the veto power, by which each of the Big Five could prevent the Security Council from taking action on a substantive issue. Three of the Great Powers at San Francisco—the United States, the Soviet Union, and Great Britain—insisted on the right of veto, and none of them would have acceded to the United Nations without it. China and France at first took a more flexible position, but the rigid stand of the Big Three soon resulted in their equally firm insistence on the veto rule.

The exact wording of Article 27 of the Charter, which established the veto power, is as follows:

1. Each member of the Security Council shall have one vote.
2. Decisions of the Security Council on procedural matters shall be made by an affirmative vote of seven members.
3. Decisions of the Security Council on all other matters shall be made by an affirmative vote of seven members including the concurring votes of the permanent members; provided that, in decisions under Chapter VI, and under paragraph 3 of Article 52, a party to a dispute shall abstain from voting.

While a major power was required to abstain from voting on resolutions related to the peaceful settlement of disputes to which it was a party, it was technically free to veto all other nonprocedural matters. In addition, the powers agreed that the decision whether a matter was substantive or procedural was itself a substantive question and hence subject to veto. Thus, by a double-veto system—one veto to decide whether the issue was substantive or procedural and the second on the issue itself—a Great Power could veto anything it chose, with the single exception of questions regarding the peaceful settlement of disputes to which it was a party. Or, to put it the other way round, all the Great Powers had to be in agreement before the Security Council could act. Clearly, it seemed that close cooperation among the Big Five would be a necessary prerequisite for an effective Security Council. Yet, the deepening split between the superpowers and the 9 vetoes cast by the Soviet Union during 1946 adumbrated to many observers a succession of paralyzing vetoes that could jeopardize the effectiveness of the entire United Nations.

In January 1966, the Security Council was enlarged from eleven to fifteen members. The four new nonpermanet members were all to be selected from the new nations of the world. An affirmative vote by the Council now required 9 votes rather than 7. The veto power of the Big Five remained unaffected by the Charter amendment.

The Soviet Union and the Veto

The Soviet Union has been responsible for 110 of the 149 vetoes cast by 1976, or about 75 percent of the total. But the figures themselves do not adequately explain the picture. One must see what effect the vetoes had on the United Nations *after* they were cast.

A Soviet veto could meet one of three different fates. First, it could "stick" completely, meaning that no significant further action on the vetoed issue was taken by other organs of the United Nations or by states outside the United Nations. For example, the Soviet veto of an investigation of the Indian invasion of Goa stuck. Second, a veto could be "circumvented" if another organ of the United Nations provided alternative machinery. In some cases, this alternative machinery could continue the effective direction of the action in place of the paralyzed Security Council. For example, the General Assembly effectively circumvented the Soviet vetoes cast during the Korean War by directing the "police action" itself. In other cases, the United Nations could try another approach but still fail to resolve the issue. For example, in 1954 the Soviet Union vetoed a resolution requesting Egypt to lift its blockade of Israeli shipping through the Suez Canal and referring the dispute to the Egyptian-Israeli Mixed Armistice Commission for negotiation. Despite the veto, Secretary-General Hammarskjöld met with the Egyptians and reached an agreement that, in effect, would have permitted Israeli cargoes to pass through the Canal. At the last moment, however, the

Egyptian government changed its mind, and the arrangement fell through. But the important point is that it was *not* the veto that prevented the successful resolution of the issue. The Secretary-General's Office had provided adequate alternatives, but the issue remained unresolved because of the action of one of the states directly involved. Thus, our criterion of a circumvented veto is not necessarily the successful settlement of an issue but the capacity of the United Nations to provide alternative machinery to fill the breach left by a paralyzed Security Council. As a third fate, a veto may be superseded either because the disputants negotiated the issue directly, as happened in the Berlin Blockade, or because changing circumstances may resolve the dispute, as when the Soviet Union decided not to protect Iraq's claim to Kuwait after a pro-Western government had taken power in Iraq. In sum, therefore, a Soviet veto can stick, be circumvented, or be superseded.

In general, one can distinguish four major areas in which the USSR has used the veto to protect and promote its national interest: vetoes cast in direct U.S.-Soviet confrontations, vetoes cast on behalf of a Communist ally, vetoes cast on behalf of a state outside the Communist bloc, and vetoes cast against candidates for UN membership. Let us now examine in greater detail the consequences of Soviet vetoes in each of these.

The Soviet Union has used the veto 18 times to protect its national interest in a direct clash with the United States.[1] It vetoed 5 resolutions calling for UN action in such cold-war confrontations as the Berlin Blockade, the Hungarian Revolution, the destruction of a U.S. RB-47 airplane (2 vetoes), and the Czechoslovak crisis of 1968. The USSR twice vetoed the election of a Secretary-General whom the United States favored strongly. It also vetoed 5 measures related to disarmament and cast 6 vetoes at various points during the UN Operation in the Congo.

Not all of these vetoes have prevented further UN action. When the General Assembly voted to extend the term of Secretary-General Trygve Lie during the Korean War, it circumvented 1 Soviet veto. When the Soviet Union vetoed an American draft resolution on the Hungarian crisis, an emergency session of the General Assembly passed a more strongly worded resolution recommending that the Secretary-General investigate the situation and suggest methods of ending the foreign intervention. Neither the Secretary-General nor a Special Committee appointed by him could secure the cooperation of the new Soviet-sponsored government in Hungary, and thus the matter was eventually dropped. From the UN point of view, however, the immediate cause of failure was not the Soviet veto. The Organization did develop compensatory if somewhat token machinery, but the attitude of the Hungarian government prevented further action. The 6 vetoes cast during the Congo Operation were all circumvented. The vetoed proposals were enacted by the Assembly in similar if not always identical language and the basic objective of the USSR—the obstruction of the Congo Operation—was not achieved. Two further issues which elicited Soviet vetoes—the Berlin Blockade and the RB-47 incident—were resolved through negotiation between the superpowers without direct UN involvement. The remaining 7 vetoes, however, did stick and no further action was taken inside or outside the world organization.

A second group of 16 vetoes was cast by the Soviet Union not to protect itself directly but to assist a Communist ally. By vetoing two resolutions the USSR prevented a UN inquiry into the new Communist government in Czechoslovakia in 1948. One veto on behalf of Albania over the Corfu Channel dispute with Great Britain was resolved outside the United Nations by an agreement of the parties to submit the issue to the International Court of Justice. Another veto—on behalf of North Vietnam against Thailand's charge of Communist infiltration—was superseded by changed circumstances. The Soviet Union vetoed five resolutions during the Korean War, but these vetoes, like those cast during the Congo Operation, did not prevent the United Nations from achieving its basic objectives. Six vetoes cast to protect Greece's Communist northern neighbors during the Greek Civil War were effectively circumvented by General Assembly action. Finally, a Soviet veto on a resolution concerning the overthrow of the Communist government in Guatemala in 1954 was superseded. In sum, only the 2 vetoes cast over Czechoslovakia were final; 11 others were circumvented by UN action; and 3 were by-passed by events outside the United Nations.[2]

Twenty-one vetoes cast by the Soviet Union may be described as proxy vetoes or vetoes cast on behalf of states with which the USSR wished to gain favor.[3] Twelve of these were used on behalf of Arab states against former colonial powers or against Israel. Five of them—1 on the diversion of the river Jordan and 4 cast at various points in the continuing Arab-Israeli dispute—were final.

The very first veto in the Security Council was cast in 1946 against a resolution expressing confidence that the British and French would withdraw their forces from Syria and Lebanon. This veto was superseded outside the United Nations as the two powers expressed their intention to withdraw and did so promptly. Another pro-Arab veto was also superseded outside the United Nations when the USSR refused to support Iraq's claim to Kuwait. The remaining 4 pro-Arab vetoes were all circumvented by UN action. Two of the 4 were cast on behalf of Egypt. One vetoed resolution concerned the passage of Israeli cargoes through the Suez Canal. As noted above, Secretary-General Hammarskjöld reached an agreement with the Egyptian government, but at the last moment the scheme failed. The second pro-Egyptian veto was cast in 1956 against a resolution calling on Egypt, the United Kingdom, and France to continue negotiations and for Egypt to submit guarantees that the Canal would be managed effectively. Despite the veto, the talks continued under the guidance of the Secretary-General. When the Canal was reopened in April 1957, Egypt deposited an instrument with the United Nations acknowledging its treaty obligations under international law and later accepted the jurisdiction of the International Court of Justice on matters of interpretation.

Two Soviet vetoes were cast during the Lebanon crisis of 1958, and both were circumvented by General Assembly action.

Six of the vetoes by proxy were used on behalf of India. The first, on the Kashmir problem, stuck. A second veto on Kashmir, cast against fuller negotiations, was by-passed when the United States succeeded in bringing India and Pakistan together for talks in exchange for U.S. aid to India during the Chinese invasion of that country. The third, on Goa, stuck. Three further vetoes were cast by the Soviet Union on behalf of India in December 1971.

These effectively prevented any Security Council action during the Indo-Pakistan War until India had attained her military objectives. A General Assembly resolution also proved futile. Hence, these 3 vetoes must be considered as final. Two vetoes cast over Indonesian independence were circumvented by Assembly action, but a veto cast in the 1964 Indonesian-Malaysian dispute has stuck. Lastly, 1 veto cast by the Soviet Union in 1974 on a technicality in the Cyprus situation was quickly superseded. In sum, therefore, 11 proxy vetoes for neutralist states have stuck; 6 were circumvented by UN action; and 4 were superseded by outside circumstances.

The largest number of vetoes, 51, was used to block the admission of new members to the United Nations. This total, however, is not as staggering as it appears, since 34 of these 51 vetoes were repeats. Italy, for example, was vetoed 6 times, and Portugal, Jordan, Ireland, Ceylon, South Korea, South Vietnam, and Japan were vetoed 4 times each. One Soviet objective in vetoing the admission of these states was to force the United States to admit such Communist states as Albania, Bulgaria, Hungary, and Rumania to the world organization. In an effort to break this membership deadlock, the two superpowers negotiated directly and in 1955 reached agreement on a package deal that made possible the admission of sixteen new members, including most of the protégés of both superpowers. In one sense, therefore, the Soviet vetoes attained their end: the admission of the Communist applicants. But in another sense, they were superseded, since all the U.S. candidates against which vetoes had been cast—save South Korea and South Vietnam—were also admitted to membership. A decision of the superpowers taken outside the United Nations effectively resolved the membership stalemate. In all, 43 of the membership vetoes were superseded by the package deal and only 8—4 against South Vietnam and 4 against South Korea—have stuck.[4]

Four early Soviet vetoes—in 1946 against Spain—do not fit into any of the above categories, but their fate is clear.[5] They were cast in order to obtain more severe action against the Franco regime for its association with the Axis during World War II. While the Assembly passed resolutions similar to some of the vetoed proposals, the rapid development of the cold war and Spain's increasing value to the West prevented further action. In effect, these vetoes were superseded by changing circumstances. The table on this page presents the above material in summary form.

An analysis of the table suggests several conclusions. First, it is a startling fact that three-fourths of the Soviet vetoes have been rendered less effective in one way or another and 23 percent have been circumvented by action of the United Nations itself. The "circumventability" of a veto depends on several factors. The identity of the veto's beneficiary is of great importance and often determines the degree of political incentive to override a veto or the degree of political caution against such action. The legal-constitutional situation may also play an important part. Here one must ask how rigid the Charter is on a given point. On the membership question, for example, the Charter seems to exclude circumvention. Some states toyed with the idea, but the World Court refused to go along with their scheme. Then, there is a point at which the legal and political issues meet: Given some latitude in the constitution and the political desire to circumvent a veto, is it *politically* possible to exploit the *constitutional* possibil-

Soviet Vetoes 1946–1976

	Stuck	Circumvented	Superseded	Total
Direct Confrontations	7 (39%)	8 (44%)	3 (17%)	18
For Communist Allies	2 (12%)	11 (69%)	3 (19%)	16
Proxy Vetoes	11 (50%)	6 (30%)	4 (20%)	21
Membership Vetoes	8 (16%)	–	43 (84%)	51
Spanish Question	–	–	4	4
	28 (25%)	25 (23%)	57 (52%)	110

ity? The Indian "liberation" of Goa is a case in point. The Soviet veto stuck in this case not because there was no alternative machinery that might have been used against it—the General Assembly could have served—but because it was clear that, in voting terms, the Assembly would have endorsed the Soviet position. The United States believed, probably correctly, that the Assembly would have supported the Soviet view of "liberation," not the Western view of "aggression." Hence, the veto served in this case as an instrument of the majority view in the United Nations rather than a device for blocking the majority position.

A second general conclusion emerging from the above table concerns the Soviet vetoes that have stuck. The Soviet Union has been more successful in direct confrontations with the United States (39 percent) and in proxy vetoes cast on behalf of neutralist states (50 percent) than in vetoes on behalf of Communist allies (12 percent). In short, along with its own direct national interest, the USSR has been better able to protect the interests of neutrals than those of allies.

It is clear from the above that, in direct superpower confrontations, the United States and other UN members acknowledge the power realities of the situation. Pushing the United Nations too far in situations like the Hungarian Revolution or the Czechoslovak crisis, for example, runs the risk of shattering it altogether. The durable character of the proxy vetoes has also been an expression of cold-war realities: First, the United States has been reluctant to seek to upset a veto cast on behalf of a neutralist state, since, like the Soviet Union, it is anxious to win neutralist support. Moreover, the political realities noted above would make it difficult to mobilize a majority for such circumvention in the General Assembly. On the other hand, the United States has taken a strong interest in circumventing vetoes cast on behalf of Communist allies when the American national interest has been at stake. The 5 circumvented vetoes during the Korean War were cases in point. In all instances, the attitude of the two superpowers has been crucial to the durability of the veto.

A third general conclusion from the record suggests that the 110 vetoes have not constituted as formidable an obstacle to the solution of international problems as one might expect. In the first place, this total is somewhat misleading, since 34 of the membership vetoes were repeats. More important, however, is the fact that in 75 percent of the cases in which a veto had been cast, some further action was forthcoming. In half of the vetoed cases, the issues were settled outside the United Nations by direct negotiations or changing circumstances. Even in these cases, however, the United Nations sometimes played a good-offices role. For example, the preliminary discussions about lifting the Berlin Blockade were held between Soviet and American officials at the United Nations.

The significant fact is that 23 percent of the vetoed issues, including important peace and security operations, were circumvented directly by compensatory UN action. In these instances, the USSR paralyzed the Security Council but not the United Nations *in toto.* General Assembly action, as in the extension of Secretary-General Lie's term in 1950, and joint action by the Assembly and the Secretary-General, as in the Congo Operation, have been the major forms of UN compensatory machinery.

On balance, the evidence suggests that the United Nations, far from being helpless in the face of the Soviet veto, has responded to the challenge with imagination and flexibility. It has moved cautiously when the direct interest of a superpower has been at stake. In three-fourths of the cases, however, either the United Nations has been able to devise means to circumvent the veto, although not necessarily to solve the problem, or the issue has been effectively settled by outside events. In short, the veto has not been an insurmountable obstacle to the resolution of international issues.

Most important, the rise of the Third World in the 1970's has been reflected in the Security Council. The Soviet Union, feeling less isolated and always intent to woo the new nations, has used the veto on fewer and fewer occasions. Between 1972 and 1976, for example, only 2 Soviet vetoes were cast. During the same period, the United States cast 12 vetoes.

Before considering the United States and the veto, it is interesting to note the fate of vetoes cast by members other than the Soviet Union: 13 by Great Britain, 7 by France, and 1 by Nationalist China.[6] Of these, only 10 British vetoes stuck. These were cast against the use of force to bring down the regimes of Southern Rhodesia and of Southwest Africa. One of these was used to block the expulsion of South Africa from the United Nations. All the others were either circumvented by UN action or superseded by events. The creation of the UN Emergency Force by the General Assembly in 1956 after British and French vetoes paralyzed the Security Council is a well-known case in point.

The People's Republic of China cast her first veto in August 1972 in order to block the admission of Bangladesh to the United Nations and her second in September 1972 on behalf of the Arab states in their confrontation with Israel.[7]

The United States and the Veto

The companion myth to the paralyzing Soviet veto is that of American self-denial. Western observers never tire of pointing out that the United States has used the veto most sparingly. Some observers go so far as to question whether the United States ever favored the inclusion of the veto power in the UN Charter. Even so well-informed a statesman as Senator John Sherman Cooper, former ambassador to India, asked in 1954 whether it was not true that the United States, at the time of the approval of the Charter, "was opposed to the veto."[8]

To assert that the United States objected to the inclusion of the veto power is incorrect. To say that the United States has used the veto power only fifteen times is literally correct but highly misleading in a broader sense. The implication would be that one superpower had selfishly put national interest above international considerations, while the other had unselfishly subordinated national interests in order to further international cooperation. The fact of the matter is that the United States has not used the veto because it has been able to protect and promote its national interest in other ways. By obtaining majority votes against resolutions it opposes, the United States has not been forced to cast vetoes. The key to this American "hidden veto" has, of course, been the composition of the Security Council. It is a fact that until the enlargement of the Council from eleven to fifteen in 1966, a majority of its members usually were military allies of the United States. In 1958, Premier Khrushchev lashed out against what, in his view, was clear American domination of the Council:

It is common knowledge that the majority in the Security Council is composed of the votes of countries dependent, in one way or another, primarily economically, on the USA. Thus, the Security Council in its present composition cannot be regarded as an impartial arbiter, and that is why it has of late ceased to play the important role in the maintenance of international peace and security which devolved upon it by virtue of the United Nations Charter.[9]

When Khrushchev made this statement, 8 votes on the Council were controlled by military allies of the United States in NATO and SEATO. Two members—Iraq and Sweden—were neutral in the East-West struggle. In the following year, Sweden was replaced by Italy, a member of NATO, and Iraq by Tunisia, another neutral.

Thus, in 1959, the United States had good reason to expect nine of the eleven Security Council members to support its position on any major East-West issue. As Norman J. Padelford has pointed out:

It is clear from the record that when the Soviet Union finds its vital interests at stake there are now no other great powers generally inclined to stand with it. Therefore, the negative vote of the Soviet delegate usually becomes a sole veto, accompanied ordinarily by the vote of whatever satellite holds a non-permanent seat on the Council. When other great powers, particularly the United States and Great Britain, find their national interests at issue they can usually persuade other permanent members to go along with them either in casting a multiple negative vote sufficient to stop a proposal without the stigma of exercising a sole veto (or near-sole veto), or to join in introducing and passing a resolution more suitable to their desires.[10]

There are numerous cases on record which suggest that the United States has used its considerable influence to persuade members of the Council to form a negative majority for its position and thus avoid having to cast a veto. For example, during the protracted controversy over the admission of new members, the United States repeatedly blocked the admission of Soviet-sponsored candidates, not by a veto, but by prevailing upon its allies to back its position. The USSR, on the other hand, had to cast 51 vetoes to block American-sponsored candidates. The U-2 episode in 1960 was another typical case of the American hidden veto in action. In May of that year, the Soviet Union brought the case before the Security Council and introduced a resolution branding the flights by American planes over Soviet territory as "acts of aggression." Two states—the USSR and Poland—voted in favor of the Soviet motion; seven states voted against: Argentina, China, Ecuador, France, Italy, the United Kingdom, and the United States—all members of the Western alliance system. Two neutralist states—Ceylon and Tunisia—abstained.

This pattern began to change somewhat in 1966, when four nonpermanent members were added to the Security Council. The passage of a resolution now required 9 affirmative votes instead of 7. Since the enlargement of the Council was undertaken primarily for the benefit of the new nations, most of which were neutralist on East-West issues, it now became more difficult for the United States to control the Council. For example, in 1966, the United States attempted to have the Vietnam question inscribed on the Council's agenda and found itself dependent upon the vote of Jordan. The move succeeded, but just barely. The days of an automatic American majority or of a hidden veto, exercised by mobilizing this majority against a Soviet-sponsored resolution, were over. U.S. influence was still very great, but now had to depend on bargaining and persuasion rather than on an absolute majority.

On March 17, 1970, the United States cast its first veto. The occasion was the 1,534th meeting of the Security Council, and the subject of the discussion was the white minority regime of Southern Rhodesia. A draft resolution submitted by Burundi, Nepal, Sierra Leone, and Zambia proposed to condemn the Ian Smith regime, urged all member states of the United Nations to sever relations with it, and also urged them to assist national liberation movements. Moreover, the draft resolution condemned the refusal of the United Kingdom to use force against the Southern Rhodesian regime. Nine states voted in favor of the draft resolution: Burundi, Nationalist China, Nepal, Poland,

Sierra Leone, Spain, Syria, USSR, and Zambia. Colombia, Finland, France, and Nicaragua abstained. The United Kingdom and the United States voted against.

The circumstances surrounding this first American veto were somewhat unusual. In the first place, a British veto alone would have killed the resolution. The United States did not have to cast a negative vote and could have preserved its vetoless record by joining the abstainers. In this particular instance, however, the American delegation wished to emphasize that it agreed with the position of the United Kingdom on the question of Southern Rhodesia. More broadly, it wanted to make the point that the United States would not hesitate to cast a veto if it felt strongly enough to do so. At any rate, America had at long last openly lost her virginity in the Security Council.

On September 10, 1972, the United States cast a second veto, this time to block a draft resolution on the Middle East that would have called for a cessation of hostilities without linking these to a murderous attack by Palestinian terrorists on the Israeli Olympic team. In effect, this was an American proxy veto cast on behalf of Israel.

In October 1972, in a major policy statement, Secretary of State William P. Rogers announced that the United States would exercise its veto power in the Security Council far more readily than it had in the past. The secretary stated that this shift in policy reflected a recent determination by the United States to pursue a more independent course. "If a resolution is a bad one, we will veto it," the secretary added.

On March 21, 1973, the United States translated this warning into reality when Ambassador John A. Scali vetoed a draft resolution on the Panama Canal. In the American view, the revision of the treaty governing the Canal was essentially a bilateral matter between Panama and the United States and the resolution, which received 13 affirmative votes with Britain abstaining, was regarded as "outside pressure."

At a deeper level, this position bore a striking resemblance to that of the Soviet Union. It seemed that the United States, when confronted with hostile majorities, would not hesitate to use the instrument which the USSR had wielded so prominently since 1945. On May 22, 1973, the United States employed the veto for the fourth time in order to block more forceful sanctions against Southern Rhodesia. Two months later, another proxy veto was cast on behalf of Israel. On October 30, 1974, the United States joined France and the United Kingdom in a triple veto to block the expulsion of South Africa from the United Nations. On June 6, 1975, a similar triple veto prevented the passage of a resolution that would have defined South Africa's occupation of Namibia as a threat to international peace. On August 11, 1975, the United States cast two more vetoes to block the admission of North and South Vietnam and on September 30, two further vetoes were cast on the same issue. Daniel P. Moynihan, the United States representative, declared that the vetoes were cast because the Security Council had not even considered South Korea's application for membership to the United Nations. The United States was ready to admit the two Vietnams if the two Koreas were admitted as well. In the American view, no partisan political tests should be applied to United Nations membership. On December 8, 1975, January 26, 1976, and March 25, 1976, the United States cast three more proxy vetoes on behalf of Israel to block what it considered unbalanced resolutions against the Jewish state. On June 23, 1976, the United States cast its fifteenth veto against the admission of Angola to United Nations membership. According to the American position, Angola failed to meet the requirements of independence while thousands of Cuban troops remained on its soil. On October 19, 1976, the United States joined France and the United Kingdom in yet another triple veto to prevent the imposition of an embargo of arms shipments to South Africa.

In considering the overall American position on the veto, one must also take notice of the considerable power the United States can exercise within UN organs before a vote is ever taken. At the present time, the United States pays over one quarter of the operating cost of the United Nations family. This contribution has been an important factor in the Organization's efforts to maintain its present precarious hold on financial solvency. If the United States were to be sufficiently displeased with a project to consider withholding even just its voluntary contributions, UN planners would debate seriously before going ahead. On occasion, the United States has actually exercised this "financial veto" in order to attain its objectives. In addition, the threat of a veto has at times been as effective as the actual casting of one. When, in 1950, the United States let it be known that it was determined to veto any candidate but Trygve Lie for the Office of Secretary-General, the threat itself was sufficient. His term was extended by the General Assembly after the USSR had cast a veto in the Security Council. Most important, the growing number of Third World nations, many of which pursue national objectives different from those of the United States, has made the casting of an American veto a somewhat more frequent event in the 1970's than it was during the cold war years.

In sum, the evidence demonstrates that the United States, like the Soviet Union, seeks to protect its national interest against any hostile action by the Security Council. During the 1950's and 1960's, the two superpowers employed different parliamentary strategies to protect these interests, but by the 1970's the United States seemed just as ready to cast a veto as the Soviet Union.

The Veto and the United Nations

It now remains to be seen what effect the interaction of the two superpowers on the veto problem has had on the political evolution of the United Nations itself.

It is clear from the above discussion that the actual exercise of the veto power has not proved to be as great a threat to the effective functioning of the United Nations as it might have been in theory. In the first place, the Security Council has tended to narrow rather than expand the scope of the veto power. It established the principle that the abstention of a Great Power was not tantamount to a veto, thus giving states the opportunity to avoid commitment on a difficult choice without preventing UN action. In the Korean police-action decision of 1950, the Security Council went even further, by declaring that the absence of a Great Power should merely be regarded as an abstention, not a veto *in absentia.* Finally, the threat of the double veto, the parliamentary device that would allow a Great Power to veto practically anything it chose, has not materialized in practice. While it still exists as a potential weapon, the double veto was used only three times, the last occasion arising in 1948.

Second, to blame the veto power for the strains and difficulties in resolving international problems is to confuse the symptoms with the causes. The Security Council veto might be viewed simply as the formal parliamentary expression of the real veto which any superpower actually has as a fact of life in a system of sovereign nation-states. The temptation of a voting assembly is to mistake its majority decisions as accurate and enforceable expressions of power realities. They are not, especially not in the nuclear age. The veto power has forced the Security Council to deemphasize majority rule as far as the superpowers are concerned in favor of the more realistic unanimity principle: slow and frequently laborious negotiations to accommodate divergent points of view until the superpowers prefer to acquiesce rather than upset the system. The veto is thus a lesson in realpolitik.

In fact, one may argue that the abolition of the veto might increase, not diminish, international tensions and the danger of war, since the majority might then be tempted to vote an action against a recalcitrant superpower. The technique of arriving at political decisions by counting votes without regard for power is a democratic luxury that the world may not be able to afford, particularly in the nuclear age. The principle of voting and living by majority decisions does make sense in a homogeneous political context, but in a world of profound schisms, negotiating with the opponent rather than outvoting him may be the wiser method of settling differences. This truth has become even more self-evident since the seating of the People's Republic of China on the Security Council. Today, consensus rather than majoritarianism is the keynote of the Council.

The third, and perhaps most important, effect of the veto has been its impact on the UN's political evolution. One reason why the veto has been less important in fact than it might have been in theory has been that other UN organs have taken up the slack created by a stymied Security Council. It is possible to chart three shifts in the locus of power among the organs of the United

Nations, all of them due at least in part to the veto. First, by 1950, owing to the threat of the Soviet veto, the Uniting for Peace procedure brought an increasing number of peace and security issues before the General Assembly. The frequency of Security Council sessions in the early 1950's declined sharply, and the scope of political issues that came before it narrowed considerably. In 1948, for example, the Council held 168 meetings; whereas in 1955, it held only 23. The Uniting for Peace Resolution—passed under strong American pressure and over vehement Soviet opposition—circumvented the paralysis of the Council and broadened the competence of the Assembly.

The Assembly, having had its own mandate enlarged in 1950, began to widen that of the Secretary-General by 1955. As we shall see in subsequent chapters, the missions of Dag Hammarskjöld to Peking in 1955, to Suez in 1956, to Lebanon in 1958, and to the Congo in 1960 and 1961 were all based on Assembly resolutions which gave the Secretary-General increasing powers to make and execute policy. Indeed, the abortive Soviet attempt to replace the Office of the Secretary-General with a veto-bound triumvirate was in essence an effort to extend the principle of the veto into a new power center: the UN Secretariat.

Beginning in 1960, however, one could observe an interesting resuscitation of the Security Council, which was based on a more circumspect use of the Soviet veto. From the experience of the preceding years, the USSR knew that if it wielded a veto on a vital matter, the Assembly and the Secretary-General were liable to step into the breach and run the operation regardless. Hence, it began to abstain on issues which it might have vetoed before, preferring to keep even an undesirable operation in the Council, where it could exercise more influence than it could if the Assembly and the Secretary-General were in control. For example, at several points during the Congo Operation, the Soviet Union abstained on resolutions to which it was doubtless opposed. "Thus, Russia might well have vetoed the Council's resolution of 21 February 1961 which strengthened the hand of a Secretary-General whom the Russians had just branded as a 'criminal.' "[11] Abstention, the Soviets reasoned, might be the better part of wisdom.

The paradoxical result of this development is that the Council has been revived by—of all things—the Assembly. As one observer put it:

The "Uniting for Peace" procedure may have seemed to rust, almost unused; but rust or not, the weapon hangs over the heads of the veto-wielding Council members. Each of these, a latter-day Damocles, is now inclined, when on the point of vetoing a resolution that might bring it down upon him, to swivel a wary eye at the ceiling and think again.[12]

Between 1946 and 1959, the Soviet Union cast 88 vetoes, or approximately 6.3 per year; from 1960 through 1976, it cast 22, or 1.5 per year, less than one-quarter as many.

In conclusion, then, the overall record suggests that there is less difference between the behavior of the superpowers in the United Nations than the 110 to 16 veto score of the USSR and United States would suggest. The United States developed over the years an effective hidden veto to protect its vital national interests, while many of the Soviet vetoes, particularly in areas not directly related to its national interest, were circumvented. In addition, the interaction of the superpowers over the veto question has led the United Nations away from the concept of majoritarianism to the more realistic principle of diplomacy in the settlement of major international disputes. Most important, however, is the fact that the circumvention of the Soviet vetoes has made the UN members use their organization in a flexible and imaginative manner. The Assembly, far from being a debating society, has exercised at times an important and significant role in several peace-keeping operations. The Secretary-General has been an active and important figure in the solution of international disputes, no lofty figurehead above politics. The United Nations has been actively engaged in solving political problems in a basically political manner—negotiation, pressure, compromise, and agreement. In this process, the Security Council has tended to become an instrument of consensus building rather than an arena for superpower confrontation.

The veto, then, has been not an insurmountable obstacle, but a constant incentive toward greater inventiveness and improvisation in international problem-solving. Perhaps more than any other single provision in the Charter, the veto has been responsible for the Charter's having remained a living document and the United Nations itself a living organization. It is true that the veto could have killed the United Nations. Thus far, the evidence suggests that it has made it stronger.

SELECTED BIBLIOGRAPHY

Bailey, Sidney D. *Voting in the Security Council.* Bloomington: Indiana University Press, 1970.

———. "Veto in the Security Council." *International Conciliation,* no. 566 (January 1968).

Boyd, Andrew. *Fifteen Men on a Powder Keg.* New York: Stein and Day, 1971.

Claude, Inis L., Jr. *Power and International Relations.* New York: Random House, 1962.

Hiscocks, Richard. *The Security Council: A Study in Adolescence.* New York: Free Press, 1974.

Jiménez de Arechaga, Eduardo. *Voting and the Handling of Disputes in the Security Council.* New York: Carnegie Endowment, 1950.

Lee, Dwight E. "The Genesis of the Veto." *International Organization* (February 1947): 33–42.

Moldaver, Arlette. "Repertoire of the Veto in the Security Council, 1946–1956." *International Organization* (Spring 1957): 261–274.

NOTES

1. In the direct-confrontation category, 7 Soviet vetoes stuck: the Atomic Energy Commission, 325th meeting, June 22, 1948; the CCA (Committee on Conventional Armaments) Work Program, 450th meeting, October 11, 1949; Arms Census Agreement, 452d meeting, October 18, 1949 (2); election of Secretary-General, 613th meeting, March 13, 1953; Arctic Inspection Proposal, 817th meeting, May 2, 1958; the Czechoslovak crisis, 1,443d meeting, August 23, 1968. Eight Soviet vetoes were circumvented: reappointment of a Secretary-General, 510th meeting, October 12, 1950; the Hungarian crisis, 754th meeting, November 4, 1956; the Congo crisis, 906th meeting, September 16, 1960; the Congo crisis, 920th meeting, December 12–13, 1960; the Congo crisis, 942d meeting, February 20–21, 1961 (2); the Congo crisis, 982d meeting, November 24, 1961 (2).

Three Soviet vetoes were by-passed either by direct negotiations between the disputants or by outside events: the Berlin Blockade, 372d meeting, October 25, 1948; the U.S. RB-47 incident, 883d meeting, July 26, 1960 (2).

2. In the veto-cast-for-an-ally category, two Soviet vetoes stuck: the Czechoslovakia case, 303d meeting, May 24, 1948 (2).

Eleven vetoes were circumvented: Greek Civil War, 70th meeting, September 20, 1946; Greek Civil War, 170th meeting, July 29, 1947; Greek Civil War, 188th meeting, August 19, 1947 (2); Greek Civil War, 202d meeting, September 15, 1947 (2); Korean War, 496th meeting, September 6, 1950; Korean War, 501st meeting, September 12, 1950; Korean War, 530th meeting, November 30, 1950; Korean War (Germ Warfare), 587th meeting, July 3, 1952; Korean War (Germ Warfare), 590th meeting, July 9, 1952.

Three Soviet vetoes were superseded: Corfu Channel Case, 122d meeting, March 25, 1947; infiltration in Indochina, 674th meeting, March 29, 1954; Guatemalan coup, 675th meeting, June 20, 1954.

3. Eleven of the Soviet proxy vetoes stuck: Palestine-Jordan River Diversion, 656th meeting, January 22, 1954; Kashmir, 773d meeting, February 20, 1957; Goa, 988th meeting, December 18–19, 1961; Israeli-Syrian dispute, 1,057th meeting, August 3, 1963; Malaysian-Indonesian dispute, 1,144th meeting, September 16, 1964; Syrian-Israeli dispute, 1,164th meeting, December 21, 1964; Syrian-Israeli dispute, 1,307th meeting, November 4, 1966; Indo-Pakistan War, 1,606th meeting December 4, 1971; Indo-Pakistan War, 1,607th meeting, December 5, 1971; Indo-Pakistan War, 1,613th meeting, December 13, 1971; Middle East crisis, 1,662d meeting, September 10, 1972.

Six of the Soviet vetoes by proxy were circumvented: Indonesia, 456th meeting, December 13, 1949 (2); Suez Canal shipping, 664th meeting, March 29, 1954; Suez Canal nationalization crisis, 743d meeting, October 13, 1956; Lebanon, 834th meeting, July 18, 1958; Lebanon, 837th meeting, July 22, 1958.

Three of the vetoes were by-passed: Syria-Lebanon case, 23d meeting, February 16, 1946; Kuwait, 960th meeting, July 7, 1961; Kashmir, 1,016th meeting, June 22, 1962.

4. Eight of the membership vetoes have stuck: South Korea, 423d meeting, Arpil 8, 1949; South Vietnam, 603d meeting, September 9, 1952; South Korea, 704th meeting, December 13, 1955; South Vietnam, 704th meeting, December 13, 1955; South Korea, 790th meeting, September 9, 1957; South Vietnam, 790th meeting, September 9, 1957; South Korea, 843d meeting, December 9, 1958; South Vietnam, 843d meeting, December 9, 1958.

Forty-three of the membership vetoes were by-passed: Trans-Jordan, Portugal, Ireland, 57th meeting, August 29, 1946; Trans-Jordan, Ireland, Portugal, 186th meeting, August 18, 1947; Italy and Austria, 190th meeting, August 21, 1947; Italy and Finland, 206th meeting, October 1, 1947; Italy, 279th meeting, April 10, 1948; Ceylon, 351st meeting, August 18, 1948; Ceylon, 384th meeting, December 15, 1948; Nepal, 439th meeting, September 7, 1949; Portugal, Jordan, Italy, Finland, Ireland, Austria, Ceylon, 443d meeting, September 13, 1949; Italy, 573d meeting, February 6, 1952; Libya, 600th meeting, September 16, 1952; Japan, 602d meeting, September 18, 1952; Laos and Cambodia, 603d meeting, September 19, 1952; Jordan, Ireland, Portugal, Italy, Austria, Finland, Ceylon, Nepal, Libya, Cambodia, Japan, Laos, Spain, 704th meeting, December 13, 1955; Japan, 705th meeting, December 14, 1955; Japan, 706th meeting, December 15, 1955; Mauritania, 911th meeting, December 3–4, 1960; Kuwait, 985th meeting, December 18–19, 1961.

5. The Spanish case, 47th meeting, June 18, 1946; the Spanish case, 49th meeting, June 26, 1946 (3).

6. The Spanish case (France and USSR), 49th meeting, June 26, 1946; Indonesian question (France), 194th meeting, August 25, 1947; membership of Mongolia (China) 704th meeting, December 13, 1955; Palestine-Suez crisis (France and United Kingdom), 749th meeting, October 30, 1956; Palestine-Suez crisis (France and United Kingdom), 750th meeting, October 30, 1956; Southern Rhodesia (United Kingdom), 1,064th meeting, September 9, 1963; Southern Rhodesia (United Kingdom and United States), 1,534th meeting, March 17, 1970; Southern Rhodesia (United Kingdom), 1,556th meeting, November 10, 1970; Southern Rhodesia (United Kingdom), 1,623d meeting, December 30, 1971; Southern Rhodesia (United Kingdom), 1,639th meeting, February 4, 1972; Southern Rhodesia (United Kingdom), 1,666th meeting, September 29, 1972 (3); Southern Rhodesia (United Kingdom and United States), 1,716th meeting, May 22, 1973.

7. Bangladesh (China), 1,660th meeting, August 25, 1972; Middle East (China), 1,662nd meeting, September 10, 1972.

8. Cited by Inis L. Claude, Jr., *Swords into Plowshares,* 3d ed. (New York: Random House, 1964), p. 135.

9. Cited by Arthur N. Holcombe, "The Role of Politics in the Organization of Peace," in his *Organizing Peace in the Nuclear Age* (New York: New York University Press, 1959), p. 97.

10. Norman J. Padelford, "The Use of the Veto," *International Organization* (June 1948): 231–32.

11. Andrew Boyd, *United Nations: Piety, Myth, and Truth* (London: Penguin Books, 1962), pp. 32–33.

12. Ibid.

The General Assembly: China and the Rise of the Third World

"Were Communist China also to become a permanent, veto-wielding member of the Security Council, that would, I fear, implant in the United Nations the seeds of destruction."
John Foster Dulles
U.S. Secretary of State
June 28, 1957

"Those who speak out against the presence of the People's Republic of China within the United Nations have missed the bus of history."
Valerian Zorin
Soviet Delegate
to the UN General Assembly
October 22, 1962

The thirty-year history of the United Nations may be roughly divided into two periods. During its first fifteen years, the United Nations was dominated by the cold war, and the major political confrontations in the General Assembly took place between East and West. During these years, relatively few new states were admitted to the World Organization because each superpower tried to prevent the admission of the friends of the other. The United States then had a relatively easy time in the General Assembly. Of the original 51 members of the United Nations in 1945, at least 35 were clearly associated with the United States, only 5 with the Soviet Union, and only 10 were nonaligned. The American delegation enjoyed a large measure of control over the Assembly and did not hesitate to use its "automatic majority" in its own national interest. By the 1960's, however, when the birth of a new nation became virtually a monthly event, the superpowers began to compete with one another to admit these states into the United Nations. A policy of competitive exclusion gave way to a policy of competitive welcome. Gradually, the major political controversies in the Assembly began to shift from an East-West to a North-South axis. By the 1970's, the situation reversed itself. As a result of the liquidation of the colonial empires, the membership of the United Nations had almost tripled. More than one hundred new nations from the Third World now enjoyed an absolute mathematical majority in the General Assembly. The major controversies over political, economic, and social issues now raged between fewer than forty developed countries and over one hundred developing countries in Asia, Africa, the Middle East, and Latin America. Since its inception a generation ago, the United Nations had almost totally changed in character. During its first fifteen years, it had served primarily as an instrument of American foreign policy. During the second decade and a half, it gradually became a vehicle for the new nations of the Third World.

This chapter consists of three parts. First, we shall trace the United Nations' transition from an East-West to a North-South axis though an analysis of superpower membership policy. Second, we shall analyze the twenty-year struggle over the representation of China. This struggle culminated in the historic watershed vote of October 1971 that signified the first major defeat of the United States in the General Assembly and marked the emergence of the Third World as a dominant force. Finally, we shall examine the impact of China on the new United Nations of the 1970's.

The Superpowers
and United Nations Membership Policy

The superpowers have had a decisive influence on the member-ship policy of the United Nations. One major criterion for admis-sion stipulated in the Charter—that a state be "peace-loving"—has often been ignored in practice. In the overwhelming number of cases, little or no attention has been paid to the Advisory Opinion of the World Court in 1948, which stated that "every application for admission should be examined and voted on sepa-rately and on its own merits."[1] Instead, if one is to understand why only nine admissions marked the first decade of the UN's existence, whereas over sixty new members joined the Organiza-tion during the second, one must examine the national policies of the superpowers. In UN admissions the change from competi-tive exclusion to accelerated entry policy was a result of super-power interaction.

During the first decade of the Organization's history, the policy of each superpower was to prevent the admission of the friends of the other. As noted in Chapter 1, the United States accomplished this goal during the early years by the hidden-veto technique, while the Soviet Union made frequent use of the veto power against pro-Western states. Each superpower at times proposed package deals which the other rejected. The United States proposed the first such deal in 1946, but it was turned down by the Soviet Union. A year later, the positions were re-versed when the United States rejected a Soviet package pro-posal. During the next eight years, the United States rejected several Soviet packages, declaring its opposition to "horse trad-ing" of this kind in principle and citing the 1948 World Court Advisory Opinion in support of its position. The United States abandoned this posture in 1955 when the superpowers agreed on a large package of sixteen new members: four Soviet-bloc nations —Albania, Bulgaria, Hungary, and Rumania; four Western na-tions—Ireland, Italy, Portugal, and Spain; and eight uncommit-ted nations—Austria, Cambodia, Ceylon, Finland, Jordan, Laos, Libya, and Nepal. This 1955 agreement ended the period of competitive exclusion in UN membership and ushered in a decade of rapid expansion.

The large majority of new members came from the emerging nations of the Third World. The United States and the Soviet Union, in a complete reversal of form, now competed in welcoming gestures where they had prevously competed in keeping the gates closed. By the mid-1970's the only states still excluded against their own wishes were the two Koreas and Vietnam. In 1954, the membership of the United Nations had totaled sixty. By the mid-1970's the total had almost tripled. A closer look at the radical difference in UN membership policy during the two decades reveals the decisive impact of the superpowers.

During the decade of competitive exclusion, 1946–1955, the United States adhered to a limited conception of its national interest. By rejecting package deals, it thwarted the ambitions of both pro-Western and neutral candidates for admission in order to exclude half a dozen Communist applicants. As a result, however, the original character and composition of the United Nations was largely preserved until 1955. This original membership included some Communist nations, but the overwhelming majority of states were pro-Western and accepted the leadership of the United States. In short, one result of the competitive exclusion policy was to perpetuate a United Nations in which the United States had virtually complete control, save for the Soviet veto power. The United States could not only obtain an automatic majority in the General Assembly but could also produce the two-thirds majority that was necessary to approve Assembly action on important matters. It was this Assembly that directed most of the Korean police action. It was to this kind of Assembly that the United States was willing to bring future peace-keeping operations under the Uniting for Peace Resolution. And it was such an Assembly that often accepted the American lead on other vital East-West questions. The passage of the Uniting for Peace Resolution in 1950 over strenous Soviet opposition—with 52 states supporting the American position, 5 against, and 2 abstentions—was a fair example of the U.S. dominance that characterized the decade of exclusion in membership policy.

The Soviet Union recognized, of course, that almost any kind of package deal was bound to improve its position within the Organization. Even a straight swap, one Communist state for one pro-Western, would strengthen the relative voting power on its side. It was also clear that an Assembly dominated by neutrals was less repugnant to the USSR than the existing one controlled by the United States and its allies. Thus, throughout the first decade, the Soviet Union sought package deals that would gain admission for its protégés but was more willing than the United States to accept members of the opposite camp and neutral states in order to obtain the deal.

It is conceivable that if the period of competitive exclusion had lasted much longer, the potential of the United Nations might have been seriously stunted. Until the membership was broadened, the Organization had no claim to universality and thus only a limited right to speak as a voice of the world community. Moreover, in time the Soviet Union might have chosen to resign from this predominantly Western club in which it was condemned to the status of a permanent minority. Thus, if the policy of competitive exclusion had continued, the United States would have retained its absolute control, but over a decreasingly effective and influential organization. With the inception of a less restrictive membership policy, the United States had to settle for a less prominent role, but in a more broadly based and representative organization.

The year 1955 signaled the end of American hegemony over the General Assembly. The United States lost its automatic two-thirds majority, although it could still command a simple majority without much difficulty. During the next decade, when the birth of a new nation became almost a monthly event, the competition between the superpowers on the membership question produced virtually the opposite result from the exclusion of the previous ten years. The superpowers now competed in welcoming the new states. The number of states permitted to join during the second decade exceeded that of the original Charter members in 1945. Some of the new African states were accorded full UN privileges before they had actually cut their teeth as national states. The superpowers acted as if the new states were ready to run internationally before they had taken more than a few steps nationally.

The logic behind the new superpower policy was obvious. Outside the United Nations, it was becoming increasingly clear that the growing number of neutralist states would play an important role in the East-West struggle, and both superpowers recognized UN membership as a good way to court new allies. Within the United Nations, the Soviet Union had to win the support of the neutralists if it was ever to escape from its position of being a permanent minority, and the United States needed the support, or at least the benevolent neutrality, of the new nations if it was to retain its position of leadership. By the mid-1970's, superpower membership policy had transformed the United Nations virtually beyond recognition. The climax of this trend was reached in 1974 and 1975 during the Twenty-ninth and Thirtieth Sessions of the General Assembly.

During those two years, the radical wing of the new Afro-Arab-Asian majority captured control of the General Assembly. Various "national liberation" groups demanded and received legitimacy. The most prominent case in point was the Assembly's decision, by an overwhelming vote, to invite Yasir Arafat, leader of the Palestinian Liberation Organization, to address the world body. When Arafat appeared, he was accorded all the ceremonial honors usually reserved for heads of state. Only 4 states out of the 138 that made up the Assembly's membership in 1974 opposed the invitation. The United States was among them. When, during the Palestine debate, Assembly President Abdelaziz Bouteflika in effect curbed Israel's right to speak by limiting the debate to one speech from each country, the United States vainly opposed this ruling. And when the Assembly in November 1974, by a vote of 89 to 8, with 37 abstentions, affirmed the right of the Palestinian people to be free and sovereign and, in a companion vote of 95 to 17, with 19 abstentions, awarded permanent observer status to the Palestine Liberation Organization, the United States was again on the side of the opposition. An effort to expel South Africa was prevented by a triple veto in the Security Council, cast by the United States, Britain, and France. But when the General Assembly, by a vote of 91 in favor, 22 against, and 19 abstentions, decided to suspend the South African delegation from its deliberations, the negative vote of the United States was not able to stop the action.

The trend spilled over from the General Assembly into one of the UN's "non-political" specialized agencies. The General Conference of UNESCO adopted several highly controversial resolutions unfavorable to Israel, including one that rejected Israel's request to participate in UNESCO's European regional grouping. Finally, on December 6, 1974, the United States delegate, John A. Scali, warned the General Assembly that when the majority rule became "the tyranny of the majority, the minority [would] cease to respect or obey it."

These Third World victories in 1974 took place as a result of an informal "deal." The Arabs and Communists joined the Africans in suspending South Africa, and the Africans and the Communists joined the Arabs in recognizing the Palestine Liberation Organization. As a result, many Western observers felt that the World Organization, which had been formed to help small nations keep the Great Powers from making war, had now made it difficult for the Great Powers to keep small nations from starting wars. The Twenty-ninth Assembly was not, however, a total defeat for the United States. The American delegation lobbied successfully to maintain United States forces in Korea under the United Nations flag and to keep the American-backed Lon Nol government of Cambodia in the United Nations, against a determined Chinese-sponsored effort to give the seat to the government-in-exile of Prince Norodom Sihanouk. The United States barely held the line, however, on the latter decision, with a vote of 56 in favor to 54 against, with 24 abstentions. Besides, the Lon Nol government collapsed a few months later and the Communist insurgents took over Cambodia.

By far the most dramatic and controversial event that took place during the Thirtieth Session of the General Assembly was a vote, taken on November 10, 1975, defining Zionism as "a form of racism and racial discrimination." By that time, there were 142 members of the world body. The vote was 72 in favor, 35 against, with 32 abstentions and 3 delegations absent.[2]

The majority, consisting of all the Communist states (save Rumania) and most Third World countries, charged Israel with white settler and military expansion policies reminiscent of the imperialist powers of a bygone era. Those states in opposition, led by the United States and the Western European powers, deplored the resolution as infamous and harmful to the United Nations cause. General Assembly President Gaston Thorn of Luxembourg declared that the vote had destroyed a climate of conciliation. And Jewish communities the world over, outraged at the vote, defended Zionism as the national liberation movement of the Jewish people.

It was indeed ironic that, thirty years after the death of Hitler, the victims of the worst excesses of racism in modern history should now be accused of a similar transgression. There was little doubt that the anti-Zionist resolution was a triumph for the forces of radicalism among the Third World, and that these forces, armed with centuries of anti-colonial fury and modern petrodollars, had now come close to making the UN General Assembly into their vehicle. But a closer scrutiny of the vote does not suggest that the General Assembly had succumbed to a wave of anti-Semitism of the Hitler variety. The reasons for the anti-Zionist vote were much more complex and are deserving of close analysis.

In the first place, a number of Third World votes were simply bought with petrodollars. Second, several African states supported the resolution for reasons of Third World solidarity without much substantive knowledge about either Israel or Zionism. As the delegate of Mauritius put it, "many people voted without knowing what Zionism is. I am confused."[3] Third, many delegations supported the anti-Zionism drive because they were against what the Palestinians told them Israel was: a white imperialist military state reminiscent of the Western colonial regimes. Fourth, United States Ambassador Daniel P. Moynihan aroused the anger of some African delegates who might have voted to defer the resolution, but who finally supported it in a fit of anti-American pique, when Moynihan endorsed a description of Idi Amin, President of Uganda and head of the Organization of

African Unity (OAU), as a "racist murderer." Fifth, Israel was perceived by many of the nations of the Third World as the protégé of the United States, which in turn was perceived by them as the military leader of all the former colonial powers in NATO. Sixth, Israel, it was pointed out, was settled largely by whites, and its early leaders were Europeans from Russia. Seventh, many states voted for the resolution because of fear of Arab oil retaliation or abstained for similar reasons as in the case of Japan. Finally, the "understanding" between the Arab and African blocs—reached during the Twenty-ninth Session—still held during the Thirtieth Session.

Thus, the anti-Zionism vote of 1975 signified the confluence of a number of factors. The most prominent were the petrodollar, opportunism, ignorance, as well as pride and prejudice. One final observation about the resolution is worthy of mention: those nations that voted in favor were largely dictatorships, both of the left and of the right, while those in opposition were largely, though by no means exclusively, the Western democracies. In the United Nations of the mid-1970's, the democracies numbered less than two dozen states and appeared almost like an endangered species.

Thus, the Afro-Arab-Asian majority is now in virtual control of the General Assembly. Heady with its new power, it is eager to push the UN to its limits—and beyond. In terms of the overall distribution of power in the General Assembly, the UN's progress toward universality has resulted in some reduction of the influence of the two superpowers and a corresponding gain for the more radical forces of the Third World. The more than one hundred developing countries, usually backed by the Communist countries, can now easily muster a two-thirds vote in the General Assembly. Secretary of State Kissinger, in July 1975, warned the Third World nations against "arbitrary tactics" and declared that, if they persisted in "procedural abuses" in the United Nations, they might inherit "an empty shell."[4] It is worthy of note, however, that serious fissures do exist even within the Third World majority. During the Thirtieth Session of the General Assembly in 1975, for example, two sets of contradictory resolutions were passed on the issues of Korea and the Spanish Sahara and no action was taken on the issue of Angola. These votes that, in effect, canceled each other out, reflected a tug of war between moderate and radical forces within the Third World.

It will take patience and understanding for the United States to adjust to all these changes. Some anger has already been made manifest. In January 1976, for example, Secretary Kissinger announced that the United States would reduce economic assistance to countries that had voted against the United States in the United Nations. It must be remembered, however, that the Assembly reflects the interests and objectives of politically motivated governments and thus reflects the politics of a world that itself changed profoundly since the years of the cold war. In every debate, there are grounds for differences; and there are merits to both sides of every argument. It is the essence of statesmanship to reconcile these competing interests and differing points of view for the common good through negotiation and compromise. Just as very few decisions of the American Congress satisfy all its members, very few decisions of the United Nations will satisfy all its members. Because the Congress may make a few bad mistakes in the eyes of some citizens, these mistakes do not justify scrapping the Constitution. Similarly, because, in the eyes of the United States, the General Assembly has made a few outrageous mistakes, these mistakes do not justify scrapping the UN Charter. In the long run, the success of the United Nations system will not depend upon the votes on some specific issues in a particular session of the General Assembly, but rather, in the words of the Charter, upon "harmonizing the actions of nations in the attainment of these common ends."

The vote to seat the People's Republic of China in October 1971 marked a real watershed in the evolution of the United Nations. It was the first major defeat for the United States, and China emerged as the self-appointed champion of the new actions initiated by the Third World. Besides, the issue of Chinese representation provides an illuminating case study of superpower interaction in the General Assembly. The long battle was fought between the United States and the Soviet Union against the background of the changing membership policy in the Assembly as described above. Both superpowers mustered powerful resources in support of their opposing positions and both attempted to adapt their tactics to a constantly changing membership. For all these reasons, we shall analyze the Chinese representation struggle in some detail.

The Superpowers and the Struggle over Chinese Representation

The problem of Chinese representation first arose in 1949 as a result of the Communist conquest of mainland China. But since the Communists had not destroyed the Nationalist regime, which had entrenched itself in Formosa, there were now two governments, each of which claimed the Chinese seat in the United Nations. In November 1949, the Communist People's Republic of China (PRC) cabled the President of the General Assembly, challenging the legal status of the Nationalist delegation and claiming that it did not speak for the Chinese people. This was followed in January 1950 by similar cables to the Security Council.[5] The Soviet Union immediately supported the Chinese Communist claims, and when the Security Council, upon strong American urging, refused to recognize them, the Soviet representative walked out in protest. Since that time, until the crucial year of 1971, the United States staked its political prestige on keeping Communist China out, and the Soviet Union, while at times showing somewhat ambiguous behavior, always voted for the entry of the People's Republic of China.

At the time of the initial claim of the PRC, forty-six nations recognized the Nationalist regime, while only sixteen, including the United Kingdom and India, recognized the new Communist government. The simultaneous existence of two governments, each claiming to represent the same state, brought up the problem of the relationship between national recognition and UN representation. Secretary-General Trygve Lie addressed himself to this issue in a legal memorandum on March 8, 1950.

The Secretary-General declared that it was "unfortunate" that "the question of representation had been linked up with the question of recognition." These were legally separable issues.

Indeed, a state might recognize one regime as the government of a member state and another as the government qualified to represent that state in the United Nations. He pointed out the unique character of the China problem, since for the first time in the history of the United Nations two rival governments were claiming the same seat. He then implied that the PRC was better qualified to occupy the Chinese seat:

It is submitted that the proper principles can be derived by analogy from Article 4 of the Charter. This Article requires that an applicant for membership must be able and willing to carry out the obligations of membership. The obligations of membership can be carried out only by governments which in fact possess the power to do so. Where a revolutionary government presents itself as representing a state, in rivalry to an existing government, the question at issue should be which of these two governments in fact is in a position to employ the resources and direct the people of the state in fulfillment of the obligations of membership. In essence this means an inquiry as to whether the new government exercises effective authority within the territory of the state and is habitually obeyed by the bulk of the population.

If so, it would seem to be appropriate for the United Nations organs, through their collective action, to accord it the right to represent the state in the Organization, even though individual Members of the Organization refuse, and may continue to refuse, to accord it recognition as the lawful government for reasons which are valid under their national policies.[6]

Mr. Lie's initiative evoked powerful U.S. resistance and provided one of the sparks that ignited the American attack on the Secretariat discussed in Chapter 3. The Soviet Union supported the Secretary-General's position, while the United States disputed it in a legal memorandum of its own:

A revolutionary government to be recognized for purposes of representation must exercise effective authority, be based on the consent of the population, be able and willing to achieve the purposes of the Charter and fulfill its obligations under the Charter and international law, and respect human rights and fundamental freedoms.[7]

The Lie memorandum and the American response to it marked the beginning of the confusion which surrounded the China issue until 1971. First, Lie's major criterion of "effective authority" was primarily a de facto political argument. The

American rebuttal emphasized the moral qualifications of the government to be represented. Thus, as Inis L. Claude has pointed out, "the treatment of the membership question as a political and moral problem [led] ultimately to the *confusion* of the issue."[8] Second, Lie's position did not make clear what would happen to the Nationalist government if the PRC were seated. Moreover, by invoking Article 4 of the Charter, which deals with the admission of members, the Secretary-General left himself open to the argument that he was confusing a problem of representation with one of admission. Finally, several nations, notably the United Kingdom, were placed in the anomalous position of recognizing the PRC on their own but dealing with the Nationalist government in the United Nations.

Strong American pressure prevented a vote on Mr. Lie's proposal. Instead, the entire debate on the Chinese representation question was transferred to the General Assembly when that body, on December 14, 1950, recommended that "whenever more than one authority claims to be the government entitled to represent a member state," the question should be considered "in the light of the Purposes and Principles of the Charter and the circumstances of each case," and that "the attitude adopted by the General Assembly should be taken into account in other organs of the United Nations and in the specialized agencies."[9] This resolution, while implying that the Assembly be a guide for other UN organs, also implied that each of the major UN organs should have the right, under its own rules of procedure, to decide on questions of representation. Hence, the state of China might be represented by the Nationalist government in one part of the United Nations but by the PRC in another.

This issue between the superpowers was now squarely joined. After boycotting the Council for a brief period, the Soviet Union returned in August 1950 to demand that the PRC be seated promptly in all organs of the United Nations as the legimate government of China and that the Nationalist government be ousted. The entire Soviet bloc, of course, supported this position, and a small number of other states also favored the seating of the PRC without, however, proposing the simultaneous ousting of the Chiang Kai-shek regime. Precisely how they would deal with the Nationalist government was not made clear. This coalition marshaled a number of arguments in favor of PRC representation in 1950. It was held that the United Nations would be more effective if it were universal and that events had shown that the PRC was in de facto control of continental China. Some states also felt that Communist China might be checked more effectively inside the United Nations than out, especially on matters of disarmament and arms control. The presence of other potentially aggressive states in the United Nations had, in any case, diluted the "peace-loving" provision in the Charter. Finally, it was argued that the Chinese veto would not add power to that of the USSR, which alone was sufficient to block Security Council action.

The opposing camp was led by the United States, which based its objections on the grounds that the PRC was an illegal, immoral, as well as a nonpermanent, government. The PRC's intervention in the Korean War and the General Assembly's finding of aggression underlined the "nonpeace-loving" character of the regime. To seat it would imply a condonement of aggression, according to this view, that might inspire other potential aggressors to try to "shoot their way" into the United Nations. In 1954, the United States, in its eagerness to keep the PRC out, asserted through Secretary of State John Foster Dulles that the veto power governing the admission of new members was also applicable, by necessary and unchallengeable analogy, to the issue of Chinese representation.[10] Indeed, the secretary of state went so far as to suggest that the veto could be eliminated on questions of admission but retained on matters of representation.[11]

From 1951 to 1960, the issue of Chinese representation came before every session of the General Assembly under the so-called moratorium device. Under this technique, the United States proposed each year that consideration of the question be deferred. This position was adopted by the Assembly at every session until 1960. See voting figures, page 40.[12]

The impact of changing UN membership policy may be seen clearly in the voting record on the China question. The absolute number of votes in favor of the moratorium remained fairly con-

Voting Patterns on Chinese Representation
under the Moratorium Device, 1951–1960

Session	For	Against	Abstaining	Absent	Total	Percent Supporting the U.S. Position
6th (1951)	37	11	4	8	60	61
7th (1952)	42	7	11	0	60	70
8th (1953)	44	10	2	4	60	73
9th (1954)	43	11	6	0	60	72
10th (1955)	42	12	6	0	60	70
11th (1956)	47	24	8	0	79	60
12th (1957)	48	27	7	0	82	59
13th (1958)	44	28	9	0	81	54
14th (1959)	44	29	9	0	82	54
15th (1960)	42	34	22	1	99	42

stant during the ten years, but since during this same period the membership of the United Nations grew by 65 percent, the relative percentage of states supporting the American position declined significantly. The U.S. position suffered its major losses in 1956 and 1960; 1956 was the first year in which the members admitted through the 1955 package deal voted on the issue. As a result, percentage support of the U.S. position dropped 10 points, and the direct opposition to the American position doubled in strength. The second major drop occurred in 1960, when seventeen new members joined the organization. Now the American position was in serious jeopardy, for the supporters of the moratorium won by only a plurality, and the combined votes of the opposition, abstainers, and absentees exceeded the U.S. position by 15 votes.

Hence, the change in UN membership policy was one factor that forced the United States to adopt new parliamentary tactics on the China question in 1961. In addition, it had become clear to many that the Communist regime was more than just a passing phase and was therefore entitled to membership. Many of the newly admitted states, which wanted expansion of the Security Council and of the Economic and Social Council, were aware that the Soviet Union would not permit revision of the Charter unless the PRC was admitted to its "rightful" seat in the United Nations. Finally, an increasing number of members felt that the United Nations could hardly expect Communist China to observe the UN Charter if at the same time the United Nations denied that nation membership status and the right to participate in UN proceedings.

On the other hand, quite apart from continued American pressure, the opposition to seating the PRC was still formidable. The PRC's position that it would accept nothing less than the expulsion of the "Taiwan clique" ruled out a "two-Chinas" solution that many members looked upon with favor. Moreover, if Peking was serious about the "restoration of China's legitimate rights" in Formosa and proceeded to "liberate" that island, then seating the PRC, in the opinion of many, would mean that "the UN should acquiesce in Communist China's design to conquer Taiwan and the 11 million people who live there and thereby to overthrow and abolish the independent government of the Republic of China."[13]

The Sixteenth General Assembly in 1961 marked the beginning of a new phase in the evolution of the Chinese representation issue. Not only had the membership of the Assembly changed, but momentous developments had taken place between the two Communist giants. Great fissures had begun to appear in the Moscow-Peking alliance, and an ideological controversy of the first magnitude was well under way. Yet, the USSR, in its public pronouncements, continued its ten-year-old agitation on behalf of Communist China.

The United States, in turn, had concluded that there was no hope of warding off a full-scale debate on the China issue. Therefore, it altered its tactics and, instead of trying to prevent debate, sought to have the issue debated in as favorable a form and climate as possible. First, the United States made a major move to obtain support for its position by agreeing to permit the simultaneous admission of Mongolia and Mauritania to UN membership. This, it was hoped, would help to win the good will of many African states on the China issue. Second, the United States was aware that a direct vote on a resolution to seat the PRC and eject the Nationalists was technically a matter of credentials, thus requiring only a simple majority vote. Hence, the American plan was to forestall such a vote by entering a draft resolution asking the Assembly to declare in advance that the China problem was an "important" question and therefore, in accordance with Article 18 of the Charter, one requiring a two-thirds majority.

The actual debate on the China question occupied twelve plenary sessions of the Assembly. During the debate, the major obstacle preventing a compromise was the attitude of the two Chinas themselves. The only thing that the Nationalists and the PRC were in agreement on was that neither would sit in the United Nations if the other China was also seated. The superpowers held to their opposing positions.

When the American-sponsored draft resolution declaring the Chinese representation issue an "important" question came to a vote on December 15, 1961, it was adopted by a vote of 61 to 34, with 7 abstentions and 3 absences. The Soviet proposal requiring the immediate seating of the PRC and the simultaneous ousting of the Chiang regime did not even get a simple majority. It was defeated by a vote of 48 against, 37 in favor, with 19 abstentions. A three-power (Cambodia, Ceylon, and Indonesia) amendment to the Soviet draft resolution, which would have provided for the seating of the PRC but did not propose the expulsion of the Nationalists, was also rejected by a vote of 45 against, 30 in favor, and 29 abstentions. Thus, the United States, by a judicious change in tactics, more than held the line in 1961.

When the Chinese question arose again at the Seventeenth General Assembly in October 1962, China had just launched her border attack on India in the Himalayas. This development undoubtedly heightened doubts about the willingness of the PRC to accept the the obligations of the Charter. India, however, continued to advocate the seating of Communist China, arguing that the "only way to check Chinese military adventurism was to make it accept its responsibilities as a member of the Organization and thereby be subject to the views and discipline of the General Assembly."[14]

The Soviet Union, despite the worsening of Sino-Soviet relations, attacked the two-Chinas solution and declared that "those who speak out against the presence of the People's Republic of China within the United Nations have missed the bus of history."[15] The United States stood fast.

When the vote was taken on October 30, it appeared that it was the Communists who had missed the bus. The Soviet resolution to eject Chiang's representatives and seat the PRC was rejected by a vote of 56 against and 42 in favor, with 12 abstentions. This vote indicated a definite shift against the PRC: The absolute number of votes against the PRC increased by 8, while those in favor increased by only 5. The 8 new votes against the PRC were cast by African nations which had abstained the previous year: Central African Republic, Chad, Congo (Brazzaville), Congo (Léopoldville), Dahomey, Ivory Coast, Niger, and Upper Volta. A spokesman for this group noted that these states still foresaw the eventual seating of Communist China but that they did not favor the exclusion of Nationalist China. He also questioned Peking's peaceful intentions in the light of the attack on India.[16] All in all, the year 1962 showed a significant reversal of the pro-PRC trend and much of the membership favoring a compromise solution. But those favoring a compromise were now closer to the American than to the Soviet position. In 1963, the voting pattern remained almost the same. An Albanian-sponsored draft resolution to oust Chiang and seat the PRC was defeated by a vote of 57 against, 41 in favor, with 12 abstentions.

No vote was taken in 1964. In 1965, an American-sponsored draft resolution declaring the Chinese representation issue an "important" question was adopted by a vote of 56 to 49, with 11 abstentions; and an Albanian proposal to seat the PRC and oust the Nationalist regime was defeated by a vote of 47 to 47, with 20 abstentions. Even though the former vote was decisive, since it ruled out the seating of the PRC by a simple majority, the United States was disturbed by the closeness of the vote on the issue itself. In 1966, however, the excesses of the Cultural Revolution had alienated some of the Afro-Asian nations, and the U.S. position gained once again. This time the vote making China an "important" question was 66 to 48, with 7 abstentions; and an Albanian proposal identical to the one advanced the previous year was defeated by a vote 56 against, 46 in favor, with 17 abstentions. An Italian-sponsored proposal to appoint a special committee to investigate the PRC's position vis-à-vis UN membership and to report to the Assembly by July 1967 was also defeated by a vote of 62 against and 34 in favor, with 25 abstentions. The patterns for 1967 and 1968 showed little change. In 1967, the votes on the three different aspects of the problem were 69–48–4, 58–45–17, and 57–32–30, respectively. In 1968, they were 73–47–51, 58–44–23, and 67–30–27.

As China began to normalize her foreign relations, UN sentiment in her favor began to rise once again. In 1969, the "important" question was adopted by a vote of 71 in favor, 48 against, with 4 abstentions, and the People's Republic was barred by a vote of 56 against and 48 in favor, with 21 abstentions. In 1970, the "important" question passed by the narrow vote of 66 in favor, 52 against, with 7 abstentions, and subsequently, a majority of 51 members actually voted to seat the People's Republic and to oust the Chiang Kai-shek regime. Forty-nine members opposed this move, and 25 abstained. Only the previously adopted resolution that it would take a two-thirds majority to seat the mainland government prevented its victory in 1970.

The moment of truth came in 1971. The China question was being debated at the very time of Presidential aide Henry Kissinger's visit to Peking to prepare President Nixon's forthcoming visit to the Chinese capital. The American position at the United Nations reflected this shift in policy. The emphasis was now placed on keeping Taiwan in rather than the People's Republic of China out. In the American view, Peking should be seated on the Security Council, while Taiwan would retain a seat in the General Assembly. Expulsion of the latter would be subject to a two-thirds vote. The United States had thus switched to a two-China, or more accurately, to a "one China, one Taiwan," position.

While it was Albania that continued to lead the fight for the exclusive right of the Peking regime to represent China, the Soviet Union strongly supported this position and emphasized the fact that it had done so for twenty-two years.

The denouement came on October 25, 1971. After a complicated procedural wrangle, the delegate of Saudi Arabia submitted a motion for postponement that was rejected by a vote of 53 in favor, 56 against, with 9 abstentions. A majority of delegates wanted a showdown right then and there. Since the United States was strongly in favor of postponement, this vote gave an indication of the final outcome. The next vote was crucial: whether the exclusion of the Chiang Kai-shek regime required a two-thirds vote. Despite intensive last-minute lobbying by the United States, the draft resolution was defeated by a vote of 59 against, 55 in favor, and 15 abstentions. The way was now clear for the Albanian draft, which was passed by an overwhelming vote of 76 in favor, 35 against, and 17 abstentions. (The voting figures are shown on this page.) After twenty-two years of diplomatic warfare, the United States had suffered its first dramatic parliamentary defeat. Peking was in, and Taiwan was out.

Voting Patterns on Chinese Representation from 1961–1971

Session	Resolution Declaring Matter "Important" Question			Proposal to Seat Peking and Exclude Taiwan		
	For	Against	Abstentions	For	Against	Abstentions
16th (1961)	61	34	7	38	48	20
17th (1962)	–	–	–	42	56	12
18th (1963)	–	–	–	41	57	12
19th (1964)			No Voting			
20th (1965)	56	49	11	47	47	20
21st (1966)	66	48	7	46	57	17
22nd (1967)	69	48	4	45	58	17
23rd (1968)	73	47	5	44	58	23
24th (1969)	71	48	4	48	56	21
25th (1970)	66	52	7	51	49	25
26th (1971)	55	59	15	76	35	17

China in the United Nations

For twenty-three years numerous Cassandras in the United States had predicted that the entry of the People's Republic into the United Nations would be a calamity for the Organization. Conversely, the Soviet Union, despite its deepening rift with China, had steadfastly defended the "restoration of her lawful right" to the seat. If one analyzes the record of the People's Republic in the Security Council and in the General Assembly thus far, one may legitimately wonder whether the long American resistance to Chinese representation was justified. The fact is that the new China managed to blend into the United Nations without undue stress or turmoil.

China's entry into the United Nations in late October 1971 occurred at a time when the World Organization was undergoing a profound transformation. The Soviet-American bipolar world had come to an end. Old alliances had begun to loosen and new ones were about to form. The old cleavage between Communists and capitalists was slowly being superseded by a new cleavage between the haves and have-nots of the world. It was almost as if a kaleidoscope had been shaken vigorously and the old patterns had disintegrated to form an entirely new constellation. A new generation had emerged with its own political priorities and its own definitions of what constituted a viable world order. In short, the postwar world was definitely over. China's entry at that very moment served as a catalyst that both reflected and accelerated a systemic change in the international order.

After five years of membership in the United Nations family, China already has a remarkable record of participation. This section will examine this record with particular attention to the main problems on the agendas of the Security Council and of the General Assembly on which China has taken positions. On the basis of this objective record an attempt to evaluate China's role in the United Nations to date will be made.

There have been five main problems that have been the concern of the Security Council since China's entry: the war between India and Pakistan; a broad range of African problems; the question of peace-keeping, with Cyprus in particular; the continuing crisis in the Middle East; and the problem of the Panama Canal.

China entered the Security Council during the Indo-Pakistan War. On that occasion the Security Council was paralyzed not because of the usual Soviet-American deadlock, but because of a confrontation between the Soviet Union and China. The three vetoes cast by the Soviet Union on behalf of her ally, India, were cast in essence against China and her ally, Pakistan. The level of discourse between the delegates of China and the Soviet Union reached levels of vituperation rarely matched in the history of the Security Council. Ironically enough, the Chinese delegate accused the Soviet Union's representative of the very transgressions of imperialism and colonialism with which the same Soviet delegate, twenty years earlier, had castigated the United States. It became clear on that occasion that the gulf between the two Great Communist Powers, China and the Soviet Union, was a great deal wider than that which separated China from the United States, or the Soviet Union from the United States. Several months after this fateful meeting, China cast her first veto against the admission of Bangladesh.

On the occasion of the Security Council's meeting in Addis Ababa, Ethiopia, in order to underline the rising importance of Third World problems, China made her first concerted and powerful bid for the ideological leadership of the smaller nations of the Third World. She vigorously supported all the resolutions that were adopted, or initiatives that were taken by the Council, against the white minority governments of South Africa and Southern Rhodesia. She emphasized again and again that she had nothing in common with the reprehensible behavior of the two superpowers, and that she, too, had suffered—as most of the nations of the Third World had suffered—from the yoke of Western incursions in the nineteenth century. Although the Soviet Union and China found themselves voting on the same side on many of these resolutions, China always took great pains to disassociate herself from the other Communist Power.

There was considerable anxiety in the United Nations that China's entry would mean the death of the last remaining major United Nations peace-keeping force still in existence, the United

Nations Force in Cyprus (UNFICYP). The Cyprus force was under the exclusive jurisdiction of the Security Council and depended for its life on extensions of its mandate, which had to be granted every six months. Since the main beneficiaries of the Cyprus force—Greece and Turkey—were both members of NATO, there was some anticipation that China, not particularly interested in making peace within NATO, would veto the operation. When the vote came, however, China abstained and has done so on every succeeding occasion, with the result that the Cyprus force continues to exist on the basis of an uneasy triangular consensus among China, the Soviet Union, and the United States.

China's appearance in the Security Council has not helped the quest for a solution to the continuing crisis in the Middle East. In fact, the spectrum of discord has widened. For the first time since their active participation in the Middle East conflict, the Palestinians found themselves a Great Power sponsor, namely China. China's greatest fear in the Middle East has been the possibility of a "collusion" between the two "establishment superpowers," the United States and the Soviet Union, with China excluded altogether. A Soviet-American compromise solution in the Middle East is the one China fears most, and hence, she has decided to back that political entity which is absolutely opposed to that compromise, the Palestinians. Nevertheless, when two new peace forces were created in 1973 and 1974 in order to separate Israeli forces and Egyptian and Syrian troops, China did not veto these initiatives, nor did she cast negative votes when the mandates of these peace forces were extended in 1974, 1975, and again in 1976.

The Security Council meeting in Panama afforded China another opportunity to underline her support for the Third World. The United States, on that occasion, was isolated in its position that the question of the Panama Canal was a bilateral affair between itself and Panama. Consequently America cast its third veto in the history of the Security Council. The other members of the Council felt that the problem was one of colonialism in the Western Hemisphere, and that it therefore deserved the multilateral attention of the United Nations. China supported this view with passion and once again, though voting on the same side as the Soviet Union, took pains to separate herself from Russia. Her objective to be the leader of the Third World became particularly clear at the Panama meeting.

China's main interest in the General Assembly has focused on six major problems: disarmament; development; environment; terrorism; the sea-bed; and finances.

China's position on disarmament problems has been plagued by a measure of ambiguity. On the one hand, she found herself unable openly to oppose a Soviet initiative for a world disarmament conference because that would have injured her position in the eyes of the Third World. On the other hand, to accede to radical disarmament would have frozen China's nuclear inferiority vis-à-vis the Soviet Union. It was difficult for China to escape from this dilemma, and finally she decided in favor of her right to continue nuclear tests, a position that was greeted by considerable displeasure in the Third World. In fact, a measure of support that the Chinese had gained among the smaller nations by virtue of her previous position on questions of colonialism was now canceled out. China has not adhered to the three main instruments of arms control that have been signed under the aegis of the General Assembly: the Outer Space Treaty, the Nuclear Non-proliferation Treaty, and the Sea-Bed Treaty. It is interesting to note, however, that China had not violated any of these treaties, in fact, and should she decide to accede to any of them, de jure, such a decision would not entail a major shift in policy.

Ambiguity has also marked China's position on the various United Nations programs pursuing economic development. In a sense, one can describe China's dilemma in this respect as an identity crisis since, on the one hand, she is an atomic Power in good standing, but on the other, she is still a poor and developing nation. China attempted to resolve this dilemma by supporting all initiatives taken by the Third World majority in the Assembly to enhance development programs and by pledging a fairly substantial sum to the United Nations Development Program.

China's role in the newly established United Nations Environment Program has been truly catalytic. China virtually stole the spotlight at the Stockholm Conference in June 1972 because the Soviet Union was absent and the United States observed a relatively low profile. Once again, China supported the position of the Third World countries, which defined environmental needs in developmental terms. The slogan "The polluter must pay" was of Chinese origin and was aimed with equal vehemence at both the Soviet Union and the United States. In this context, China also raised a fundamental philosophical question by pointing out that the United States, which has approximately 6 percent of the world's population, consumes over 50 percent of the world's ecological resources. The world, in China's view, could afford only one United States of America. But what if China decided to emulate the industrial model? The ecology of the planet would not be able to sustain it. The spectacle of 800 million poor Chinese may be a national tragedy, but the spectacle of 800 million rich Chinese would·be a planetary catastrophe. By raising these fundamental questions, China underlined the urgency of the environmental crisis and the need for a global approach to it. When the question of the location of the new Environmental Secretariat arose in December 1972, China strongly supported the Third World position of placing it in Nairobi, Kenya, which the United States opposed and on which the Soviet Union abstained. It was dramatic to note how, on that occasion, the old cleavage between the capitalist and Communist states was eclipsed by a new cleavage between the rich and the poor.

Similar fundamental questions were raised by China on the question of terrorism. The Chinese stated quite bluntly that national liberation groups, including the Palestinians, were justified in the use of force against the "establishment" Powers such as South Africa and Rhodesia, which were regarded by China as the real terrorists. In this connection, the Chinese resuscitated the old scholastic doctrine of the "just war," but conveniently sidestepped the thorny problem of defining it.

In her quest to become the major spokesman of the smaller nations, China supported their ambitious claims to territorial waters extending, in some cases, up to two hundred miles. On this occasion, the Chinese once again took the opportunity to chastise the superpowers. Perhaps the most interesting new initiative taken by China on this topic, however, was her position that the United Nations itself, rather than any single state, should have access to the resources of the sea-bed and of the ocean floor.

China played a constructive role in the bitter dispute between the Soviet Union and the United States over the American move to reduce the United States assessment to the regular budget from 31 to 25 percent. The Soviet Union had taken the position that, instead of being lowered, the American contribution should be raised to 38 percent. In the context of this debate, the Chinese came forward with an unprecedented offer to raise their contribution gradually over the next few years from 4 to 7 percent. When taken together, with the contributions of the two Germanys, which amounted to approximately 8 percent of the budget, it seemed that the deficit created by the American reduction was more than offset by contributions from China and the two Germanys.

China's entry into the United Nations coincided with the election of the fourth Secretary-General. On legal grounds alone, had China chosen to do so, she could have vetoed the election of a new Secretary-General. Not only did she acquiesce in the election of Mr. Kurt Waldheim, but she also displayed considerable sensitivity to the fate of a large number of Chinese nationals who were recruited into the Secretariat over the period of twenty-three years during which China was represented by the Chiang Kai-shek régime in Taiwan. Most of the staff members are still in the Secretariat and continue to perform their duties with a minimum of friction. The Mainland Government, in turn, is slowly bringing its own people into the Secretariat. For the time being, one of the places in the world where Chinese Communists and Chinese Nationalists manage to co-exist in the same physical location without any upheaval is the United Nations Secretariat.

Conclusions

An overall perspective of China's role in the United Nations demonstrates that she, like most other members of the world body, has pursued her national interests. She has tended to employ the United Nations as yet another instrument toward that objective. In that pursuit, her behavior has been pragmatic rather than ideological. It is interesting to note, for example, that although Maoist guerrillas were active in East Pakistan, China chose to support the Government of West Pakistan in its civil war. In that sense, China has placed Machiavelli above Mao Tse-tung.

It is useful to remember that of all the members of the United Nations, China probably has the least experience with a multilateral organization and the innumerable compromises and accommodations that membership in such a body entails. In the light of this fact, China's diplomats have done remarkably well in a relatively short time to learn the arts of negotiation and compromise. Like many other members, they have found themselves, at times, on the horns of dilemmas from which they had to extricate themselves. The conflicting objectives of wooing the Third World and of pursuing nuclear development are cases in point. China has managed to deal with these dilemmas with a fairly high degree of sophistication.

In retrospect the overall record suggests that China has been able to fit into the structure of the United Nations without excessive turbulence. Certainly, on several issues China's impact has been negative, but on many more the effect has been constructive. There is little doubt that, on the balance sheet, the credits exceed the debits. Perhaps, most significantly, China drew the world's attention to the urgency of the ecological problem. Since most Member States have a tendency to bring their problems to the United Nations at a very late stage and to make the United Nations a kind of receiver in bankruptcy, subsequently blaming it for that bankruptcy, China's initiative in this regard must be considered as a major contribution. Moreover, as the Great Powers continue to relegate the United Nations to the sidelines and negotiate the great policy issues outside of it, the fact that at least one major Power has taken up the cause of smaller nations, which feel increasingly ignored on the current global scene, is an auspicious development. Finally, from China's point of view, it is important to remember that for two thousand years she has considered herself to be the center of the universe, superior to all other nations whom she regarded as "barbarians." Then, in the nineteenth century, the scales were suddenly reversed: the "barbarians" invaded China and parceled her out among themselves. China's entry into the United Nations signifies the first time in her history that she has been compelled to deal with other states on the basis of sovereign equality.

SELECTED BIBLIOGRAPHY

Alker, Hayward R., Jr., and Bruce M. Russett. *World Politics in the General Assembly.* New Haven: Yale University Press, 1965.

Bailey, Sydney D. *The General Assembly of the United Nations.* rev. ed. New York: Praeger, 1964.

Hovet, Thomas, Jr. *Africa in the United Nations.* Evanston, Ill.: Northwestern University Press, 1963.

————. *Bloc Politics in the United Nations.* Cambridge, Mass.: Harvard University Press, 1960.

Kay, David A. *The New Nations in the United Nations, 1960–1967.* New York: Columbia University Press, 1970.

Rudzinski, Aleksander W. "Admission of New Members: The United Nations and the League of Nations." *International Conciliation,* no. 480 (April 1952).

Steiner, H. Arthur. "Communist China in the World Community." *International Conciliation,* no. 533 (May 1961).

Stoessinger, John G. *Nations in Darkness: China, Russia, and America.* New York: Random House, 1975.

NOTES

1. Advisory Opinion of the International Court of Justice on Condition of Admission of New Members to the United Nations, May 28, 1948. International Court of Justice, *Reports of Judgements, Advisory Opinions and Orders,* 1948, pp. 57–66.

2. *New York Times,* 11 November 1975.

3. Ibid., 12 November 1975.

4. Ibid., 15 July 1975.

5. Leland M. Goodrich, *The United Nations* (New York: Crowell, 1959), p. 100.

6. UN Doc. S/1466; Security Council, *Official Records,* Fifth year, Supplement 4, January 1-May 31, 1950.

7. Cited in Goodrich, op. cit., p. 101.

8. Inis L. Claude, Jr., *Swords into Plowshares,* 2d ed. (New York: Random House, 1959), p. 104. (Italics Claude's.)

9. Cited in H. Arthur Steiner, "Communist China in the World Community," *International Conciliation,* no. 533 (May 1961): 389–454.

10. *New York Times,* 9 July 1954. Cited by Claude, op. cit., p. 105.

11. Testimony of Mr. Dulles on January 18, 1954, *Charter Review Hearing,* Part I, pp. 7, 13, 18, 20. Cited by Claude, op. cit., p. 106.

12. Steiner, op. cit., p. 447.

13. Address by Adlai Stevenson, delegate of the United States to the Sixteenth General Assembly, December 1, 1961. In Richard P. Stebbins, ed., *Documents on American Foreign Relations* (New York: Harper & Row for the Council on Foreign Relations, 1961), p. 499.

14. *The United Nations Review* (November 1962): 33.

15. Ibid., p. 32.

16. Ibid., p. 33.

The Secretary-General: The American and Soviet Attacks on the Secretariat, 1952 and 1960

"Startling evidence has disclosed infiltration into the United Nations of an overwhelmingly large group of disloyal United States citizens, many of whom are clearly associated with the international Communist movement."

Presentment of U.S. Federal
Grand Jury, December 1952

"Everyone has heard how vigorously the imperialist countries defend the attitude of Mr. Hammarskjöld. Is it not clear whose interests he interprets and executes, whose 'saint' he is?"

Premier Nikita Khrushchev
UN General Assembly
October 3, 1960

"It may be true," said Dag Hammarskjöld shortly before he died, "that in a very deep, human sense there is no neutral individual, because everyone, if he is worth anything, has to have his ideas and ideals. ... But what I do claim is that even a man who is in that sense not neutral can very well undertake and carry through neutral actions because that is an act of integrity."[1] This statement, which was made in response to Premier Khrushchev's blunt assertion that no man could be neutral, probably best expresses the philosophical conception of the UN Secretary-Generalship.

One of the greatest fears of the founders of the United Nations was that the new World Organization would be no more than the sum of its parts—a group of delegates each loyal to his own nation and perceiving the world through the particular lenses of his own nationality. The men at San Francisco were deeply convinced that one important road to international order could be constructed by providing the United Nations with a nucleus of men and women who, for the duration of their tenure as world civil servants, would be loyal to the world community and not seek or receive instructions from any national government. It was this notion of international loyalty-building that provided the rationale for the Office of the Secretary-General and for his staff, the UN Secretariat.

The Office of the Secretary-General of the United Nations is not without precedent. The League of Nations had made provision for such a post. Its first incumbent, Sir Eric Drummond, a British civil servant, was primarily an administrator who made it his policy to remain aloof from the political disputes that were sapping the lifeblood of the League. Albert Thomas, on the other hand, the Director-General of the League's International Labor Organization, set quite another precedent. Not content with anonymous administrative responsibilities, he ventured into the uncharted lands of international statesmanship and took stands on controversial policy issues. Weighing these two precedents and seeing value in both, the UN architects endowed the Office of the UN Secretary-General with political as well as administrative powers. The Secretary-General was not only to be the chief administrative officer of the United Nations, but in the words of the Preparatory Commission in 1945, his Office was to represent

a quite special right which goes beyond any power previously accorded to the head of an international organization. The Secretary-General more than anyone else will stand for the United Nations as a whole. In the eyes of the world, no less than in the eyes of his own staff, he must embody the ideals and principles of the Charter.[2]

This conception of the Office led to the inclusion in the Charter of Articles 98 and 99, which set forth the Secretary-General's significant political powers. Under Article 98, the Secretary-General may be entrusted with broad discretionary powers by the major organs of the Organization. And under Article 99, "the Secretary-General may bring to the attention of the Security Council any matter which in his opinion may threaten the maintenance of international peace and security." The founders of the United Nations thus clearly intended the Secretary-General to be an international statesman, a kind of conscience of the world. In order to equip him adequately for this role, they gave him what, in some respects at least, amounted to the power of acting as a twelfth member of the Security Council.

Each of the superpowers at different times was involved in a frontal attack against the Office of the Secretary-General. In 1952, rampant forces of anticommunism in the United States aimed their attack on the authority of the Secretary-General as chief administrative officer of the Organization; in 1960, the Soviet Union attempted to paralyze the political initiative of the Secretary-General as international statesman with its "troika" proposal. The Secretariat and the Secretary-Generalship withstood both assaults, but not without major crises which shook the United Nations. A comparative analysis of these two events sheds important light on the U.S.-Soviet confrontation at the United Nations and its effects on the political evolution of the World Organization.

The American Attack

The first Secretary-General of the United Nations was Trygve Lie of Norway. Lie used his political powers abundantly and took positions in conflicts among the major powers from the very start. In 1946, he submitted a memorandum on his own initiative regarding the power of the Security Council to retain on the agenda an item on Soviet troop withdrawals from Iran. Two years later, he supported the European Recovery Program and opted in favor of the partition of Palestine. Soon thereafter, he became embroiled in political controversies of the first magnitude. Early in 1950, Mr. Lie advocated the seating of the Chinese Communist delegation in the United Nations and provoked the extreme displeasure of the United States. Several weeks later, he strongly supported American initiative in the police action to repel aggression by North Korea and went so far as to label the North Koreans as the aggressors. While this action reconciled the United States, it provoked the implacable hostility of the Soviet Union. When, in late 1950, the question of Lie's reappointment came up, the United States threatened to veto the appointment of any other candidate, while the Soviet Union declared with equal conviction that it would not tolerate Lie. The United States prevailed upon the General Assembly to "extend" his term for another three years. Yet, ironically, it was not from the Soviet Union but from the United States that the major attack on the Secretariat came during Trygve Lie's extended term.

The U.S. attack on the Secretariat during 1952 and 1953 had its roots in the American political conditions at the time. Early in 1950, the trial of Alger Hiss had raised the specter of Communist infiltration in positions of high official responsibility. Shortly thereafter, Senator Joseph McCarthy launched an attack on the State Department, claiming that it was infested with Communists. Although a special Senate subcommittee, the Tydings Committee, called McCarthy's charge "a fraud and a hoax" as early as July 1950, a connection was made in the public mind between these charges and recent setbacks in U.S. foreign policy, as in China.

At the same time, the United States was undergoing a difficult period of readjustment in the United Nations. The early, if overoptimistic, hopes for global peace through the World Organization had given way to the harsh realities of the cold war. The extensive use of the Soviet veto was resented by many Americans. The rising voices of colonial peoples put the United States into an embarrassing position between its revolutionary heritage of independence and its important NATO allies. Most important, the United States was bearing the brunt of a costly and bloody war in Korea and its protracted peace negotiations. These two trends—the fear of Communist infiltration, inspired by McCarthy, and disillusionment with the United Nations—were important ingredients in the American attack on the Secretariat.

During the summer of 1952, a Special Federal Grand Jury was impaneled in New York to investigate possible violations of U.S. laws by American citizens working in the UN Secretariat. The refusal of several staff members to answer questions about affiliations with the Communist party attracted the attention of the American public and of Secretary-General Trygve Lie.[3] On October 13, 1952, the day before the opening of the Seventh General Assembly, the Internal Security Subcommittee of the Senate Judiciary Committee moved to New York and opened public hearings on the activities of U.S. citizens employed by the United Nations. During these subcommittee sessions, held October 12–15, twenty-four current and four former employees of the United Nations testified. Of the twenty-four current employees, seventeen invoked the Fifth Amendment on questions related to past or present associations with the Communist party.[4] Of the seven current employees who did not invoke the Fifth Amendment, three admitted past membership in the Communist party, and a fourth was implicated by the testimony of an outside witness.[5]

Immediately following this testimony, Secretary-General Lie took rapid steps to try to stem the rising tide of American criticism. Because of the varying tenures of the UN employees and their different behavior before the Senate subcommittee, the Secretary-General was faced with three separate dilemmas. First, should he dismiss the three temporary American employees who admitted that they had once been Communists? Second, should he fire the seven temporary employees who had invoked the Fifth Amendment? And third, how should he deal with the ten permanent UN officials who had invoked their U.S. constitutional privilege of silence and who, as international civil servants, were protected by immunities?

Secretary-General Lie took a clear and immediate stand to discharge those temporary employees who admitted past Communist affiliations. First, he argued, an American Communist was not a representative American citizen, since the United States had declared the party subversive and dedicated to the forcible overthrow of its government. Second, because the UN Headquarters was in the United States, the Secretary-General felt that "it was plain common sense not to want any American Communists in the Secretariat."[6] He explained the presence of the few Communists by stating that haste in the hiring of personnel in 1946 had made adequate screening of applicants very difficult and that his requests to the Department of State and FBI for information on U.S. applicants at first had met with no response. When, in 1949, the State Department finally agreed to examine records of U.S. applicants for UN jobs, it still refused to provide the Secretary-General with adequate information upon which he could base an independent judgment. For example, not only had the evaluations been extremely slow in coming through, but they had usually been one-word summaries, such as "questionable" or "reject." The Secretary-General had not been willing to dismiss an employee on the basis of such limited material. Moreover, not until March 1, 1952, had the Secretary-General been empowered to dismiss temporary staff members without giving any other reason than that such action would be in the best interests of the Organization. Thus, he could not have dismissed UN employees on the basis of the U.S. reports even if he had wanted to.

The problem of temporary UN employees who refused to answer the Internal Security Subcommittee's questions was more complicated. Yet, the Secretary-General was of the opinion that these employees, too, should be dismissed. He defended his action as follows:

United Nations immunity extended only to acts of Secretariat members in their official capacity. It did not extend to their outside activities or private lives. I felt strongly that a United Nations official should cooperate fully with investigations conducted by an official agency of his own government, at least in those countries where Western democratic traditions protected him from the exercise of arbitrary power. . . . Furthermore by virtue of the very fact that a United Nations official was an international civil servant, special obligations were imposed upon him to conduct himself vis-à-vis the Member governments at all times in a manner above just reproach. This latter opinion was fully shared by the General Assembly when it adopted Article 1.4 of the Staff Regulations, which read:

> Members of the Secretariat shall conduct themselves at all times in a manner of conduct befitting their status as international civil servants. They shall not engage in any activity that is incompatible with the proper discharge of their duties with the United Nations. They shall avoid any action and in particular any kind of public pronouncement which may adversely reflect on their status. While they are not expected to give up their national sentiments or their political and religious convictions, they shall at all times bear in mind the reserve and tact incumbent upon them by reason of their international status.

I believed that to plead a privilege against self-incrimination, though it was a constitutional right, would be clearly in violation of Article 1.4, except in extraordinary circumstances.[7]

Lie also felt that these UN officials had to be discharged because they "tended under the circumstances to discredit the Secretariat as a whole, to cast suspicion on all the staff—and, still more serious, imperil the position of the Organization in the host country."[8] He therefore dismissed those Americans with temporary contracts who had invoked the Fifth Amendment. In all cases of dismissal, however, the Secretary-General first ascertained to his own satisfaction that the employees had, in fact, been connected with subversive organizations at one time.

The controversy centered on the third group: the ten staff members with permanent contracts who had refused to answer certain questions. Lie immediately placed the involved personnel on compulsory leave while he considered his next move. To aid him in reaching a decision, the Secretary-General, on October 27, constituted a special three-man panel of eminent international jurists, consisting of Messrs. E. S. Herbert, W. D. Mitchell, and P. Veldekens. This body, on November 29, 1952, recommended "the dismissal from the United Nations staff of all active members of the U.S. Communist Party or other organizations officially declared subversive."[9] They further recommended that all UN employees of U.S. nationality who refused to answer questions about their past or present Communist party membership should be dismissed because their action created a "suspicion of guilt." They claimed that such a refusal to answer questions was a fundamental breach of Article 1.4 of the Staff Regulations and that the Secretary-General was therefore empowered to dismiss the ten staff members with permanent contracts who had refused to cooperate with the Senate subcommittee. Finally, they advised the Secretary-General to be guided by the views of the host country in security matters.

Acting upon the advice of the jurists, Lie notified the employees that he would have to dismiss them if they did not state their intention to answer questions within three days. This they declined to do, and so, on December 4, they were formally discharged. Once again, however, Lie made a private investigation regarding each dismissal.

The discharge of the employees was ill-timed. Just two days before, on December 2, the Federal Grand Jury, which had held hearings throughout this period, made its public presentment. It declared that "startling evidence [had] disclosed infiltration into the United Nations of an overwhelmingly large group of disloyal United States citizens, many of whom [were] closely associated with the international Communist movement."[10] Previous criminal records and morals charges of American UN officials were also publicized. The Grand Jury presentment concluded by saying that it had found that "in some of the most flagrant and obvious cases of disloyalty, the State Department [had given] a clean bill of health."

Unfortunately, the dismissal of the Secretariat employees two days after the Grand Jury report seemed to confirm the presumption that the United Nations was indeed harboring subversives. Ironically, Lie's action had been based entirely upon the performance of the Secretariat employees at the Senate subcommittee hearings, since no copy of the Grand Jury proceedings had been available. In addition, the Grand Jury presentment, while it leveled a general charge against the United Nations, did not return a single indictment. As Trygve Lie later noted: "Had there been any meaningful evidence of illegal subversive activity against any member of the Secretariat, it would have returned indictments in accordance with its duty. It did not return even one; but its 'presentment' made a blanket and indiscriminate finding of 'Guilty.' "[11]

Lie's troubles did not end with the dismissals; they had only begun. Sentiment throughout the United States was rising against the United Nations as well as the State Department, which allegedly had cleared some of the persons involved. On January 1, 1953, the State Department, perhaps in an effort to relieve the heat on itself, supplied the Internal Security Subcommittee with a list of thirty-eight UN Secretariat employees who had received "adverse comments" in their loyalty reports. At the time the list was released, twenty-seven of the thirty-eight were no longer employed by the United Nations.[12] On January 7, 1953, Senator Pat McCarran introduced a bill to prevent citizens of questionable loyalty from accepting employment in the United Nations and proposed a procedure whereby any American applying for a UN job would first have to be cleared by the FBI and other U.S. security agencies. At one point, U.S. investigators actually moved into UN buildings to check existing UN employees of U.S. nationality. In psychological and symbolic terms, this was probably more damaging than the establishment of routine procedure for clearing new applicants for the staff. Lie, in an attempt to reassure the American public, stated in his report of January 30 that "the UN work[ed] in a glass house, not only physically, but in every respect. It [was] not a profitable place for spies and saboteurs. No military secrets [were] ever handled by the Secretariat."[13] Nevertheless, both the Grand Jury and two Senate subcommittees continued investigations of UN personnel in 1953.

In all, twenty temporary and permanent employees had been discharged from the UN Secretariat during 1952 for admitting past membership in the Communist party or for invoking the Fifth Amendment. One additional staff member, who invoked the Fifth Amendment at hearings early in 1953, was also dismissed. These twenty-one employees brought their cases before the UN Administrative Tribunal, an impartial appeal board for aggrieved UN employees. On September 1, 1953, the Tribunal ruled that one of the ten temporary employees had been fired in breach of contract and that ten of the eleven permanent employees had been fired illegally. The Tribunal ordered reinstatement in four cases and compensation in lieu of reinstatement in the other seven.[14] Thus, the Secretary-General was faced with a new dilemma: How should he react to the decision of a UN Tribunal which had ruled against the obvious wishes of a superpower?

Lie decided not to reinstate any of the discharged Secretariat members. The Administrative Tribunal therefore reconsidered these four cases and, on October 13, 1953, fixed total compensation for the entire group of eleven. They were awarded full salary up to the date of the Tribunal's judgment plus $300 each for legal costs. Total compensation for the illegal firing was fixed at $170,-730, plus pension rights in one case.[15] The United States bitterly contested this ruling and held that the General Assembly was not obligated to accept it. The Assembly, in turn, on December 9, referred the question to the International Court for an advisory opinion.[16]

On July 13, 1954, the International Court of Justice, in a 9-to-3 opinion, with the American justice in dissent, supported the ruling of the Administrative Tribunal.[17] Total compensation was eventually fixed at $179,420.[18] The U.S. Congress declared that no American funds paid to the United Nations could be used to pay compensation to the dismissed officials.[19] Thus, Lie faced yet another problem: how to pay the compensation costs? To cooperate with the American government in meeting the issue presented by Congress, the money was paid not out of the UN's regular budget but out of the Tax Equalization Fund. Since this Fund was supported not by contributions from member states but by the UN staff in order to equalize tax burdens, the device adopted met the congressional stipulation.

One additional hurdle remained: the U.S. requirement that American citizens applying for positions with the United Nations be cleared first by the U.S. government. After the crisis had passed, an arrangement for security clearances was worked out between the American government and the United Nations. Under this agreement, each applicant must be processed by the U.S. security system. The American government reserved to itself the right to give information and advice to the Secretariat on the basis of its investigations but not to dictate personnel policy. In practice, nevertheless, it did not prove difficult, on at least one occasion, for the Secretary-General to decline the "advice" of Washington. In 1954, for example, Ambassador Henry Cabot Lodge sharply criticized the Director-General of UNESCO for not dismissing summarily all Americans on his staff who had received negative loyalty reports.[20] In recent years, there have been no major clashes over the issue, but it is nevertheless true that the U.S. government wields significant potential power over UN personnel policy, which may border on an infringement of the Secretary-General's role as the UN's chief administrative officer.

The entire episode, if looked at in perspective, suggests several important conclusions. First, it is important to remember that the State Department and the executive of the U.S. government did not launch the attack. It was precipitated by the extremists in the American public and by reactionary elements in the Congress. The executive was caught in the middle between domestic pressures and international responsibilities. The pressure exerted on the executive branch made it necessary to urge the Secretary-General to give in to the demands. Second, the Secretary-General largely complied with all the American demands, though not always in the summary fashion demanded of him. The crisis was composed of five separate parts: the discharge of temporary employees, the discharge of permanent employees, the decision of the Administrative Tribunal to reinstate four employees, the payment of compensation, and the security-clearance system. The United States had its way on each point, except the payment of compensation, although the United Nations did meet congressional stipulations regarding the method of payment. Whatever the intrinsic merits of the case, the Secretary-General found it virtually impossible to resist the pressure of the American superpower. As one authority put it, "[The Secretary-General] believed that the Communist problem in the Secretariat was objectively a molehill, but recognized that it had become a subjective mountain which had to be removed if the United Nations was not to be destroyed by the withdrawal of American public support."[21]

Third, and perhaps most important, the Secretariat recovered its balance. It gave ground on certain important points during the crisis, but the fundamental principles of the international civil service and the independence of the Secretary-General were not destroyed. The Secretariat weathered the American attack in 1952 and 1953, just as it had endured the Soviet three-year boycott of Trygve Lie from 1950 to 1953 and would endure the Soviet assault to be analyzed below. But there was irony as well as pathos in the American attack, because at that time the Secretary-General was already under heavy censure and even boycott by the Soviet bloc. As Trygve Lie poignantly wrote, looking back on the period:

Their [the Soviets'] three years' boycott had been the crudest form of pressure against the independence of the Secretary-General, and the most flagrant violation of Article 100 of the Charter; and there had been continuous vilification and abuse of me and my staff by the Soviet press since 1950. The central theme of it all had been that the Secretariat was dominated by Americans, and that they and I were in all respects tools of Wall Street and Washington. In the light of such charges, it was indeed ironic that the Secretariat should have been subjected at the same time to attacks in the United States for exactly opposite reasons.[22]

The Soviet Attack

The setting in which the Soviet Union mounted its assault on the Secretary-General in 1960 was very different from that of 1952. The membership of the Organization had almost doubled as a result of the influx of many new nations from the developing areas of the world. These were beginning to wield considerable power in the General Assembly. The tensions between the two superpowers had not abated, but numerous minor crises and at least two major ones—in Hungary and Suez—had been weathered short of catastrophe. The United Nations itself had evolved novel techniques of keeping the peace by interposing buffer forces between the major contestants in the Middle East and in the Congo. The Office of the Secretary-General itself had undergone a significant political evolution since the election of its second incumbent, Dag Hammarskjöld, in 1953. It was this new role of the Secretary-General that prompted the Soviet attack. Hammarskjöld's background was very different from that of his predecessor. He had been an economist and chairman of the Swedish National Bank as well as deputy minister for foreign affairs. He had never been a member of a political party and was known to have a "passion for anonymity." In short, he was a civil servant, not a politician. Unlike Lie, Hammarskjöld at first chose not to take overt political initiative. Public diplomacy was replaced by "quiet diplomacy." This is not to say that the ferocity of the East-West struggle left the new Secretary-General untouched. But Mr. Hammarskjöld's approach to political disputes differed in two important respects from that of his predecessor. First, he always attempted to gain authority for his actions from the Security Council or the General Assembly, even though this authority was often broad and vaguely worded. Second, most of his diplomatic maneuvers were carried on behind the scenes, away from the searchlight of publicity. The former habit gained him the confidence of the major powers, while the latter made possible agreements without serious loss of face for any nation. A quick survey of Hammarskjöld's major activities before the Congo crisis erupted reveals how active quiet diplomacy can be.

In 1954, the Secretary-General flew to Peking to negotiate the release of eleven American airmen who were interned there as UN personnel. Virtually no publicity was released about the trip, but a year later the airmen were released. In 1956, during the Suez crisis, the Secretary-General improvised the UN Emergency Force which helped restore the *status quo ante bellum* in the Middle East. After his unanimous election to a second five-year term of office, there developed a growing tendency in both the General Assembly and the Security Council to grant the Secretary-General broad powers for the exercise of his quiet diplomacy. Thus, the Assembly requested Hammarskjöld to facilitate the withdrawal of foreign troops during the Lebanese crisis in 1958. And when, in mid-1960, the Belgian withdrawal from the Congo left the new republic strife-torn and threatened by superpower intervention on the model of the Spanish Civil War, the talents of the Secretary-General were called upon once more. Acting under the authority of the Security Council, he organized a UN Force, excluding the superpowers, which was to restore peace and order in the Congo until responsible self-government could be established. When the Congo was threatened by civil war through the secession of the province of Katanga, Hammarskjöld—again after securing Security Council authoritization—entered Katanga at the head of the UN Force to prevent a major conflagration.

As the Congo crisis developed further, however, Hammarskjöld began to run into major difficulties. A power struggle erupted between the two leading political figures in the Congo—President Joseph Kasavubu and Premier Patrice Lumumba. Kasavubu, conservative and mildly pro-Western, "dismissed" Lumumba, and Lumumba—radical, volatile, and virulently anticolonial—in turn "dismissed" Kasavubu. The Secretary-General refused to embroil the United Nations in this internal struggle, but the superpowers took opposing sides, the United States throwing its support behind Kasavubu and the Soviet Union behind Lumumba.

The Soviet Union had attempted to shore up Lumumba's position by sending transport planes, trucks and arms. The Secretary-General requested that these shipments cease, since they were contravening his plan to insulate the Congo from superpower involvement. When Andrew W. Cordier, Hammarskjöld's special representative in the Congo, decided to close airports and radio stations in order to prevent the spread of inflammatory propaganda and the extension of civil war, the Soviet Union again accused the Secretary-General of neocolonialism. And when, in early September 1960, Ceylon and Tunisia proposed a resolution in the Security Council that "no assistance for military purposes be sent to the Congo except as part of the UN action," the Soviet Union vetoed it.[23] Thus, the stage was set for a massive attack by the Soviet Union against the Office and person of the Secretary-General.[24]

The Fifteenth Session of the General Assembly opened in September 1960 with a gathering of heads of states unprecedented since the days of the Congress of Vienna. The two superpowers were also represented by their respective national leaders. On September 22, President Eisenhower fully endorsed the actions of the Secretary-General in the Congo. But on the following day, Premier Khrushchev led the Soviet assault.

The Soviet premier claimed that the Secretary-General was pro-Western and that the UN executive was not representative of a true balance of forces in the world. He declared that Hammarskjöld was abusing the prerogatives of his office and that the Congo Force was aiding the aims of the colonialists. Finally, he urged the replacement of the Secretary-Generalship with a three-man directorate:

The conditions appear to be ripe for abolishing the post of Secretary-General, who is now the sole administrator of the Office, the sole interpreter and executor of Security Council and General Assembly decisions. . . .

It is necessary that the executive agency of the United Nations reflect the actual situation now obtaining in the world. The United Nations includes member states of the military blocs of the Western powers, socialist states and neutralist countries. . . .

We deem it wise and fair that the United Nations executive agency consist not of one person, the Secretary-General, but of three persons enjoying the confidence of the United Nations—representatives of the states belonging to the three basic groups mentioned above.

In short, we think it would be wise to replace the Secretary-General, who is now the sole interpreter and executor of the decisions of the Assembly and the Security Council, by a collective UN executive agency consisting of three persons, each representing a definite group of states. This would provide a definite guarantee that the activity of the UN executive agency would not prove detrimental to one of these groups of states. The UN executive agency would then be a truly democratic body; it would truly safeguard the interests of all UN member states, irrespective of their social and political systems.[25]

This troika proposal, as it was quickly dubbed, was immediately seen by most of the assembled delegates as a thinly disguised attempt to emasculate the Office of the Secretary-General. A three-man directorate in which each triumvir would have a veto over the actions of the Organization would clearly reduce UN effectiveness to the lowest common denominator. It would extend the veto power into the Secretariat and turn it into a kind of "super Security Council." Moreover, it would make it possible for one of the triumvirs to interrupt a UN operation in midstream, something which had never been possible before. Finally, the division of the triumvirate into three camps not only seemed arbitrary and imprecise but would mean that the three Secretaries-General would merely reflect the cold war rather than try to transcend it. On the whole, the troika seemed the perfect formula for total paralysis.

Hammarskjöld's reply to Khrushchev's invitation to "resign in a chivalrous manner" was dignified and eloquent. He stated that he was not beholden primarily to the Great Powers, but "to all the others" who depended upon a strong and effective United Nations. He told the Assembly that he would rather see the Office of the Secretary-General "break on strict adherence to the principles of independence, impartiality, and objectivity than drift on the basis of compromise."[26] He noted that it would be easier to resign than to resist the assault of the Soviet Union but declared that his resignation would mean a Soviet veto of any successor and thus the end of an effective UN executive. "The man does not count, the institution does," he concluded.

The Assembly affirmed the Secretary-General's stand with a resounding vote of confidence of 83 in favor, 11 against, and 5 abstentions. The Soviet proposal did receive some consideration from the new nations. Premier Nkrumah of Ghana offered a plan to equip the Secretary-General with three deputies, chosen from the East, West, and neutralist blocs, each with "clearly defined authority" in UN affairs. This would have meant the introduction of the troika at a somewhat lower level. And Prime Minister Nehru of India proposed an advisory committee from different geographic areas, a sort of inner cabinet whose views and perhaps even approval would have to be sought on any important matters. None of these suggestions was adopted, however. The United States in particular hoped that the troika was dead. But a Moscow editorial noted that "the seeds have been sown and would bear fruit." The Soviet Union had not abandoned its plan but merely postponed its attack until a more propitious moment.

The announcment of the murder of Patrice Lumumba in Katanga province in February 1961 brought forth a renewed Soviet attack on the United Nations in general and on the Secretary-General in particular. On a level of vituperation rarely matched even by previous Soviet attacks, the Secretary-General was held personally responsible for Lumumba's murder. The USSR demanded that the Congo Force be withdrawn within a month and called for the removal of "Dag Hammarskjöld from the Office of Secretary-General as an accomplice and organizer of the murder of leading statesmen of the Congo Republic, who [had] stained the name of the United Nations." For its part, "the Soviet Government [would] not maintain any relations with Hammarskjöld and [would] not recognize him as an official of the United Nations."[27]

Hammarskjöld now found himself in the position of former Secretary-General Trygve Lie, from whom the Soviets had also withdrawn recognition when his actions had gone against their will. Nevertheless, Hammarskjöld repeated his pledge of October 3, 1960, not to resign so long as the uncommitted countries wished him to remain.[28] The USSR not only continued its attacks on the Secretary-General but now broadened its troika proposal to cover the Secretariat as a whole. Insisting that there were "no neutral men," the Soviet Union demanded greater Afro-Asian and Soviet representation in the Secretariat, particularly at the higher levels. The United States stood solidly behind the Secretary-General.

Dag Hammarskjöld presented his own political testament in the Introduction to his last Annual Report in August 1961. He distinguished between two views of the United Nations: The Organization could be conceived as a "static conference machinery," or it could be a "dynamic instrument" that could take executive action and resolve or forestall conflicts. In his Report, he clearly favored the latter view, thus rejecting the implications of the troika. Khrushchev responded by stating that "even if all the countries of the world adopted a decision that did not accord with the interests of the Soviet Union, the Soviet Union would not recognize such a decision but would uphold its rights, relying on force."[29]

The tragic death of Dag Hammarskjöld on the eve of the opening of the Sixteenth General Assembly not only plunged most of the delegates into profound grief but caused considerable anxiety, since the Soviet Union had a veto over the election of a successor. Actually, however, the Soviet leadership was quite aware that it could not get the troika plan through the Assembly but hopeful that it would be able to effect a drastic cutback in the power of the Office by holding out for a modified triumvirate— the rotation of the Secretary-Generalship among three undersecretaries representing the major blocs.

The United States now attempted to rally the General Assembly behind its view that the Secretary-General's authority must not be compromised and that a single person be named in an acting capacity until a new Secretary-General could be elected. President Kennedy expressed this view forcefully before the Assembly:

However difficult it may be to fill Mr. Hammarskjöld's place, it can better be filled by one man rather than by three. Even the three horses of the troika did not have three drivers, all going in different directions. They had only one, and so must the United Nations executive. To install a triumvirate, or any rotating authority, in the United Nations administrative offices would replace order with anarchy, action with paralysis, and confidence with confusion.[30]

In response, the Soviet Union, on September 27, proposed that the post of Secretary-General be left vacant and that four undersecretaries—from the United States, the Soviet Union, Africa, and Asia—collectively take charge of the functions of the Office, rotating a temporary chairmanship among themselves. This plan found little, if any, support in the Assembly.

Most of the membership supported a single successor, to be elected in the customary manner. On October 1, the Soviet Union backed down another step and suggested a compromise in which an acting Secretary-General would be elected who would operate "in the spirit of accord" with three undersecretaries, one from each political bloc. This lower-level troika also found no support. Finally, in intense negotiations between U.S. Ambassador Adlai Stevenson and Soviet Ambassador Valerian Zorin, it was agreed that the undersecretaries would have no veto over the Secretary-General's actions and that—since no exact number of undersecretaries could be agreed upon—the Secretary-General himself would choose a limited number *after* his election to serve as his principal advisors. This selection was to be based on geographic distribution rather than on ideological blocs. On November 3, 1961, the General Assembly, upon recommendation of the Security Council, unanimously named U Thant of Burma Acting Secretary-General for the remainder of Hammarskjöld's term.

This decision postponed the troika issue until April 10, 1963, when Hammarskjöld's term of office was to expire. But Soviet reservations about Acting Secretary-General U Thant apparently were dispelled by his conciliatory mediation during the Cuban crisis of 1962. After private superpower negotiations, the Security Council unanimously recommended, and the General Assembly unanimously approved, the election of U Thant to a full term as Secretary-General retroactive, according to his own wish, to his designation as Acting Secretary-General on November 3, 1961.

Three possible explanations suggest themselves for the Soviet relinquishment of the troika plan. In the first place, the proposal found little or no support among the uncommitted nations, and the Soviets were fearful of defying the wishes of that large and influential group of nations, most of which happened to agree with the American point of view. Second, UN policy in the Congo after Hammarskjöld's death was run by the "Congo Club," headed by two American Secretariat officials—Ralph Bunche and Andrew Cordier—who simply continued the Secretary-General's policy in the Congo. The Soviets probably thought that a neutralist Acting Secretary-General might be more tractable than leadership of the Secretariat by American officials for an indefinite period. Finally, the Soviet Union retained the power to veto the election of a permanent Secretary-General after the expiration of Hammarskjöld's term. All in all, however, the appointment of U Thant for a full five-year term marked a threefold Soviet concession: "instead of a 'troika,' a single individual was named; he was not required to make any prior commitments to the states sponsoring him; his authority was not circumscribed either by agreement or by the impinging prerogatives of political deputies."[31] The institution of the Office of the Secretary-General as designated under the UN Charter had survived another assault by a superpower.

Conclusions

Both the American and the Soviet attacks on the Secretariat were the result of fear that the Secretary-General was favoring the other superpower. The heart of the position of certain powerful American critics in the early 1950's was the contention that U.S. nationals of questionable loyalty in the UN Secretariat were helping the Communist cause, while the heart of the Soviet position in the early 1960's was the insistence that the Secretary-General was supporting American policy in the Congo. Each superpower saw the influence of the other in the actions of the Secretariat, and each attacked that institution in an attempt to protect its national interest.

The differences between the two attacks, however, are perhaps more significant than the similarities. First, the sources of the attacks were different. The American executive did not mount the assault as an act of U.S. policy but permitted the United Nations to be exposed to the pressure of extremist elements in Congress and did little to protect the integrity of the Secretariat. The troika proposal, on the other hand, clearly emanated from the Soviet government as an official act of national policy. Second, the goals of the superpowers differed. The United States never questioned the institution of the UN chief executive, although the Congress was prepared to infringe on the independence of the international civil service. The Soviet Union, however, wanted not only to remove the incumbent Secretary-General but to emasculate the Office. Third, the circumstances of the two cases were entirely different. One involved personnel policy and affected few if any UN members besides the United States; the other was a frontal attack on the very institution of the Secretary-General and aroused the passions of most of the membership. Finally, the United States basically won its battle, whereas the Soviet Union lost, a fact that provides an interesting illustration of the relative power positions of the superpowers in the United Nations at these two different periods. In 1952, the American government was the host country, the largest financial contributor, commanded a two-thirds majority in the General Assembly, and fought its battle on an issue that in the General Assembly, and fought its battle on an issue that most members regarded as a private matter between the United States and the United Nations. In 1960 and 1961, the Soviet Union, on the other hand, confronted an enlarged Assembly with a proposal that affected everyone and that, according to most members, had no basis in the Charter.

Perhaps most important, however, is the fact that the UN Secretariat weathered both attacks. The principle of independence of the Secretariat was reaffirmed, and UN personnel policy today no longer has the haphazard quality of the early days. Similarly, the troika was shelved, and the capacity of the Secretary-General as a political mediator and international statesman has continued to evolve. In short, at times both superpowers have been involved in attacks on the Secretariat in order to protect their national interests but in each case the negative effect was temporary. Indeed, a case may be made for the proposition that, particularly in the Soviet affair, the attack provided the momentum for a subsequent reaffirmation of the integrity of the Secretariat by a large majority of member states, which left the Office with stronger and more articulate support than before.

SELECTED BIBLIOGRAPHY

Bailey, Sydney D. *The Secretariat of the United Nations.* New York: Carnegie Endowment, 1962.

Foote, Wilder T., ed. *Dag Hammarskjöld, Servant of Peace: A Selection of His Speeches and Statements.* New York: Harper & Row, 1962.

Gordenker, Leon. *The UN Secretary-General and the Maintenance of Peace.* New York: Columbia University Press, 1967.

Lash, Joseph P. *Dag Hammarskjöld, Custodian of the Brushfire Peace.* Garden City, N.Y.: Doubleday, 1961.

Lie, Trygve. *In the Cause of Peace.* New York: Macmillan, 1954.

Rovine, Arthur W. *First Fifty Years: The Secretary-General in World Politics, 1920–1970.* New York: Humanities Press, 1971.

Urquhart, Brian. *Hammarskjöld: The Diplomacy of Crisis.* New York: Knopf, 1972.

Zacher, Marc. *Dag Hammarskjöld's United Nations.* New York: Columbia University Press, 1969.

NOTES

1. Cited in Wilder Foote, ed., *Dag Hammarskjold, Servant of Peace: A Selection of His Speeches and Statements* (New York: Harper & Row, 1962), p. 351.

2. Cited by H. C. Nicholas, *The United Nations as a Political Institution* (New York: Oxford University Press, 1959), p. 153.

3. Report of the Secretary-General on Personnel Policy (January 30, 1953), UN Doc. A/2364, p. 19.

4. Ibid., p. 10.

5. Ibid.

6. Trygve Lie, *In the Cause of Peace* (New York: Macmillan, 1954), p. 388.

7. Ibid., pp. 395–396.

8. Ibid., p. 397.

9. *New York Times,* 1 December 1952.

10. *New York Times,* 3 December 1952.

11. Lie, op. cit., pp. 400–401.

12. UN Doc. A/2364, op. cit., p. 10.

13. Ibid., p. 55.

14. Report of the Secretary-General on Personnel Policy (November 21, 1953), UN Doc. A/2533, p. 17.

15. Ibid.

16. The vote was 41 to 6, with the United States and 12 other members abstaining. Res. 785, VIII (December 9, 1953).

17. "Effect of Awards of Compensation Made by the U.N. Administrative Tribunal, Advisory Opinion of July 13th, 1954," *ICJ Reports* (1954): 47.

18. Richard P. Stebbins, ed., *The U.S. in World Affairs* (New York: Harper & Row for the Council on Foreign Relations, 1953), p. 398.

19. House Congressional Res. 262, 83d Congress (August 20, 1954).

20. *New York Times,* 17 October 1954.

21. Inis L. Claude, Jr., *Swords into Plowshares,* 3d ed. (New York: Random House, 1964), p. 187.

22. Lie, op. cit., p. 404.

23. Draft Resolution submitted to the Security Council by Tunisia and Ceylon on September 16, 1960 (S/4523), defeated on September 17 by a vote of 8 to 2 (USSR and Poland), with France abstaining.

24. For a more complete discussion and analysis of the United Nations in the Congo, see Chapters 5 and 6.

25. Address by Premier Nikita Khrushchev to the General Assembly, September 23, 1960; cited in Richard P. Stebbins, ed., *Documents on American Foreign*

Relations, 1960 (New York: Harper & Row for the Council on Foreign Relations), pp. 563–569.

26. *New York Times*, 27 September 1960.

27. Text of the Soviet Government's Statement on the Death of Patrice Lumumba, February 14, 1961, in Richard P. Stebbins, ed., *Documents on American Foreign Relations, 1961* (New York: Harper & Row for the Council on Foreign Relations), pp. 337–340.

28. Statement to the Security Council, February 15, 1961; *New York Times*, 16 February 1961.

29. Alexander Dallin, *The Soviet Union at the United Nations* (New York: Praeger, 1962), p. 205.

30. Address by President Kennedy to the General Assembly, September 25, 1961, in Richard P. Stebbins, ed., *Documents on American Foreign Relations, 1961* (New York: Harper & Row for the Council on Foreign Relations), pp. 473–484.

31. Dallin, op. cit., p. 176.

PART TWO

The Superpowers
and United Nations
Peace-Keeping Operations

The Middle East Crises of 1956, 1967, and 1973 and United Nations Peace-Keeping Forces

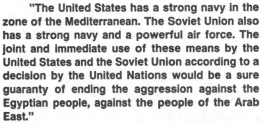

"The United States has a strong navy in the zone of the Mediterranean. The Soviet Union also has a strong navy and a powerful air force. The joint and immediate use of these means by the United States and the Soviet Union according to a decision by the United Nations would be a sure guaranty of ending the aggression against the Egyptian people, against the people of the Arab East."

Letter from Soviet Premier Bulganin
to President Eisenhower,
November 5, 1956

"The President has just received a letter from Chairman Bulganin which had been previously released to the press in Moscow. This letter—in an obvious attempt to divert world attention from the Hungarian tragedy—makes the unthinkable suggestion that the United States join with the Soviet Union in a bi-partite employment of their military forces to stop the fighting in Egypt."

Response by the White House
to Chairman Bulganin's letter,
November 5, 1956

Perhaps the most important responsibility of the United Nations lies in its avowed intention, proclaimed in the Charter, "to save succeeding generations from the scourge of war." The United Nations has already had considerable experience with a variety of peace-keeping operations, a great deal more, in fact, than the League of Nations had during its entire lifetime. All of them have been distinctive, and few generalizations are possible about them as a group. There was the Korean police action in the early 1950's, which actually was a war fought to a stalemate. UNEF in 1956 was the first international peace force, followed soon by ONUC, the far more ambitious and complex experiment in peace-keeping in the Congo. In 1964, the Security Council dispatched a peace force to Cyprus. In 1973, the Council authorized UNEF II, a modest force that served as a buffer between Israeli and Egyptian troops in the wake of the October war. And in 1974, a small force was interposed between Israeli and Syrian troops on the Golan Heights. In addition, the United Nations has sent into the field a number of observers and presences: Kashmir, Palestine, Lebanon, Laos, and Yemen are only some of the places which have benefited from these minor peace-keeping operations. There has been, indeed, a permanent procession of such activities, created and directed by the world organization.

In all of these experiments in peace-keeping, the superpowers have been involved either directly or indirectly. This analysis will limit itself to the interaction between the superpowers in Africa and in the Middle East. Hence, we shall consider four of the most significant peace-keeping operations mounted by the United Nations during the 1960's and 1970's: the UN Congo Force, the two UN Emergency Forces in the Sinai, and the UN Disengagement Observer Force in the Golan Heights. Since the problem of financing UNEF I and the Congo Force almost bankrupted the United Nations, and since the dispute between the superpowers over payments was mainly responsible for this, the final chapter of Part Two concludes with an analysis of that crisis.

The Middle East Crises
of 1956, 1967, and 1973
and the Superpowers

One of the strangest phases in the relationship between the two superpowers occurred in the winter of 1956 in the Middle East. During that "winter of discontent" three different yet interrelated struggles were approaching a climax: The hostility between Israel and the Arab states was escalating toward open combat; the new nationalism of Egypt was becoming increasingly belligerent toward Anglo-French colonialism; and the competition between the Soviet Union and the United States overarched the entire Middle East.

The crisis was precipitated in the summer of 1956, when President Gamal Abdel Nasser of Egypt nationalized the Suez Canal Company, abrogating in the eyes of Britain and France the International Convention of Constantinople of 1888, which had provided that "the Suez Maritime Canal shall always be free and open, in time of war as in time of peace, to every vessel of commerce or of war without distinction of flag." The Egyptian leader defended his act by stating that the Canal was within Egyptian territory and that the time had come to announce Egypt's "Declaration of Independence from Imperialism."In an emotional speech, he hailed the nationalization as a symbolic act which would set Arab nationalism on its course from the Atlantic to the Persian Gulf. Britain and France, aghast at this unexpected move, lodged a strong protest against the seizure of "an international waterway" and against the violation of what the two Western nations considered to be their legal rights in the area. For Britain, as well as for Egypt, the Suez Canal was a symbol. While for Egypt it represented the growing power of the new nationalism, for Britain control of the Canal symbolized her status as an empire and as a world power. To the French, who blamed Egypt for supporting the Algerian rebellion against France, seizure of the Canal served as a last straw. For Britain and France alike, the issue at stake was not merely the rational one of safeguarding the economic rights of their shareholders in the Suez Canal Company or of protecting a key economic life line. Far more important was their emotional reaction to the seemingly insolent nationalism represented by the Egyptian move. Thus, the stage was set for a violent encounter between nationalism and colonialism.

During the weeks that followed Nasser's action the conflict broadened. Britain and France sounded out the official American reaction to the situation. Prime Ministers Eden and Mollet, contemplating the use of force against Nasser, were partially reassured by the fact that Secretary of State Dulles also appeared outraged by Egypt's action. The British and French foreign ministers compared Nasser's action to Hitler's behavior at Munich and stated in the strongest terms that this type of Western appeasement must not be allowed to occur again. Secretary Dulles replied that "force was the last method to be tried, but the United States did not exclude the use of force if all other methods failed."[1] From this statement Eden inferred that the United States would, at best, present a united front with Britain and France in a show of force against Nasser and, at worst, remain benevolently neutral.

Britain and France now prepared for military action. They hoped to mount a lightning attack against Egypt, occupy the Canal, depose Nasser, and then negotiate with his successor from a position of strength. In the course of these preparations, it became increasingly evident to the two Western powers that they shared a common interest with Israel. The new Jewish state, harassed by border clashes and made increasingly insecure by Nasser's pronouncements "to drive Israel into the sea," could be used as the cutting edge of the Anglo-French punitive expedition against Egypt. "Collusion" between Britain and France on the one hand and Israel on the other has not been substantiated, but circumstantial evidence points in that direction. At any rate, Israel invaded Egyptian territory on October 29, 1956, and rapidly advanced toward the Suez Canal. On the following day, Britain and France issued an ultimatum to Israel and Egypt calling for a cessation of fighting and demanding the occupation of Suez and other key areas. The ultimatum was rejected by Egypt, and on October 31, British and French airplanes bombarded Cairo. What had begun as an armed conflict between two Middle Eastern nations now assumed the proportions of a direct Western attack against the new nationalism.

The superpowers entered the picture on October 30. On that day, the United States called for a meeting of the Security Council and, to the consternation of Britain and France, introduced a resolution calling upon Israel to leave Egypt without delay and asking all member states to "refrain from the use of force or threat of force."[2] This resolution was immediately vetoed by Britain and France. At the same meeting, the Soviet Union asked the Security Council to pass a draft incorporating some parts of the defeated U.S.-sponsored resolution. Nationalist China and Iran suggested adding still other parts of the defeated resolution, and the USSR agreed. At the next meeting, the Council voted on the Soviet-Chinese-Iranian draft. Again this proposal was vetoed by Britain and France.[3]

As the Security Council stood paralyzed and the Anglo-French action continued, the tension between the superpowers mounted steadily. Premier Bulganin, in a news conference in Moscow, warned of the possibility of a third world war and declared that Soviet "volunteers" were ready to aid the Egyptian forces. He proposed that the United States and the Soviet Union restore the peace in the Middle East through a joint show of force. This suggestion was rejected as "unthinkable" by President Eisenhower. Simultaneously, a Soviet draft resolution proposing a joint U.S.-Soviet force to be established under Article 42 was rejected by the Security Council under strong American pressure.[4] The United States was eager to see the Anglo-French action ended, but it was equally eager to prevent the establishment of a Soviet presence in the Middle East.

On November 1, the Security Council, at the instigation of the Yugoslav delegation, invoked the Uniting for Peace procedure and called an emergency session of the General Assembly. The United States and the Soviet Union both supported this move, and only Britain and France cast negative votes. In the

Assembly, on November 2, the United States adopted a sternly condemnatory attitude toward the Anglo-French military action. "The United States," declared President Eisenhower, "was not consulted in any way about any phase of these actions, nor were we informed of them in advance."[5] Secretary of State Dulles condemned the resort to force by Britain, France, and Israel, which could "scarcely be reconciled with the principles and purposes of the United Nations to which we have all subscribed."[6] In this attitude, the United States found support from a not particularly welcome source—the Soviet Union.

The USSR, in a vehement denunciation of the Anglo-French action, urged the Assembly "to condemn the armed attack by the United Kingdom, France, and Israel against Egypt as an act of aggression incompatible with the purposes and principles of the United Nations; to demand the immediate cessation of hostilities and the withdrawal of armed forces; and to appoint a United Nations commission to supervise the carrying out of the recommendations of the General Assembly."[7]

The two superpowers were able to agree on a compromise resolution sponsored by the United States urging a cease-fire and a withdrawal of all forces behind the armistice lines. The resolution was adopted by a vote of 64 in favor, 5 opposed, and 6 abstentions. One of those abstaining was Lester Pearson of Canada, who claimed that the resolution had made "one great omission": it had not provided for a vital instrument to prevent another explosion in the Suez area—"a truly international peace and police force."[8] After sounding out key delegations and the Secretary-General, Mr. Pearson, on November 3, introduced a draft resolution requesting the Secretary-General to submit a plan within forty-eight hours for the creation, "with the consent of the nations concerned," of an emergency international force "to secure and supervise the cessation of hostilities." The United States gave the plan its strong support, declaring that it was interested in a solution that would "meet the immediate crisis as well as do something that would go to the causes and into the more long-range subjects."[9] The Soviet Union felt that more coercive action would be preferable but did not object strongly to the Canadian plan. Thus, the General Assembly, on November

3, approved the Canadian draft resolution by a vote of 57 to 0, with 19 abstentions.[10] The abstainers included the Soviet bloc, Britain, France, Israel, Egypt, Australia, New Zealand, the Union of South Africa, Portugal, Austria, and Laos.

Thus, the United States, instead of observing a benevolent neutrality toward the British, French, and Israeli actions, had taken a leading role in the General Assembly in calling for a cessation of fighting and the immediate withdrawal of the Anglo-French-Israeli forces from Egypt. To the consternation of many of its allies in NATO, the United States found itself side by side in the United Nations with its great antagonist in the East-West struggle. Thus, under joint pressure of the superpowers in the Assembly, Britain had to yield. Confronted by UN resolutions charging her with aggression, dismayed by the actions of the United States, and troubled by an increasingly hostile opposition at home, Prime Minister Eden terminated his abortive venture. France had no choice but to follow suit, and the "gentle persuasion" of the United States resulted in the withdrawal of Israeli forces shortly thereafter. As Secretary-General Hammarskjöld set about improvising an international peace force, most delegates in the General Assembly felt that a world conflagration had narrowly been averted.

If one takes stock of the roles the superpowers played in the Suez crisis up to this point, it is apparent that the United States faced the most difficult choice: What action did its national interest dictate? Where did its national interest really lie? It was confronted in the most acute way possible with the dilemma of whether to support the colonial powers or the new nationalism. Its actual decision to side with Egypt inevitably alienated Britain and France and put the most severe strains on the NATO alliance. Sir Anthony Eden was compelled to resign, and throughout Britain as well as France a growing body of anti-American sentiment became vocal. Indeed, in the view of a number of observers, such as former Secretary of State Dean Acheson, American policy in the crisis came close to losing the United States its two closest allies, splitting the NATO alliance, and thus exposing Western Europe to the domination of communism.[11] On the other hand, if the United States had sided with Britain and France against

Egypt, its risks would have been no less heavy. The new nations of Africa, Asia, and the Middle East would have quickly concluded that when the chips were down the United States was at heart no less a colonial power than its Western European allies. In disillusionment, the new nationalism would have veered away from the United States toward the Soviet Union. Probably the least amount of animosity would have resulted if the United States had abstained from the conflict altogether. Yet even then both sides would likely have found reason for objecting to America's role.

As one observer has pointed out, "the criticism of the American stand came essentially to this point: the United States had chosen to behave like a collective security power, not like an ally. In the Middle Eastern situation, Uniting for Peace had prevailed over NATO."[12] Yet, the American rejection as "unthinkable" of a Soviet proposal for joint superpower intervention in the Middle East suggests strongly that the American position was not determined by the abstract considerations of the collective-security ideal. There was, first, a sense of outrage, felt by both the president and secretary of state because the British and French had not bothered to consult their NATO ally on so important a matter as military action in the Middle East. Second, from a purely military standpoint, the punitive expedition seemed to be foundering and thus could not be presented to the General Assembly as a *fait accompli*. The United States, by supporting the Anglo-French venture or even by taking a neutral view of it, would have risked the ill will of a large majority of the UN membership and, in addition, would have been in an embarrassing position if the military action failed or bogged down. Most important, the United States feared the intervention of the Soviet Union in the Middle East through "volunteers" and the risk of sparking a major war through direct superpower confrontation in the contested area.

All this does not deny the possibility that some of the reasons which motivated the United States may have been of a genuinely moral nature. As the American government stated, the United States acted as it did because it insisted on the principle that the same standard of international law and morality should apply to all nations, friends and foes alike. Yet even this seemingly unassailable moral reason rested upon ambiguities. It could be argued, for example, that a moral action might under certain circumstances result in immoral consequences. Thus, the moral behavior of the United States in the Suez crisis ran the risk of leading to the disintegration of NATO and the immoral result of opening Western Europe to Soviet pressure. Conversely, if the United States had decided upon the immoral step of supporting the British and French military expedition against Egypt, the outcome might have been the quite moral one of restoring the legal economic rights of the Western powers and of reestablishing the Suez Canal as an international waterway. The point here is *not* that the United States acted either morally or immorally. It is, rather, that among other things, the Suez affair demonstrated how subtle and indeterminate the relationship between ethics and power in international relations can be.

The Soviet Union's national interest in the Suez crisis was much easier to determine. From its point of view, the only unusual aspect was its alliance with the United States in the United Nations. In order to dissociate itself from this somewhat unwelcome association, the Soviet Union interpreted the action of the United States not as helpful to Arab nationalism but, rather, as a nefarious scheme to replace British and French imperialism with American imperialism. In contrast, it pointed to itself as the only true champion of the new nationalist cause. The Soviet offer of "volunteers" was designed to underline its firm commitment to the new nationalism. Indeed, from the Soviet Union's point of view, the Suez crisis constituted a great windfall in the East-West struggle: The British and French appeared to be digging their own graves in the Middle East, and the United States seemed to be doing its best to help them. Thus, by appealing to the cause of Arab nationalism, the Soviet Union saw its opportunity to eject Western influence from the Middle East and gain a foothold of its own. The fact that Israel was allied with the two colonial powers made it easier for the Soviet Union to inflame Arab nationalism. Typically, therefore, the Soviet Union showed itself ready to use every facet of this colonial struggle to advance its own cause in the East-West battle. From the melee, communism emerged with a clear-cut gain.

The main losers in the Suez affair were clearly the two colonial powers, Britain and France. In humiliation, they had to watch Nasser snatch a political victory from a military defeat. Abandoned by their traditional ally, they had to admit that they could no longer act like Great Powers and that, in the last analysis, their initiative in international politics depended upon the decision of the United States. The new nationalism had inflicted a painful defeat upon them, and the very issue which they had set out to rectify by force of arms—the internationalization of the Suez Canal—now seemed beyond redemption. For all practical purposes, the Suez crisis terminated Anglo-French authority in the Middle East. Suez had become another Dien Bien Phu.

The greatest victory in the Suez crisis was won by Arab nationalism. Nasser now was clearly master of the Suez Canal. The two great superpowers had both supported him. The prestige of the Egyptian leader reached its zenith immediately after the Suez affair, although it was somewhat tarnished by the military disaster of Egyptian arms. Not only did Nasser triumph in the showdown with Western colonialism, but his other great foe, Israel, had also been compelled to withdraw as a result of American pressure. The political logic of the East-West struggle, by becoming the decisive factor in the crisis, thus operated to advance the cause of Arab nationalism to greater strength and prestige than it had ever possessed or than Nasser could ever have hoped to gain on his own.

Israel emerged with certain important gains: It had demonstrated its military superiority over Nasser. Yet, it was prevented from capitalizing on its advantage by strong U.S. pressure to withdraw. In the end, all the territories it had occupied had to be given up.

While each state in the Suez crisis had its national interest to protect, each actor was also a participant in the three-struggle pattern outlined above. What were the results there? In the East-West struggle, the Soviet Union clearly had come off best. It had created a more attractive image of itself in the Arab world. The promulgation by the United States of the Eisenhower Doctrine in March 1957—pledging American assistance against communism to Middle Eastern countries—was testimony to increasing American awareness of this latest Soviet gain. In the second struggle, that of nationalism versus colonialism, the winner was clearly the new nationalism. After Suez, the Great Power role of Britain and France in the Middle East was clearly at an end. The Eisenhower Doctrine attempted to salvage what was left of Anglo-French influence. In the third struggle, between Arab nationalism and Israeli nationalism, both countries emerged stronger from the crisis: Israel because of its formidable military prowess, Egypt because of its political triumph over Britain and France.

Interdependence among the major actors again was the keynote of the Arab-Israeli War of 1967, although the specific alignment of forces was quite different. This time the two superpowers took opposing sides, while Britain tended to favor Israel, and France leaned toward the Arabs.

The decade between the two crises had seen a number of border incidents but no major eruption. In early 1967, however, tension began to mount. President Nasser's Arab neighbors accused the Egyptian leader of hiding behind the UN Emergency Force in order to avoid a confrontation with Israel. Sensitive to this charge, on May 18, Nasser demanded that UNEF leave the positions in Sinai that it had occupied for more than ten years. Whether the Egyptian leader initiated this move primarily to assuage his Arab critics, or whether he really intended to clear the field for military action, is not certain. At any rate, Secretary-General U Thant complied with the demand, reasoning that UNEF could no longer remain in the area if the consent of the host government were withdrawn. Hence the UNEF contingents were removed from Sinai, the Gaza Strip, and from Sharm El-Sheik overlooking the Straits of Tiran. Almost simultaneously, Israel, Syria, and Jordan began to mobilize their armed forces and to mass them on their respective borders. On May 20, military control over the Gaza Strip reverted to Egypt, and the Arab League issued a joint declaration that was signed by twelve of its members, with only Tunisia abstaining, stating that an attack on one would be considered an attack upon all. Israel responded by calling up the reserves, and on May 22, Egypt ordered total mobilization. During this early phase of the crisis, the superpowers indicated their positions but still refused to become vitally involved.

The second phase of the crisis began on May 23, when President Nasser announced a blockade of the Gulf of Aqaba, thus cutting off Israel's only southern port at Elath. Israel immediately responded by defining the blockade as an act of war that entitled it to take appropriate action. Egypt maintained that the Straits of Tiran were within her territorial waters and thus could be closed to states with which she was at war.

At this juncture, the East-West struggle was superimposed upon the competing nationalisms of Israel and the Arab states. On May 23, President Lyndon B. Johnson presented the American position. He described the blockade as "illegal and potentially disastrous to the cause of peace" and affirmed that "the right of free, innocent passage through the international water [was] a vital interest of the international community." In effect, the president supported the settlement that had been reached after the Suez crisis of 1956. Because Egypt was determined to overthrow that settlement, the American position in effect came down on the side of Israel.

On the following day, the Soviet Union declared that Israel was to blame for the dangerous aggravation of tensions in the Middle East. The forces of imperialism, represented by "a handful of colonial oil monopolies" and backed by commercial interests in the United States and Britain, were the chief culprits behind the scene, in the Soviet view. The USSR further proclaimed its support for the Arab states in their "just struggle for national liberation against colonialism."

The other major powers, Britain, France, and Communist China, also took their stands in the escalating crisis. Britain supported the United States on the right of free passage of all nations through the disputed straits; France declared herself to be "not committed in any way and on any subject" on the side of "any of the states involved"; and China, supporting the Arab cause, also accused both the United States and the Soviet Union of "strangling the just struggle of the Palestinian people."

In the meantime, the two main protagonists edged closer to the brink. On May 25, Israel's ambassador, Abba Eban, flew to London and Washington in order to ascertain what the two Western powers would do to end the blockade. Both offered vague assurances but counseled restraint. On May 28, Syria and Iraq signed a military agreement calling for the cooperation of their armies against Israel; on the following day, President Nasser announced that Soviet Premier Aleksei Kosygin had sent him a pledge to guarantee the Egyptian blockade. On May 30, King Hussein, described several weeks earlier as a "Hashemite Harlot" by President Nasser, placed Jordan's armed forces under Egyptian control in the event of war with Israel. Thus, by the end of May, the brink was reached, and Israel confronted the armies of Egypt, Syria, and Jordan.

On the morning of June 5, heavy fighting broke out between Israel and Egypt. In four days of lightning warfare, Israel defeated the armies of her three main Arab antagonists. In Egypt, she captured the Sinai up to the east bank of the Suez Canal and also lifted the blockade of Aqaba by capturing Sharm El-Sheik. The Gaza Strip also fell into Israeli hands. In bloody fighting with Jordan, Israel occupied the Old City of Jerusalem and all of Jordan west of the Jordan River. Finally, Israel also captured portions of Syrian borderlands from which Arab guns had harassed Israeli settlements. On June 9, the short but violent war came to a halt with a cease-fire resolution passed by the UN Security Council.

During the next phase, the conflict moved from the military arena of the Middle East to the political forum of the United Nations. Both the Security Council and the General Assembly debated the issues, the latter in a four-week emergency special session. In the world forum, Israel insisted on recognition by the Arab states and an end to belligerency as conditions of withdrawal from the occupied Arab territories. She was supported in this view by the United States and Britain. The Arab states demanded unconditional withdrawal and full reparations and insisted that Israel be condemned as an aggressor. Soviet Premier Kosygin supported the Arab demands from the rostrum of the General Assembly. France inclined toward the Arab position, and the small nations were about evenly divided. Neither superpower was able to muster a two-thirds majority for its respective position, and thus the General Assembly adjourned in a mood of frustration after two resolutions calling upon Israel to rescind its annexation of Old Jerusalem were ignored. The one concrete UN measure was the dispatch of a small number of cease-fire observers to the Suez Canal.

An analysis of the changes in power constellations after the war reveals some suggestive comparisons and contracts with the 1956 crisis. In the first place, the Soviet Union had backed a loser this time, whereas she had been on the winning side a decade earlier. Most of the military hardware that the USSR had shipped to the Arab states had been captured or destroyed in the four days of war. Nor was the Soviet Union able to turn anticolonial sentiments to its advantage in the United Nations, because many of the smaller nations also identified themselves with Israel. On the other hand, the defeat of the Arab states now made these states more than ever dependent upon the USSR, which promptly resumed arms shipments to them.

The role of the United States was once again problematical. She was on the winning side, and superficially her policy seemed successful. But on a deeper level, it was clear that the swiftness of Israel's victory had saved the United States from having to make some very difficult decisions. Had the war gone badly for Israel, the United States might have been forced to intervene and risk a confrontation with the Soviet Union.

Britain and France, the two main losers in the 1956 affair, were only marginally involved this time. A new power factor in the equation, however, was Communist China, which accused the United States and the Soviet Union of conspiring together in the Middle East.

Israel, which had to withdraw in 1956, this time was determined not to yield its military gains except in exchange for an end to belligerency. This the Arabs were unwilling to concede, and therefore, in the view of many observers, the 1967 war had exacerbated the deeper causes of the conflict.

Thus, by mid-1967, the balance of power in the Middle East had been definitely altered. Although Israel had won her military victory essentially unaided, the political constellation clearly showed once again the interdependence of the two great struggles of our time. One superpower tried to exploit the Arab-Israeli War by describing it as a struggle between Arab nationalism and Western imperialism. In this effort, the USSR failed where it had succeeded in 1956, when the two superpowers found themselves on the same side. And the United States, eager to pacify the struggle, was saved from the decision to intervene by Israeli arms. Thus, the connection between the two world struggles might have widened the theater of war had the conflict between the two main antagonists been inconclusive or gone the other way.

So far as the UN's role in the conflict was concerned, both Israel and the Arab states were profoundly disappointed. Israel perceived the United Nations as hostile, and the Arabs tended to regard it as useless. Be that as it may, there was little doubt that —in the light of the numerous Middle East resolutions that had gone unimplemented—the currency of UN resolutions was in danger of serious devaluation.

Israel's swift and decisive victory in 1967 had left a legacy of shame and bitterness on the Arab side. Diplomacy had not been able to dislodge the Israelis from the five territories that they had captured from three Arab countries in June 1967: Sinai and the Gaza Strip from Egypt; Old Jerusalem and the West Bank from Jordan; and the Golan Heights from Syria. The UN Security Council had been able to adopt only a single resolution on the Middle East over a period of six years. That resolution, which was passed on November 22, 1967, linked a promise of secure and recognized boundaries to Israel with a promise of withdrawal from occupied territories to the Arabs. But neither side was willing to take the first step and, therefore, the entire situation remained frozen. No face-to-face negotiations between Arabs and Israelis ever took place. The Arabs gazed across the cease-fire line with increasing fury and frustration as Israel made plans to populate the territories with Israeli settlers. Israel seemed bent on de facto annexation, and the Arabs seemed equally determined to prevent it.

Anwar Sadat, who became Egypt's new president after the death of Nasser in 1970, gradually and without much fanfare prepared for an Arab counterattack. Unlike Nasser, the less flamboyant Sadat did not divide the Arab world, but doggedly worked toward a consensus. The Soviet Union, unwilling to give the Arabs offensive weapons, did replace the military hardware that had been captured or destroyed by Israel in 1967. The Soviets also trained Egyptian and Syrian commanders in Soviet military strategy and tactics in order to prevent a repetition of the debacle of the Six Day War. By 1973, the Arabs were encouraged to believe that at least some of the lost territories could be regained by force of arms. Thus, the stage was set for yet another violent encounter.

On Yom Kippur, the Jewish Day of Atonement, Syria and Egypt launched a well-coordinated surprise attack against Israel. In the north, in an effort to regain the vantage point over Israeli settlements in the valley below, Syria attacked the vital Golan Heights. In the Sinai, Egypt threw a major military force across the Suez Canal capturing Israeli positions on the East Bank and sending Israel's defenders backward into the desert.

By the end of the first week of war, Israel had stemmed the Arab onslaught, but the myth of its invincibility had nevertheless been shattered. Egypt had managed to insert almost 100,000 men on the East Bank of the Suez Canal and the fiercest tank battles since World War II raged in the Sinai Desert and the Golan Heights. Casualties were heavy on both sides. Buoyed up by the successes of Syria and Egypt, other Arab countries joined in the battle. Iraq and Jordan supplied troops for the Syrian front, and Saudi Arabia and other oil-rich Arab sheikdoms placed increasing pressure on the United States to abandon its support of Israel.

As casualties mounted and both sides suffered staggering losses in war material, the superpowers entered the arena. The Soviet Union began to resupply the Arab states with ammunition and light weapons. When the United States decided to do the same for Israel, the Soviet Union escalated its supply operations to tanks and planes. This, too, was matched by the United States. Thus, by the end of the first week, the war had reached a new and dangerous plateau. Not only was the armor of both sides locked in a death struggle, but the fragile détente between the Soviet Union and the United States hung in the balance.

During the second week of the war, Israel gradually gained the upper hand on both the Syrian and Egyptian fronts. After fierce tank battles in the Golan Heights, the Israelis not only threw back the Syrians, but embarked on the road to Damascus. On the Egyptian front, the Israelis inserted troops on the West Bank of the Suez Canal on Egyptian territory. Their aim was to encircle the Egyptian troops on the East Bank in Sinai and to cut off their retreat across the Canal back to Egypt. After massive air and tank battles, the Israeli objectives were attained. The Egyptian troops were trapped in two large pockets in Sinai and the Third Army was at Israel's mercy for its supply of food and water. At this juncture with the balance shifting rapidly in Israel's favor, the superpowers intervened once more.

On October 21, acting with great urgency to protect its Egyptian ally, the Soviet leadership agreed on a formula for a cease-fire resolution with Secretary of State Henry Kissinger. This resolution, which was rushed through the UN Security Council on the following morning under joint Soviet-American sponsorship, provided for a cease-fire in place and called on all parties to start immediate negotiations toward implementing the 1967 Security Council plan for peace in the Middle East. The cease-fire began shakily, with the Egyptian forces trapped behind Israeli lines trying to break out and Israel seeking to destroy the Egyptian forces once and for all. A second cease-fire call still did not end the fighting. As a result, the Soviet Union proposed that a joint Soviet-American peace force be dispatched to the Middle East. The United States rejected this proposal because it feared the possibility of a military confrontation in the area. The Soviet Union then declared that it would introduce its own troops into the area unilaterally. To counteract this Soviet threat, the armed forces of the United States were placed on military alert by President Richard Nixon.

During the "alert" crisis, a compromise was worked out. The Security Council approved a third resolution sponsored by the nonaligned countries that authorized the Secretary-General to send a UN buffer force to the area. The first UN troops began to arrive from Cyprus on October 27. By then, all fronts were quiet. The precarious Soviet-American détente had held after all.

The Middle East Peace Forces and the Superpowers

The UN Emergency Force (UNEF) could not have come into existence without the approval, or at least the tacit consent, of the two superpowers. Yet both were carefully excluded from participation. UNEF was never meant to be a fighting army, but rather a symbol of the UN's involvement which, it was hoped, would bring about the neutralization of the disputed area. The direct involvement of one of the superpowers would have meant the necessity of inviting the other as well. Hence, neither was invited by the Secretary-General, and UNEF thus became the first genuine international peace force not dominated by a Great Power.

When Secretary-General Hammarskjöld and Lester Pearson began to build the Force, they decided to appoint Major General E. L. M. Burns, chief of staff of the UN Truce Supervision Organization in Palestine, as head of the new UN Command. The next vital decision concerned the composition of troops to be sent. To the delight of leading UN officials, twenty-four members agreed to make troops available for the enterprise, with offers ranging from 1,180 from Canada to 250 from Finland. However, this delight began to give way to embarrassment when, in order not to jeopardize relations with Egypt, it became necessary to reject some of the offers. For example, the Canadian contingent, especially a battalion of the Queen's Own Rifles, resembled the British too much in appearance. Pearson tactfully decided to use them as maintenance and administrative personnel in roles where they would be least conspicuous. New Zealand troops were politely rejected because New Zealand had voted with Britain and France in the General Assembly on the Suez affair. Pakistan was considered unsuitable because it was a member of the Baghdad Pact and an irritant to India. Troops from the Soviet bloc— Czechoslovakia and Rumania—were not "rejected" but simply not "activated." Finally, 6,000 troops from ten countries—Brazil, Canada, Colombia, Denmark, Finland, India, Indonesia, Norway, Sweden, and Yugoslavia—were ready for action.

The composition of the Force was very important, since its admission to the contested area depended upon the permission of Egypt. Though this condition was distasteful to many members of the Assembly as well as to UN officials, it was, according to the Secretary-General, the "very basis and starting point" of the entire operation. In effect, Egypt therefore had a veto over the national make-up of the Force and could, as well, determine the length of its stay in the Suez area. On November 12, Egypt granted UNEF permission to enter. Shortly thereafter, Britain, France, and Israel were persuaded to withdraw from Egyptian territory, and UNEF proceeded to neutralize the contested boundary zones. Its function became essentially that of a buffer between Israel and Egypt.

The United States fully supported the UNEF experiment, which served the American national interest in two ways: First, the United States was eager to heal the rift between itself and its two NATO allies, Britain and France; and second, it was equally eager to remove any pretext for unilateral Soviet intervention in the Middle East. Thus, the United States saw its national interest well served by placing the responsibility for a solution in international hands. No American troops were included in UNEF. Had the United States assumed a more active role, the suspicion of the Soviet Union and the Afro-Asian nations would no doubt have been aroused. Hence, American involvement was limited to the marginal one of providing transport planes, uniforms, helmets, and other kinds of materiel and logistical support for the Force. On the matter of the direction and control of UNEF, the position of the United States was at all times congruent with that of the Secretary-General.

The Soviet view of UNEF was critical. However, its opposition always remained muted and never reached the proportions of active obstruction. Part of the criticism was of a legal nature. The Soviet Union maintained that only the Security Council, acting under Chapter VII of the Charter, had the power to establish an international police force.[13] The creation of UNEF by the Assembly under the Uniting for Peace procedure therefore came under Soviet fire. On the other hand, in the Suez case, this procedure was invoked by the Assembly to overcome not a Soviet but a British and French veto. Hence, while the Soviet Union was in general deeply hostile to the extension of the Assembly's mandate into the area of peace and security, in this specific instance its national interest dictated abstention on the vote to establish UNEF and only relatively mild criticism thereafter. The USSR was also suspicious of UNEF on political grounds. It had fears that UNEF would permanently remove the Suez Canal from Egyptian control and possibly aid Britain and France in the goal of reestablishing their authority. And finally, it voiced concern that the Force was an American scheme to displace Anglo-French influence with American power.

In May 1967, President Nasser abruptly demanded that UNEF be withdrawn from the borders that it had patroled for over a decade. Secretary-General U Thant complied with the Egyptian demand, though with serious misgivings, and the Force was promptly removed.

U Thant's decision was a very controversial one. The Secretary-General was widely criticized for giving in too hastily to Egyptian pressure. Critics pointed out that although it was true that UNEF's presence on the Egyptian border depended on the consent of the Egyptian government, the Secretary-General could have stalled by requesting an emergency session of the Security Council or of the General Assembly and thus gained time. The Israeli ambassador to the United Nations, Abba Eban, stated caustically that "the umbrella was removed at the precise moment when it began to rain." The Secretary-General defended his action by pointing out that there would have been no legal basis for maintaining the Force on Egyptian soil without that nation's consent. Moreover, the Force had never been permitted to patrol the Israeli side of the border, and when the Israeli government was asked whether it would invite the UNEF troops to its side after they left Egypt, Israel replied that it would refuse to do so. Both governments were within their rights, the Secretary-General asserted. A further complication in the picture was the fact that two nations that had given contingents to UNEF—India and Yugoslavia—were removing their forces even before the Secretary-General had given the order to withdraw. Moreover, several UNEF soldiers were killed by Egyptian troops with the threat that, unless UNEF was promptly withdrawn, it would be regarded as an "army of occupation." Finally, the Secretary-General reasoned that if he did not comply with the request of a sovereign government, consent for the admission of a peace-keeping force in a future crisis might be infinitely more difficult to obtain. Given all these conflicting considerations, the Secretary-General made his difficult and fateful choice.

The second UN Emergency Force (UNEF II) was established immediately after the conclusion of the Yom Kippur War, in late October 1973. UNEF II was deployed by the Security Council for an initial six-month period, subject to renewal, along the disengagement line that had been negotiated between Israel and Egypt by Secretary Kissinger. UNEF II differed from its predecessor in three important respects. First, it was placed under the exclusive mandate of the Security Council. This meant that it could not be terminated *during* each six-month period except with the unanimous consent of the permanent members. Each of the Big Five, however, had the power to prevent its prolongation every six months when the Security Council voted on the renewal of the mandate. Thus, UNEF I could be killed at any time by the host country, but UNEF II could be killed only at regular six-month intervals by the veto of a permanent member. Second, while the troop composition of UNEF II consisted primarily of small neutral countries, Poland became a part of the Force in addition to Austria, Sweden, Finland, Ireland, Ghana, Senegal, Kenya, Nepal, Panama, Peru, Canada, and Indonesia. Thus, a Warsaw Pact nation for the first time became a member of a UN peace force. In addition, the United States and the Soviet Union sent a small number of observers into the cease-fire area. Another precedent was set when the Soviet Union agreed to share the $30 million assessed budget that was authorized by the Security Council for the first six-month period, as well as several subsequent appropriations of between $30 million and $40 million each. China, however, decided not to participate in the votes either authorizing or extending the peace force nor did she choose to share in the costs, even though these were defined as regular "expenses" in accordance with Article 17 of the Charter. In October 1976, the Security Council agreed to extend the mandate of UNEF II for a full year at an annual cost of approximately $83 million.

UNEF II operated at a level of approximately four thousand men under the direction of a Finnish commander, Major-General

Ensio Siilasvuo. The Security Council maintained tight political control, and, despite some minor areas of friction, the Force operated very effectively. When violence erupted in Ireland, however, the Irish contingent was withdrawn. UNEF II, like its predecessor, still consisted of borrowed troops that could be recalled at will by their national governments.

In May 1974, in the wake of the disengagement arrangement that had been worked out by Secretary Kissinger between Israel and Syria, the Security Council established a small UN Disengagement Observer Force (UNDOF). The new force was to draw its contingents from UNEF: 500 Austrians, 350 Peruvians, 100 Canadians, and 100 Poles were transferred for patrol duty to the Golan Heights. Once again, the Security Council authorized an initial six-month period and once again China did not vote. UNDOF's expenses were subsumed under the UNEF budget. A formula was worked out under which those nations that contributed troops to UNEF or UNDOF received reimbursements so that they did not have to shoulder a double burden of both manpower and money. UNDOF acquitted itself well under the leadership of Brigadier-General Gonzalo Briceño Zevallos of Peru who exercised his command under the watchful eye of the Security Council. In late November 1974, after a trip by Secretary-General Waldheim to the Middle East, Syria acquiesced in a six-month extension of UNDOF's mandate to patrol the Golan Heights, and the Security Council approved the prolongation. Another six-month extension was granted in May 1975. In November 1975, Syria agreed to yet another, but only on the condition that the Palestine Liberation Organization would be invited to participate in the Security Council's Middle East deliberations. The condition was met by a vote of 13 to 0. Thus, by the mid-1970's, UN peace-keeping operations had clearly become the exclusive province of the Security Council.

Conclusions

The escalation of the Suez crisis of 1956 may be seen in three concentric circles: the crisis began between two competing forms of nationalism—Arab and Israeli; when Britain and France attacked Egypt in retaliation against President Nasser's nationalization of the Suez Canal, the local struggle merged into the larger one of nationalism versus colonialism; and immediately thereafter, the superpower conflict entered the picture. The speed of the escalation process impressed the need for UN action upon the membership, and the involvement of the superpowers in the crisis made it clear that their political support for, or at least acquiescence in, such action would be essential. Yet, given the explosiveness of the situation, it seemed best to exclude them from actual physical participation. These twin premises became the basis of UNEF.

The UNEF experience demonstrated that the United Nations was capable of responding to a major challenge with extraordinary resourcefulness. The framers of the Charter had assumed that concerted military action by the Great Powers would nip any conflict in the bud. Actually, however, in the Suez crisis the peace depended not on how quickly the superpowers' armed forces would be brought to the scene but on how successfully they could be kept at arm's length. Neither superpower was asked to contribute troops to UNEF. The United Nations adjusted its peacekeeping machinery to the original intentions of the Charter.

The abstention of the superpowers from active participation in UNEF points up a striking dilemma for any international force. In order to be an effective instrument of collective security and a powerful military force, it must include one or more of the Great Powers. But if it does, it is likely to find itself dominated by a superpower, as was the case in Korea, and to suffer a proportionate loss of its international character. Hence, a truly international force that excludes the superpowers can hardly be more than a "buffer" or at best "an intermediary technique between merely passing resolutions and actually fighting."[14]

Despite the fact that the superpowers were excluded from actual peace-keeping activities in UNEF, the success of the operation largely depended upon their political attitudes. The United States gave UNEF its strong support from beginning to end, and the Soviet Union, though highly ambivalent about the Force, never actively obstructed its operations. Thus, the General Assembly and the Secretary-General were able to conduct the action in a relatively smooth manner until the withdrawal of the Force in 1967.

In a more fundamental sense, however, the differing relations of the superpowers in 1956 and 1967 vitally affected the capacity of the United Nations to deal with the two crises. In 1956, the fact that the United States and the Soviet Union found themselves temporarily on the same side contributed in large measure to the passage of the Assembly resolution authorizing the establishment of UNEF. In 1967, the fact that the superpowers were clearly on opposite sides prevented the world organization from playing more than a marginal role in the conflict. In 1973, the two Great Powers once again were on opposite sides, but the policy of détente that both pursued dictated a compromise that led them to the United Nations.

Thus, UNEF II and UNDOF were creatures of superpower détente. Secretary Kissinger succeeded in disengaging Israeli forces from Egyptian and Syrian troops, and the two UN peace forces helped in the process of *keeping* these hostile armies disengaged. The Soviet Union could have sabotaged this American initiative, but chose not to do so for reasons of its own. Nor did China cast a veto. Structurally and financially, the two new peace forces in Sinai and in Golan were on a somewhat more solid footing than UNEF I had been. Yet their lifeblood continued to derive not so much from these structural and financial improvements, welcome though they were, but from the improvement in the climate between the two giants in world politics, the Soviet Union and the United States.

SELECTED BIBLIOGRAPHY

Burns, Arthur Lee, and Nina Heathcote. *Peace-Keeping by UN Forces: From Suez to the Congo.* New York: Praeger, 1963.

Claude, Inis L., Jr. "The United Nations and the Use of Force." *International Conciliation*, no. 532 (March 1961).

Cox, Arthur M. *Prospects for Peacekeeping.* Washington, D.C.: Brookings, 1967.

Frye, William R. *A United Nations Peace Force.* Dobbs Ferry, N.Y.: Oceana, 1957

Goodrich, Leland M. *Korea: A Study of United States Policy in the United Nations.* New York: Harper & Row, 1956.

James, Alan. *The Politics of Peace-Keeping.* New York: Praeger, 1969.

Lall, Arthur. *The UN and the Middle East Crisis of 1967.* New York: Columbia University Press, 1970.

Rikhye, Indar, et al. *The Thin Blue Line: International Peacekeeping and Its Future.* New Haven, Conn.: Yale University Press, 1974.

Rosner, Gabriella. *The United Nations Emergency Force.* New York: Columbia University Press, 1963.

Wainhouse, David D. *International Peace Observation.* Baltimore: Johns Hopkins Press, 1966.

NOTES

1. *Full Circle: The Memoirs of Anthony Eden,* cited by Herbert Feis in *Foreign Affairs* (July 1960), p. 600.

2. UN Doc. S/3712 (October 29, 1956).

3. UN Security Council, *Official Records,* 11th Year, 750th Meeting (October 31, 1956).

4. Ibid., 755th Meeting (November 5, 1956).

5. "Radio and Television Address by President Eisenhower, October 31, 1956," in U.S. Department of State, *United States Policy in the Middle East,* p. 49.

6. "Statement in the UN General Assembly by Secretary of State Dulles (November 1, 1956)," ibid., pp. 151–157.

7. UN General Assembly, *Official Records,* 1st Emergency Special Session, 562d Meeting (November 1, 1956), p. 18.

8. Ibid., p. 36.

9. UN General Assembly, *Official Records,* 563d Meeting (November 3, 1956), pp. 55–71.

10. UN Doc. A/3290 (November 4, 1956).

11. Dean Acheson, *Power and Diplomacy* (Cambridge, Mass.: Harvard University Press, 1958), pp. 109–116.

12. Inis L. Claude, Jr., *Swords into Plowshares,* 2d ed. (New York: Random House, 1959), p. 460.

13. UN General Assembly, *Official Records,* 1st Emergency Special Session, 567th Meeting (November 7, 1956), pp. 127–128.

14. Lester Pearson, "Force for UN," *Foreign Affairs* (April 1957), p. 401.

The Congo Crisis and the United Nations Operation in the Congo

"Does independence come wrapped in paper or do we get it at the bank?"

An anonymous Congolese

Phase One: Superpower Consensus

The Congo crisis of the early 1960's affords a second illuminating case study of superpower interaction in the area of peace and security operations. Historians may differ with Mr. Hammarskjöold's view that the UN's task in the Congo was the most important responsibility that the world organization had to shoulder in the first fifteen years of its lifetime, but most will agree that the Congo problem sorely strained the UN's diplomatic, military, and financial resources. The two superpowers played major roles throughout the entire drama.

Belgian rule in the Congo had for fifty years been based on the assumption that a paternalistic concern for the physical well-being and economic needs of the indigenous population would prevent the rise of a nationalist movement. When, in January 1959, violent nationalist riots erupted in Léopoldville, the Congolese capital, it became clear that this assumption had been incorrect. The Belgian government, interpreting these riots as a harbinger of impending disaster, decided to end its colonial rule as rapidly as possible. Independence for the Congo was slated for June 30, 1960. During the last year of Belgian colonial rule, little attempt was made to prepare an indigenous elite for the imminent responsibilities of self-government. Only a handful of Congolese had enjoyed a university education, and the overwhelming majority of the Congo's 14 million people were illiterate. Most were under the impression that on Independence Day all Belgian property would revert to the Congolese population. As one Congolese phrased the question, "Does independence come wrapped in paper or do we get it at the bank?"[1]

Thus, on June 30, 1960, the colony of the Belgian Congo was suddenly transformed into an independent nation, a newborn infant left on the world's doorstep. The government that took over the Congo was headed by President Joseph Kasavubu and Premier Patrice Lumumba. Both had been members of the Congolese National Movement. Kasavubu, the more conservative of the two, was not excessively hostile toward Belgium and the Western powers. The office of the presidency which he came to occupy was largely an honorific post. Lumumba, the premier, had been a more ardent nationalist than Kasavubu and was resolved to sever all relations with Belgium after independence. Both these men were challenged in their views by Moise Tshombe, premier of the provincial government of Katanga. Tshombe had been backed by the Belgian government during the colonial period. He was a wealthy man, conservative, and pro-Belgian. Thus, the new Congolese leadership held political views along the entire spectrum—from Lumumba's uncompromising anticolonialism to Tshombe's pro-Belgian sentiments.

A few hours after its Declaration of Independence, the new government faced a crisis which threatened its very survival. The Congolese Army of 25,000 men, which had never had an African officer corps, rose up, demanding the ouster of its Belgian officers and pay increases for the enlisted men. Many disappointed civilians who had expected to inherit all Belgian possessions on Independence Day joined in the mutiny. During the following days the mutiny spread through the rest of the Congo. In the major cities lawlessness prevailed, and thousands of Belgians fled. On July 11, Tshombe declared that Katanga was seceding from the rest of the country and forming a new state allied with Belgium. Since Katanga Province was the wealthiest part of the Congo, possessing the country's richest mineral deposits, this act of secession threatened the life of the new state. Moreover, the provincial government of Katanga requested Belgian military help in order to suppress the violence that was engulfing it along with the rest of the Congo. Belgian troops reentered Katanga for the purpose of restoring order. But on the following day, the Belgian government charged that since the new Congolese government of Premier Lumumba had been unable to protect the lives and interests of the remaining Belgian population, Belgian troops would march into Léopoldville as well. When the Belgians reentered the capital, shooting broke out between them and Congolese soldiers. At this point the Lumumba regime began to blame the riots not on the Africans but on the Belgians. The premier accused Belgium of aggression and stated that the colonial power had conspired with Tshombe to engineer the secession of Katanga Province in order to find a justification for the reimposition of colonial rule. What had started as only a local conflict thus quickly took on the dimensions of a major struggle between nationalism and colonialism.

On July 13, 1960, members of the Lumumba regime cabled the U.S. government for aid, but both Premier Lumumba and President Kasavubu immediately disavowed this appeal and stated that it had been meant as a request for a UN force composed of military personnel from neutral countries. Nevertheless, the earlier request touched off a sequence of events that turned the Congo into a battleground for the superpowers. Soviet

Premier Khrushchev immediately announced that the Congolese soldiers had been perfectly right in their mutiny against the Belgian officers. He also claimed that the United States and the Western colonial powers in NATO had conspired to send Belgian troops into the Congo to reimpose colonial status under the pretext of restoring order. UN Secretary-General Dag Hammarskjöld called an emergency meeting of the Security Council and urged authorization for the dispatching of a UN military force to the Congo. During the Council session the Soviet Union condemned Belgian "armed aggression" and accused the United States of collusion with colonialism. The United States denounced the Soviet accusation as "outrageous and untrue." The Security Council, in an 8-to-0 vote, called on Belgium to withdraw its troops from the Congo and authorized the Secretary-General to organize a UN Operation in the Congo—ONUC—to be patterned on the model of the Middle East Force established during the Suez crisis of 1956. Both the Soviet Union and the United States voted for the resolution, while Britain, France, and Nationalist China abstained.

Thus, the first UN resolution on the Congo reflected at least a temporary consensus between the superpowers. It was in the national interest of the United States to interpose the authority of the United Nations between East and West and to prevent the Congo from becoming another battlefield in the cold war; it was in the Soviet interest to speed the withdrawal of the Belgian forces and thus to play its self-appointed role as champion of anticolonialism. As in the Suez case, the ultimately divergent national goals of the two superpowers did not prevent them from permitting common UN action. Moreover, the solid backing of the African states for the resolution encouraged both superpowers to stand clear.

The superpower consensus thus established was tenuous, however. Premier Khrushchev revealed the continuing basic conflict in national interests when he announced that the Soviet Union was considering direct intervention in the Congo. He stated that this might become necessary, since he had received a telegram from President Kasavubu and Premier Lumumba stating that their lives were in danger and that they might "be compelled to ask for intervention by the Soviet Union if the Western camp [did] not desist from aggression against the sovereignty of the Congo Republic."[2] The Soviet leader pledged Russia's support to Lumumba and told the West, "Hands off the Congo!" On July 24, the Soviet delegation to the United Nations demanded the evacuation of the Belgian "aggressors" within three days. The U.S. representative, Henry Cabot Lodge, countered with the declaration that the United States "would do whatever may be necessary to prevent the intrusion of any military forces not requested by the United Nations."[3] The Security Council barred unilateral intervention and urged the speedy withdrawal of Belgian forces. In the meantime, ONUC was gradually replacing the Belgian troops. The two superpowers were carefully excluded from the international contingent. Almost 20,000 troops from twenty-nine nations, including Morocco, Tunisia, Ghana, Ethiopia, Mali, Guinea, Ireland, Sweden, and India—all under the UN flag—were deployed throughout the Congo to prepare the way for the more arduous task of building a responsible and viable Congolese government.

Even while UN troops were arriving in the Congo, further complications developed. Tribal antagonisms erupted into local wars; South Kasai, following the example of Katanga, seceded from the central government; and Moise Tshombe not only refused to dismiss his Belgian advisers and troops but announced that he would meet with force any attempt by the United Nations to enter Katanga.

In the light of all these developments, Hammarskjöld thought it necessary in early August to return to the Council for a clarification of his mandate. The consensus between the superpowers continued to hold. Both the United States and the Soviet Union voted for a resolution sponsored by Tunisia and Ceylon which declared that "the entry of the United Nations Force into the province of Katanga [was] necessary" and demanded the immediate withdrawal of Belgian troops from the province.[4] The resolution was adopted by a vote of 9 to 0, with France and Italy abstaining. The United States voted for the resolution with some misgivings because of the strong action against Belgium; the Soviet Union, which wanted even stronger action, had introduced a draft resolution that would have imposed upon the Secretary-General the obligation "to take decisive measures, without hesitating to use every means to that end," to remove the Belgian troops. But in the end, the Soviet Union, too, supported the Ceylon-Tunisia resolution.

Phase Two: The Breakdown of Consensus

The consensus between the superpowers broke down when, in the autumn of 1960, the new Congolese government disintegrated into factions. A power struggle between Premier Lumumba and President Kasavubu erupted. In September, the two leaders fired each other from their respective positions. In the melee, a young pro-Western colonel, Joseph Mobutu, took command of the armed forces. As a result, the position of the political leader most sympathetic to the USSR was undermined. Under Mobutu's rule, many Belgian administrators returned to the Congo as unofficial advisers.

The superpowers now took opposing positions on the two rival factions in the Congo government. The United States pressed the United Nations to recognize the Kasavubu-Mobutu government, while the Soviet Union began to support the deposed Lumumba with aircraft and trucks. The UN representative who was in charge of this critical phase of ONUC's operations in the summer and fall of 1960 was Andrew W. Cordier, executive assistant to Dag Hammarskjöld. Cordier's overriding concern was to uphold the Charter and to restore law and order in the wartorn Congo. In order to stop both Kasavubu and Lumumba from inflaming popular feelings even further and to prevent the outbreak of civil war, he decided to close all Congolese airports, to immobilize troops, and to shut down the national radio in Léopoldville. Three years later, Mr. N. T. Fedorenko, the Soviet delegate in the Administrative and Budgetary (Fifth) Committee of the General Assembly, was to declare that, by this action, "Cordier had adopted a decision that broke Lumumba's back" and had thus started the United Nations on its pro-Western course in the Congo.[5] Similarly, many highly placed

U.S. officials later pointed to Cordier's decision as having "stopped the Russians." Cordier himself defended his action on the grounds that it had *not* been taken *against* one of the rival factions or *against* one of the superpowers but *for* the law of the United Nations and the Charter.[6]

After the closure of airports and radio stations by the United Nations, the Soviet Union accused the United Nations of neocolonialism and proposed a draft resolution directing the United Nations to cease any interference in the internal affairs of the Congo and to hand over the airports and radio stations to the central government. Only Poland supported this resolution. Ceylon and Tunisia abstained and proposed a substitute resolution which endorsed the policies and actions of the Secretary-General. This resolution was vetoed by the Soviet Union.[7] The consensus between the superpowers had now broken down completely, paralyzing the Security Council. The General Assembly was immediately called into emergency session.

The superpowers now attempted to line up majorities for their opposing positions in the General Assembly. The United States led the forces seeking "to affirm and strengthen the mandate already given to the Secretary-General by the Security Council." The Soviet Union, on the other hand, took the position that "the United Nations Command and the Secretary-General personally have unmasked themselves as supporters of the colonialists."[8] After intensive and often acrimonious debate, an overwhelming majority of the Assembly supported the Secretary-General's policy, appealed to members to refrain from unilateral action in the Congo, and created a Conciliation Commission made up of African and Asian representatives in order to pacify the internal dissensions in the Congolese government.[9]

The General Assembly also considered another important matter at this time: Who should represent the Congolese government in that body? The Republic of the Congo had been admitted to membership on September 20, but the question of seating its representatives had been left to the Credentials Committee. Several days later, Guinea proposed that, pending a decision of the Credentials Committee, representatives of the Lumumba government should be seated. This proposal was supported by

Ceylon, Ghana, India, Indonesia, Mali, Morocco, and the United Arab Republic, all of which had troops in the Congo. It was also vigorously defended by the Soviet Union.

The Guinean proposal brought a sharp protest from Kasavubu, who immediately set out to plead his case at UN Headquarters in New York. On November 8, he appeared on the rostrum of the General Assembly and demanded the seating of his representatives. He was supported in this demand by the United States, which claimed that the Lumumba government did not have effective and stable control of the country or the ability to fulfill its international obligations. The Assembly debate was adjourned briefly, pending the return from the Congo of the Conciliation Commission. But on the Credentials Committee, which had been given a separate mandate after the vote of the Congo's membership, the West had a clear majority. The United States proposed the accreditation of the Kasavubu delegation, and, after two days of heated debate, the motion was adopted in committee by a vote of 6 to 1. Lumumba's supporters now had to bring their fight into the General Assembly.

Both superpowers lobbied intensively for their positions, especially among the African members of the Assembly. The United States was backed solidly by all the NATO powers, most of the Latin-American states, and a majority of the French-speaking African members, although a considerable number of African and Asian states which had endorsed the Congo policy of the Secretary-General now balked and either abstained or voted against it. The final vote on the critical accreditation issue was 53 in favor of seating the Kasavubu delegation, 24 opposed, and 19 abstentions. The U.S. position emerged victorious.

The Congo Operation continued, but now it was clear that one of the superpowers no longer felt that it served its national interest. Though it could still be said that ONUC was impartially assisting the legitimate government of the Congo to restore order, it was obvious that the Soviet Union believed the Kasavubu government to be pro-Western. For this reason, the USSR vetoed the continuation of ONUC in the Security Council and, when the Secretary-General carried on the operation under Assembly authority, mounted the attack against him and his Office discussed in Chapter 3. The United States, of course, insisted that it was supporting a disinterested UN operation that sought to restore peace and order in the Congo. One wonders, however, what American policy might have been had the Credentials Committee and the General Assembly seated Lumumba instead of Kasavubu.

Phase Three:
The United Nations' Show of Force

On February 13, 1961, it was announced that Patrice Lumumba had been killed by hostile tribesmen in Katanga. This event, which convulsed the Congo and threatened to plunge it into civil war, led to a partial restoration of superpower consensus in the Security Council. On February 21, the Council, in a 9-to-0 vote with the Soviet Union and France abstaining, passed its strongest resolution to date, urging that "the United Nations take immediately all appropriate measures to prevent the occurrence of civil war in the Congo, including . . . the use of force, if necessary, in the last resort."[10] The resolution also called for "an immediate and impartial investigation" of Lumumba's death. The United States had some misgivings about the implications of the use of force, even "in the last resort," but the fact that most of the African and Asian states solidly supported the resolution helped persuade the American delegation to vote for it. The Soviet Union, also fearful of alienating the African states if it vetoed the "force in the last resort" resolution, abstained. Thus, with the reluctant approval of one of the superpowers and the tacit consent of the other, the Security Council—no longer veto-bound— resumed political direction of the Congo Operation. The African states had thus been instrumental in restoring a partial consensus between the superpowers.

During the spring and summer of 1961, the Congo presented a picture of extreme confusion. Kasavubu had appointed Cyrille Adoula as prime minister of the Congolese government, but the Adoula government was unable to control the entire country. Lumumba's vice-premier, Antoine Gizenga, established the "legitimate government" of the Congo in Stanleyville. And ONUC forces, in their efforts to integrate Katanga into the central government, ran into mounting resistance not only from the Katangese forces of Moise Tshombe but from French, Belgian, and South African mercenaries. There were numerous casualties on all sides. Finally, on September 17, in an effort to persuade Tshombe to desist, the Secretary-General decided to go himself to Katanga but was killed during a night flight when his airplane crashed near Ndola, in Northern Rhodesia. The tragic event imperiled the entire operation. Nevertheless, top officials in the UN Secretariat continued Hammarskjöld's work. On September 21, a provisional cease-fire was agreed upon, but ratification did not follow until five weeks later. The Security Council met on November 13, ten days after the election of U Thant as Acting Secretary-General. The continuing need to resolve the problem of Katanga resulted in an even stronger resolution than the one of February 21. With no negative votes and only France and the United Kingdom abstaining, ONUC was now authorized "to take vigorous action, including the use of the requisite measure of force for the immediate apprehension of all foreign military and paramilitary personnel and political advisers not under the United Nations command, and mercenaries."[11] Both superpowers strongly supported this antisecessionist resolution. The United Nations was now clearly committed to support Adoula's central government against the secessionist efforts of both Tshombe and Gizenga.

In early December, Acting Secretary-General U Thant directed UN forces to reestablish law and order in Elisabethville, the capital of Katanga. This initiative resulted in heavy fighting. The United Nations moved in heavy reinforcements for an all-out offensive to gain control in Katanga. But some Western powers, notably Belgium and Great Britain, still hesitated to see Tshombe suppressed. Apart from the considerable financial interest both countries had in Katanga, Tshombe was considered the only pro-Western anti-Communist, whereas Gizenga was seen as a serious Communist threat to the Congo, and the central government as being at best merely neutral. There were supporters of the Tshombe regime even in the United States. Britain refused to supply bombs to the United Nations to be used against Katanga. Some Western opinion viewed the danger of Communist influence as the greater threat, while the anticolonial African and Asian nations saw Tshombe as the tool of "imperialism" and therefore the major danger. The Soviet Union backed the anti-Tshombe forces.

The United Nations was now determined not to stop until the secession was ended. UN forces, supported by jet fighters, pressed on; and on December 20, Tshombe signed the Kitona Agreement, acknowledging the authority of the central government and promising to comply with the UN resolutions requesting the removal of foreign mercenaries. But talks to implement this agreement were not begun until March 1962, and in June, after a second breakdown of discussions, it appeared that Tshombe still had no intentions of ending his secession. In late July, U Thant submitted a plan for the reunification of the Congo, consisting of a 50-50 sharing of revenues from Katangese mines, integration of the Katangese army with that of the central government, and the discontinuance of separate representation abroad, in return for which Katanga would receive considerable local autonomy. U Thant intimated that if this plan was not accepted economic pressures would be used, possibly extending to a complete trade and financial boycott. But neither Belgium, Britain, nor the United States wanted pressures to go beyond the economic sphere, and Tshombe's conditional acceptance of the plan sufficed to avert any economic sanctions. In October, the West became preoccupied with the Cuban crisis and seemed content to let Congolese matters drag on. But the Chinese attack on India gave rise to Indian pressures to obtain the release of her troops in the Congo, numbering over 5,000 men, to fight in the Himalayas. Moreover, the weakening of Premier Adoula's position, occasioned by the central government's inability to enforce its authority in Katanga, created a need for the early settlement of the Katangese secession. Finally, ONUC, which cost $120 million a year, was leading the United Nations into serious financial difficulties. These are discussed in Chapter 6.

By December 1962, U Thant's plan to incorporate Katanga into the central government had not yet been carried out. Thus, the pressure for economic measures against Tshombe increased. Adoula had been requesting such measures since August, but at that time both Britain and Belgium had been opposed. Nor had the United States actively supported such a move. Now Belgium shifted its stand, in return for a promise from the central government to grant Katanga a large share of the mining revenue. The United States, too, threw its support behind Adoula. But Britain and the Union Minière still refused to go along. Fighting again broke out in late December, but Elisabethville was captured by UN forces on December 28, and the important mining center of Jadotville fell a week later. At first it appeared that Tshombe was going to fight to the end and pursue a scorched earth policy which would ruin Katanga, but he surrendered his last stronghold at Kolwezi in return for a general amnesty for Katanga's officials. By the end of January 1963, the resistance was ended, but the situation continued to be tense throughout the rest of the year. In mid-1964, the last ONUC contingents were withdrawn from the Congo, and the problems of reconstruction and reconciliation among the many warring factions reverted to the Congolese government. Ironically, Moise Tshombe emerged as the new premier of the Congo after the withdrawal of ONUC.

The only UN presence remaining in the Congo after June 1964 was the UN Civilian Operation. This undertaking had begun in July 1960 side by side with the UN's peace-keeping function. It aimed to keep intact transport and communications, sustain a decent level of public health, further education and public administration, and develop industry and agriculture. During the latter part of ONUC's work, the Civilian Operation became almost indistinguishable from a large and very ambitious technical-assistance program. Most of the Operation was financed from the UN Congo Fund. This Fund was supported by voluntary contributions from twenty governments. The United States at first contributed almost three-fourths and later about one-half of the expense. The remainder was paid by other Western countries. The Soviet Union made no contribution.

The problem of putting the Congo back on its feet politically and economically had been a staggering one. Indeed, maintaining ONUC in the Congo for four years had nearly bankrupted the

United Nations. Like the King's men, the United Nations could not put the Congo back together again. But the presence of the Organization had at least brought a solution within reach. And it had prevented a major clash between the superpowers in the heart of Africa.

Conclusions

The Congo crisis, like the Suez crisis before it, may be seen in three concentric circles. It began as a local conflict among several warring factions or competing forms of nationalism. When the new Congolese government attacked the intervention of Belgium as an act of aggression, the tribal struggle merged into the larger one of nationalism versus colonialism. Finally, the superpower conflict entered the picture as the last and widest of the circles, with the Soviet Union gaining its first foothold in the Congo through Lumumba and the United States striving to oust the USSR by supporting the United Nations and Kasavubu.

The overall record demonstrates that the two superpowers considered their national interests better served through UN action than through UN paralysis. The United States permitted the United Nations to act because it hoped to neutralize a no man's land in Africa from the East-West struggle and because it was impressed with the powerful African backing for UN action. The Soviet Union permitted the United Nations to act because it, too, wanted to woo the Africans in the United Nations and because a veto would have brought about immediate action in the Assembly, where the USSR had much less power and influence. Only when the Congo Operation began to go directly against the interests of one of the superpowers was a veto cast. And when the UN's policy became more acceptable, the Soviet Union once again stood clear.

Flexibility once again was a keynote. Political control of the Congo Operation passed from the Security Council to the General Assembly and the Secretary-General and finally reverted full circle to the Council. The Secretary-General had to adapt the Operation to a constantly changing UN mandate and to constantly changing attitudes on the part of not only the superpowers but other key states in the Organization. When one considers that ONUC at various times was bitterly attacked by the USSR, opposed by France, and seriously questioned in influential quarters in Britain and the United States, one realizes that the Operation probably could not have survived without an extraordinary degree of adaptability to political developments. And, as in the Suez precedent, an additional element of flexibility characterized ONUC: The peace was kept not by activating the superpowers but by carefully excluding them from the actual physical conduct of the Operation. It is true that ONUC had to be launched with the political support of both superpowers, yet it was able to survive against the will of one of them, and it was conducted without the troops of either.

SELECTED BIBLIOGRAPHY

Burns, Arthur Lee, and Nina Heathcote. *Peace-Keeping by UN Forces: From Suez to the Congo.* New York: Praeger, 1963.

Fabian, Larry L. *Soldiers Without Enemies: Preparing the United Nations for Peacekeeping.* Washington, D.C.: Brookings, 1971.

Gordon, King. *UN in the Congo.* New York: Carnegie Endowment, 1962.

Harbottle, Michael. *The Impartial Soldier.* New York: Oxford University Press, 1970.

James, Alan. *The Politics of Peace-Keeping.* New York: Praeger, 1969.

Lefever, Ernest W. *The Crisis in the Congo: A UN Force in Action.* Washington, D.C.: Brookings, 1965.

O'Brien, Conor Cruse. *To Katanga and Back.* New York: Simon & Schuster, 1963.

Urqhuart, Brian. *Hammarskjöld: The Diplomacy of Crisis.* New York: Knopf, 1972.

NOTES

1. *New York Times,* 10 July 1960.
2. *New York Times,* 24 July 1960.
3. Ibid.
4. UN Doc. S/4426 (August 9, 1960).

5. UN Press Release GA/AB/842 (May 22, 1963).
6. Interview with Dr. Andrew W. Cordier (March 18, 1963).
7. UN Doc. S/4526 (September 17, 1960).
8. UN General Assembly, *Official Records,* 4th Emergency Special Session, 858th Plenary Meeting (September 17, 1960).
9. General Assembly Res. 1474 (ES-IV) (September 20, 1960).
10. UN Doc. S/4741 (February 21, 1961).
11. UN Doc. S/PV 982 (November 24, 1961), pp. 71–75.

The United Nations Financial Crisis and the Superpowers

"The Western powers and their accomplices were alone responsible for the expenses occasioned by those illegal operations [UNEF and ONUC] which are now the cause of the United Nations' financial difficulties, and it is they that should bear those costs, so that the prestige of the United Nations might be maintained."

Nikolai T. Fedorenko
Soviet Delegate
to the Fifth Committee,
May 1963

"Mr. Chairman, there is a confrontation. There is a confrontation not between countries. There is a confrontation by the Soviet Union with the advisory opinion of the World Court. There is a confrontation of the Soviet Union with the acceptance of that opinion by the General Assembly. There is a confrontation by the Soviet Union with the solvency of the United Nations. In short, Mr. Chairman, there is a confrontation between the Soviet Union and the United Nations."

Francis T. P. Plimpton
United States Delegate
to the Fifth Committee,
May 1963

While the United Nations was engaged in major peace-keeping responsibilities, there was never a shortage of Cassandras predicting that the Organization would end with a bang. However, during the height of the UN Operation in the Congo, there existed a real possibility that it might have ended with a whimper. A fiscal crisis developed in the early 1960's that became a threat to the life of the Organization. The cause of this crisis was the refusal of the Soviets and others to pay for the two operations that the United Nations had mounted to keep the peace: the UN Emergency Force in the Middle East (UNEF) and the UN Congo Force (ONUC).

Never had so many people argued so much about so little money. The financial crisis was in reality a political crisis over the proper role for the United Nations to play in the national policies of its member states, particularly the superpowers. Only secondarily was it a crisis over the costs of UN membership.

The United Nations Emergency Force

As we have seen, the General Assembly authorized UNEF by a vote of 64 to 0, with 12 abstentions, in November 1956 and, after much delicate negotiation, over 6,000 men—contingents from ten countries (Brazil, Canada, Colombia, Denmark, Finland, India, Indonesia, Norway, Sweden, and Yugoslavia)—were ready for action. But it was clear that unless the question of financing was solved, the Force would not get beyond the paper stage. Hence the Secretary-General, in his proposals to the General Assembly, gave the matter of financing the Force his most careful attention.

On November 21, 1956, the Secretary-General recommended that a special account outside the regular budget be set up for UNEF and that the costs of the Force be shared by the member states on the basis of the scale of assessments to be adopted for the 1957 budget. In addition, he suggested an initial appropriation of $10 million to meet the immediate cash needs of the Force.

On December 3, the Secretary-General faced the problem of allocating the balance of the expenses of the Force and indicated to the Assembly that the only equitable way of meeting the costs henceforth was to share them according to the 1957 scale of assessments. Although UNEF costs were financed under a special account, the Secretary-General nevertheless considered them as "United Nations expenditures within the general scope and intent of Article 17 of the Charter."[1] Some states disagreed sharply with this proposal, however, and it profoundly divided the Fifth Committee of the Assembly. The superpowers took opposing positions immediately.

The U.S. delegate agreed with the Secretary-General and pointed out that the Committee's decision would be of crucial importance for the future of the Organization. He was supported by most of the Western nations. This view was sharply challenged by the delegate from the Soviet bloc, who insisted that the entire cost of the Operation should be borne by those countries which had precipitated the crisis—Britain, France, and Israel.

Between these two opposing views, yet a third emerged: Most of the smaller nations claimed that everyone should pay something but that the Great Powers, which had special privileges under the Charter, should also shoulder special responsibilities and pick up the major portion of the bill.

This formula won the day in the General Assembly and was adopted by a vote of 62 in favor, 8 against, and 7 abstentions. Only the Soviet bloc voted against. Under the terms of the resolution, everyone was expected to contribute, but nations with limited capacity to pay received rebates of up to 50 percent of their assessments. The United States pledged itself to make voluntary contributions in order to cover the deficits created by these rebates.

The decision to assess the member states by this rebate formula did not solve the problem of financing UNEF. The heart of the problem was how to collect the assessments. Each year, arrears and defaults amounted to roughly one-third of the total assessment. The largest single debtor was the Soviet Union, which justified its nonpayment with two arguments: first, that "the aggressors must pay" and, second, that UNEF was illegal in a fundamental sense, since only the Security Council had the right to authorize peace-keeping operations.

The Secretary-General's position was clear: All member states had a legal obligation to pay. This view was supported by a majority of the membership and most adamantly by the United States.

Although the numerous arrears and defaults had put the United Nations into serious financial straits by 1960, UNEF never threatened the financial structure of the Organization itself. It was the Congo crisis which was to shake that structure to its very foundations.

The United Nations Congo Force

After the two superpowers had both voted for the authorization of a peace force in the Congo in the Security Council on the night of July 13–14, 1960, and a tenuous consensus had thus been attained, the Secretary-General set about to put together and finance the new Force. On October 24, 1960, the Secretary-General estimated the cost of the Congo Force for 1960 at $66,-625,000. Once again, he defended the principle of collective responsibility as the most equitable method of sharing the financial burden. The United States supported him, but the Soviet Union stated its intention not to contribute to any part of ONUC's expenses, since, in its opinion, "the main burden ... should be borne by the chief culprits—the Belgian colonizers."[2] The rest of the money should be raised through voluntary contributions.

At this point, the Secretary-General presented his view to the Fifth Committee. After strongly endorsing the principle of collective responsibility, Mr. Hammarskjöld deplored the tendency of some delegations to approve courses of action for the United Nations without following through financially:

Will this organization face the economic consequences of its own actions and how will it be done? Further, if it is not willing to face the financial consequences of its own decisions, is it then prepared to change its substantive policies? There is no third alternative.

He then pointed up the resulting dilemma:

The Secretariat finds itself in a difficult position. On the one hand, it has to pursue "vigorously" the policy decided upon by the General Assembly and the Security Council. On the other hand, it is continuously fighting against the financial difficulties with which these decisions under present circumstances face the Organization. Of course, the Organization cannot have it both ways.[3]

Finally, the Fifth Committee, by a vote of 45 in favor, 15 opposed, with 25 abstentions, approved a draft resolution proposed by Pakistan, Tunisia, and Senegal and supported by the United States. The resolution recommended an ad hoc account of $48.5 million for the expenses of ONUC, to be assessed on the basis of the 1960 scale; stressed that these assessments would be "binding legal obligations" on member states within the meaning of Article 17 of the Charter; called on the government of Belgium to make a substantial contribution; and recommended that voluntary contributions be applied to reduce by up to 50 percent the assessment of states with the least capacity to pay. On December 20, this recommendation was adopted by the General Assembly by a vote of 46 in favor, 17 opposed, with 24 abstentions.

The second round was fought over the 1961 assessment of $100 million. Again, the Fifth Committee was deeply divided. Since the sum under consideration was the largest ever to be assessed by the United Nations for a single operation and since the decision would obviously have far-reaching consequences, more fundamental and elaborate arguments were raised by the superpowers than over the 1960 assessment. Moreover, the very solvency of the Organization depended on the outcome of the discussion. The United States once again favored the principle of collective responsibility on the basis of the 1960 assessment, although it offered to waive its reimbursement rights of over $10 million and to make a voluntary cash contribution of up to $4 million to be used to reduce the assessments of governments with limited capacity to pay.

The Soviet Union insisted that since ONUC was a Security Council "action" in the sense of Article 48 of the Charter, the General Assembly had no right to reach a decision on the matter. Article 11 of the Charter provided that any question involving peace and security on which action was necessary must be referred to the Security Council by the Assembly. Hence, in the Soviet view, ONUC financing should be governed not by Article 17 but by the unanimity principle in the Security Council. The Secretary-General stated in rebuttal that once the Security Council had taken a decision, the implementation costs fell clearly within the meaning of Article 17 and therefore within the bailiwick of the Assembly. The Soviet position, he argued, would have the effect of extending the unanimity principle of the Big Five to matters of finance, which would clearly lead to the paralysis of the entire Operation in the Congo.[4]

Finally, the Fifth Committee adopted a draft resolution, originally sponsored by Ghana, Liberia, Pakistan, and Tunisia, and supported by the United States, which apportioned $100 million for the period January 1 to October 31, 1961, according to the 1960 assessment scale, "pending the establishment of a different scale of assessment" to defray ONUC's expenses.[5] This time reductions of up to 50 percent were granted the poorer nations in order to obtain the necessary two-thirds majority in the plenary Assembly. Voluntary contributions were to be applied to offset the resulting deficits. The Big Five and Belgium were called upon to make substantial voluntary contributions. The final vote, taken at dawn on the last day of the session, was 54 in favor, 15 against, with 23 abstentions. The Soviet bloc, Mexico, and Belgium cast negative votes, while France and South Africa abstained and subsequently refused to contribute.

The third round was fought in December 1961 over the 1962 ONUC budget. The Fifth Committee delegates went over much the same ground as in the previous debates and recommended an appropriation of $80 million to cover ONUC costs from November 1, 1961, to June 30, 1962. On December 20, 1961, the General Assembly, by a vote of 67 in favor, 13 against, with 16 abstentions, appropriated this amount, with the same provisions for reductions that were approved in April.

The only nation which made voluntary contributions in cash to the Congo Operation was the United States. The sums contributed between 1960 and 1962 totaled more than $30.6 million and were used to cover the deficits created through rebates given to the poorer nations.

At the time of the opening of the Sixteenth General Assembly in 1961, UNEF and ONUC arrears had brought the United Nations to the brink of bankruptcy. In the case of UNEF, forty-one members owed all or part of their assessments for the 1960 budget, bringing arrears to almost 25 percent, and sixty-five members owed all or part of their 1961 assessments, bringing the combined shortage to almost 30 percent of the total. In the case of ONUC, sixty-six members had accumulated a combined shortage of nearly 40 percent of the 1960 budget, and only twenty-four had paid their 1961 assessments.[6] The accumulated arrears for UNEF and ONUC by the end of 1961 exceeded $80 million, which was a sum larger than the annual regular budget. Two of the five permanent powers of the Security Council—the Soviet Union and France—had declared their intention not to make payment, and a third—Nationalist China—had defaulted.

As a result, the two peace-keeping operations had become heavily dependent on one of the two superpowers—the United States. Although the United States was assessed less than one-third of the 1961 UNEF budget, in effect, since its voluntary contribution was used to offset the reductions granted to fifty-one countries with limited capacity to pay, it was paying 43 percent of the total. In 1962, these reductions were increased, and the United States assumed responsibility for a portion of the assessment of seventy-nine member states, which brought its share of the total cost to 48 percent. In the case of ONUC, the United States had assumed this larger share from the very beginning.

Such dependence on one superpower was not desirable, and, more important, the failure of other states to pay their assessments was reaching alarming proportions. The UN debt now exceeded $100 million. In April 1961, a Working Group of Fifteen was established which attempted to construct a special scale of assessment for peace-keeping operations. On November

15, 1961, this Working Group reported its findings to the Fifth Committee. In essence, the report was a catalog of individual opinions largely retracing the ground that had been covered in earlier debates on UNEF and ONUC financing. Only one positive recommendation emerged from the discussions—a suggestion to ask the International Court for an advisory opinion on the applicability of Article 17 of the Charter to peace-keeping operations. In order to settle at least one argument in the financing controversy, the Assembly decided, on December 20, 1961, by a vote of 52 in favor, 11 opposed, with 32 abstentions, to ask the International Court for an advisory opinion on the question: Did the expenditures authorized by the General Assembly for UNEF and ONUC constitute expenses of the Organization within the meaning of Article 17 of the Charter?[7] Acting Secretary-General U Thant had warned the Assembly at that time that the United Nations was faced with imminent insolvency if arrears and current assessments were not paid promptly. He estimated that by June 30, 1962, the gap between the debts of the Organization and its available net cash resources would exceed $100 million. Quite obviously, drastic emergency action was necessary to finance the peace-keeping operations beyond June 1962.

The Bond Issue:
The United Nations as Borrower

On December 20, 1961, the General Assembly also adopted Resolution 1739, authorizing the Secretary-General to issue bonds in the amount of $200 million. The resolution provided that the bonds were to bear interest at 2 percent a year and that the principal was to be repaid in twenty-five annual installments by including in the regular budget each year beginning in 1963 an amount sufficient to pay installments of principal and interest charges. The bonds were to be offered to member states of the United Nations, members of the specialized agencies and of the International Atomic Energy Agency, and, if the Secretary-General with the concurrence of the Advisory Committee on Administrative and Budgetary Questions should so determine, to nonprofit institutions or associations. The sale of bonds was to continue until December 31, 1963.

The debate in the Fifth Committee which preceded the passage of Resolution 1739 was animated and frequently heated. The superpowers took opposing positions. Strong support for the bond issue came from the delegates of the United States, Canada, Australia, Ireland, Ethiopia, Ghana, Ceylon, Burma, and the Netherlands. Philip M. Klutznick of the United States said that if all members paid their arrears on the peace-keeping operations, the Organization could forget about the proposal; but since the exact opposite seemed to be true, the Committee could not leave the Acting Secretary-General with a political mandate and no means to carry it out. Any amount less than $200 million would be insufficient to put the UN house in order. The proposal was to be seen as a one-time emergency arrangement to keep the Organization alive. The opposition was led by A. A. Roschin of the Soviet Union, who declared that the deficit in the United Nations existed not because certain states failed to pay their contributions but because UNEF and ONUC were illegal under the Charter. A bond issue would make the United Nations a tool of the bondholders. It was a maneuver to enable the United Nations to engage in similar illegal peace-keeping activities in the future.

The passage of the bond resolution by the General Assembly was only the first step in securing the $200 million loan for the United Nations. In many member nations only legislative approval could authorize subscription to the bond issue. Most crucial, of course, was to be the decision of the Congress of the United States. When the U.S. delegate to the United Nations voted in favor of the bond resolution, he stated at the time that only the Congress could authorize the purchase of such bonds and that his vote was to be considered as subject to this condition. Indeed, the fiercest legislative battle over the bond issue took place in the Congress of the United States.

On January 30, 1962, President Kennedy sent a special message to Congress to appropriate $100 million for the purchase of the bonds. Exhaustive hearings on the bill were held in the Senate Committee on Foreign Relations during February and March.

The bond issue was defended by top-level members of the administration, including Secretary of State Dean Rusk; Assistant Secretary of State for International Organization Affairs Harlan Cleveland; the U.S. Representative to the United Nations Adlai Stevenson; and the U.S. Representative to the Economic and Social Council Philip Klutznick. The merits of the bond plan were seriously questioned, however, by several members of the Committee on Foreign Relations, particularly Senators George D. Aiken (Republican, Vermont) and Bourke B. Hickenlooper (Republican, Iowa). These debates in the committee were perhaps the most crucial phase in the history of the bond issue.

There were several strong arguments adduced in favor of the bond proposal. First, it was claimed that the bond issue would ensure the principle of collective responsibility, since the principal and interest payments on the bonds would come out of the regular budget, thus compelling nations to pay or risk the loss of voting privileges in the General Assembly. Second, it was asserted that the United States would save money in the long run because, since the bonds would be paid back out of the regular budget over a twenty-five-year period, the United States would contribute to UNEF and ONUC operations on the basis of 32 percent instead of 48 percent as heretofore. Third, since the Secretary-General would be permitted to sell bonds not only to member states of the United Nations but also to members of specialized agencies and possibly to nonprofit institutions, the bond issue offered the prospect of new financial resources. Germany and Switzerland, for example, two nonmembers, would, it was hoped, purchase some of the bonds. Fourth, it was argued that the twenty-five years permitted for repayment would make each annual installment small enough for the burden on some of the smaller countries not to be unreasonable. Finally, the administration defended the view that the bond proposal appeared to be the best temporary device for financing the two peace-keeping operations until a pay-as-you-go plan could be agreed upon. Moreover, the bond issue was not to be deemed a precedent for UN financing, nor was it intended to relieve nations in arrears of their responsibilities toward the two peace-keeping operations. The proceeds were expected to be large enough to carry UNEF and ONUC until the end of 1963.

While no member of the committee proposed that the United States withhold emergency financial assistance from the United Nations, there was considerable concern about whether the bond technique was the wisest course of action. Senators Aiken and Hickenlooper suggested as an alternative that the United States should make a three-year loan of $100 million, with an annual interest rate of 3 percent, to help the United Nations over its financial emergency. The two senators, who received considerable support in the committee, questioned the bond device on a number of grounds. First, it was felt that even though the bond issue was not to become a precedent, it would nevertheless encourage further fiscal irresponsibility by member states that were in arrears. Many might decide that if the United States bought one-half of the bonds, this amount would suffice and thereby relieve them of their own responsibilities. Hence, a short-term loan coupled with a vigorous attempt to collect arrears on past assessments would be preferable. The bond issue would simply postpone the moment of truth and encourage irresponsible nations to shift their burdens to others. Second, support for the bond issue in the General Assembly itself had not been overwhelming. While it was true that 58 nations had voted in favor of the bond resolution, 13 had voted against it, and 33 had abstained or had been absent, indicating that perhaps as many as 46 states did not support the bond proposal. Finally, it was feared that a bond issue would be merely a disguised form of assessment under which subscribing states would first pay up the arrears of delinquent states; then, when the bonds came due, the redemption money would come not from the states in arrears but from those which had both paid their assessments faithfully and subscribed to the bonds as well.

After weighing these conflicting considerations, the Committee on Foreign Relations, by an 8-to-7 vote, reported favorably on the bond bill. The alternative of a straight $100 million loan was narrowly rejected. The majority, however, decided to protect the United States by including the proviso that the president would be authorized to purchase $25 million worth of bonds without limitation but that the purchase of additional bonds up to a total of $100 million would have to be matched by the aggregate amount purchased by other nations. Furthermore, in order to ensure repayment of the bonds, it was decided to deduct from the annual contributions of the United States to the regular budget amounts corresponding to principal and interest payments owed to the United States. Finally, it was made clear that the bond issue was not to set a pattern for the future financing of peace-keeping operations but was to be regarded as an extraordinary one-time remedy for the financial ills of the United Nations.

The narrowness of the vote was a source of considerable anxiety to the administration. It was feared that a hostile majority would develop on the floor of the Senate. Even if the bill did pass the Senate, passage in the House of Representatives was highly uncertain. Consequently, the White House supplanted the State Department as the intermediary with the Senate, in the hope of achieving an overwhelming Senate majority for the president's proposal. The result was agreement on a revised form of the bill; the money was to be designated as a loan but still made available for the purchase of UN bonds by the president at his discretion. This compromise, in which the president maintained the substance of his proposal and the senators won their semantic point of designating the fund as a loan, produced a favorable vote on the Senate floor of 70 to 22. The bill as finally passed retained the original matching proviso as well as the condition that bond repayments be deducted annually from the U.S. contribution to the regular budget. It also included a clause to the effect that the United States should use its best efforts to promote a pattern of UN financing that would make unnecessary any future large-scale borrowing.

The telling argument against a straight $100 million loan that finally won over the opposition was the fact that such a loan would certainly have precipitated a financial crisis after three years. It would have been like a pistol pointed at the head of the United Nations, since, in all likelihood, the world organization would have had no resources to repay the loan at the end of the three years. Moreover, the Senate shared the hope of the administration that the bond plan would compel all members to pay their share of the costs of peace-keeping operations. The Aiken-Hickenlooper loan project would not have furthered the principle of collective responsibility. The battle in the U.S. Senate over the bond proposal was not solely, not perhaps even primarily, the result of a difference of opinion over the respective merits of a bond issue or a straight loan. The bond controversy became a catalyst and brought into the open a good deal of doubt, suspicion, and ambivalence about the United Nations as a whole. The role of the United Nations in Katanga, the rising power of the African and Asian nations in the General Assembly, and the increasing intransigence of the Soviet position—all these stimulated a broad reassessment of the world organization. The difficulties which the bond proposal experienced in the U.S. Senate were largely to be explained in terms of a genuine and serious questioning of the role of the United Nations—especially its peace-keeping function—in the foreign policy of the United States.

The battle in the House of Representatives was no less intense. In September 1962, that body, by a vote of 256 to 134, settled on a bill which permitted the United States merely to match bond purchases of other UN members up to $100 million. The Senate version would have permitted outright U.S. purchase of $25 million. In the last analysis, the more restrictive version was adopted by the Congress. Hence, the full $200 million worth of bonds authorized by U Thant could be raised only if members other than the United States should buy $100 million.

By late 1965, sixty-five states had subscribed to the bond issue, many of them subject to legislative approval. The total amount purchased had reached almost $150 million, of which the United States had bought almost $75 million. Only in the United States had the condition of legislative approval posed a serious threat. Everywhere else, parliaments approved the pledges of their delegations with relative ease.

Superpower Showdown

It had always been clear to even the strongest supporters of the bond issue that the measure would have to be regarded as a stopgap emergency device pending a permanent solution of the problem of financing peace-keeping operations. One ray of hope appeared when, on July 20, 1962, the World Court declared in a 9-to-5 Advisory Opinion that the costs of UNEF and ONUC were to be considered as legally binding obligations upon the entire membership. The Seventeenth General Assembly, on December 19, 1962, after a debate which covered familiar ground, decided to "accept" the Advisory Opinion by a vote of 76 in favor, 17 against, and 8 abstentions. As a result, a considerable number of smaller nations cleared their accounts, but the Soviet Union and France refused to abide by the Opinion. Since France was paying for UNEF, it became increasingly obvious to all concerned that the first major nation to fall under the penalty provisions of Article 19 would be the Soviet Union. Under the terms of this Article, member states delinquent in their assessed contributions for two years or more could lose their votes in the General Assembly unless that body specifically waived the penalty.

In the meantime, the General Assembly reestablished the Working Group and increased its membership from fifteen to twenty-one. The enlarged Working Group continued to search for a solution to the impasse. The Soviet-bloc countries stuck to their contention that only the Security Council had the right to impose assessments for peace-keeping operations. The United States stiffened its position and declared its opposition to any special scale of assessments for UNEF and ONUC for the last six months of 1963 which would involve an assessment percentage for the United States in excess of 32.02 percent. The new U.S. position was based on the assumption that the regular scale made ample adjustments for low per capita income countries and the belief that the financing of UNEF and ONUC for the last six months of 1963 should be handled on an ad hoc basis by methods which would not necessarily constitute a pattern for the future.

The bond money was virtually exhausted by early 1963. Hence, the Assembly had to meet in emergency session in May 1963. It assessed $42.5 million for the two peace forces for the last six months of 1963 according to the regular scale, with a 55 percent reduction to the developing countries. In December, it appropriated $17.75 million for UNEF for 1964 but decided to allot only $15 million to carry ONUC through June 1964.

While conditions in the Congo had improved somewhat, the Assembly's action was taken with at least one eye on its own problems. The accumulated Soviet debts for UNEF and ONUC were rapidly reaching the point at which the USSR would run the risk of losing its vote in the General Assembly under Article 19 of the Charter. The Assembly had no desire to precipitate a major political and constitutional crisis at a time when its military and financial problems in the Congo were still considerable. It was hoped that after the Congo Operation was concluded, some compromise might be arranged concerning the Soviet payments and that the Article 19 crisis could be avoided. Thus, the Assembly was in an increasingly conservative mood, and the combined cash appropriations for UNEF and ONUC for 1964 amounted to less than one-fourth of those appropriated for 1963.

The threat of a constitutional and political crisis over Article 19 had another and perhaps, in the long run, more important impact upon the Assembly than reducing the appropriations for ONUC in late 1963 and 1964. New threats to the peace arose in 1962 in West New Guinea, in 1963 in Yemen, and in 1964 in Cyprus, and the United Nations had to make some provisions to meet its responsibilities. In West New Guinea, the United Nations established the UN Temporary Executive Authority (UN-TEA) and arranged to have the costs shared jointly by the Netherlands and Indonesia. Similarly, in 1963, the expenses of a UN Observer Group in Yemen were split between Saudi Arabia and Egypt without cost to the United Nations. The expenses of the UN peace-keeping force in Cyprus were met by voluntary contributions every three months. In September 1964, Secretary-General U Thant had a hard time raising the modest sum of $7 million needed to keep the 6,400-man force in Cyprus for another three-month period. The original motive behind the move to split the costs between the involved nations in UNTEA and in Yemen was probably to spare the United Nations additional financial strain at this critical juncture and to try to wrap up the Congo Operation *before* Article 19 fell on the Soviets, in the hope that the latter would make some sort of voluntary payment once the Operation was over. In these three cases, however, the United Nations took an important step away from the collective-responsibility principle upon which it had insisted previously. In two cases it was only the involved countries that paid. In Cyprus the voluntary contributions further underscored the disintegration of the collective-responsibility principle. In sum, in an effort to postpone a showdown on this principle, the United Nations, with U.S. support, created three precedents that undermined it.

By 1964, even the Secretary-General admitted that "if the UN does not settle its past, it may not have much of a future." In June 1964, the last UN troops left the Congo, and the Operation to which the USSR had been so much opposed was thus brought to an end. It was now hoped that some compromise could be reached on the Soviet debt. The usual September opening of the General Assembly was postponed until December 1 in order to give diplomats an opportunity to work behind the scenes. The United States, unsure of the support of the Afro-Asian countries and fearful of a showdown, decided not to fight the issue on its merits and would have agreed to a voluntary, unspecified Soviet payment sufficiently large to escape the sanction of Article 19. The United States and other members proposed numerous face-saving compromises to the USSR which would permit that country to make a payment without yielding its basic position that the peace-keeping operations were illegal violations of the Charter. However, no compromise was reached, and as December 1 approached, positions hardened. The United States took the stand that the penalty should go into effect automatically and was determined to enforce it against the Soviet Union if the latter withheld payment. The USSR, on the other hand, insisted that a decision to suspend a member from voting could be obtained only by a two-thirds vote of the members present and voting. It based its case on Article 18 of the Charter which requires a two-thirds majority for Assembly decisions on "important" issues, including "the suspension of the rights and privileges of membership." A week before opening day, the United States declared that it would withhold pledges to the Special Fund until the Soviet Union paid enough of its arrears to avoid the application of Article 19; and the latter stated that, if it were stripped of its voting rights, it would leave the United Nations.

In order to avoid a head-on collision between superpowers, the Secretary-General proposed on opening day that the Assembly conduct its business on a "no-objection" basis, that is, without taking formal votes until some compromise on the debt issue could be hammered out. This proposal was accepted and established an uneasy truce between the superpowers during which further possibilities for compromise could be explored. The Afro-Asian nations proposed a "rescue fund" to which all members, including those in arrears on their peace-keeping assessments, would make voluntary contributions. After protracted and laborious negotiations, the Soviet Union committed itself to the Secretary-General to pledge an unspecified voluntary contribution but refused to name the amount and date of payment, demanding in return that the Assembly resume normal business and voting procedure. The United States refused to accept this proposal, describing it as a "pig in the poke." In effect, the Soviet Union demanded the right to vote now and pay later, while the United States insisted that the Soviet Union pay first and vote later.

In the meantime, the tenuous "no-vote" procedure threatened to break down when a sharp disagreement arose over one of four nonpermanent Security Council seats to be filled by December 31, 1964. While three candidates were unopposed, the fourth seat was hotly contested by Jordan and Mali. Since neither candidate was prepared to yield, the President of the Assembly, Mr. Alex Quaison-Sackey, proposed a special "consultation" procedure which, in effect, was tantamount to voting, with the single difference that the location of the ballot box was outside the Assembly hall. When three of these "straw polls" failed to break the deadlock, the two candidates reluctantly agreed to split the term.

New Year's Day of 1965 added France and ten other states to the list of members that were in danger of losing their voting rights under Article 19. Thus the crisis assumed more serious proportions, since, by now, over 10 percent of the membership, including two Great Powers, fell under Article 19. The no-vote procedure continued, but under it none of the important agenda items could be touched. Shortly before the Assembly was to adjourn, the delegate of Albania threatened the precarious superpower truce by demanding an immediate resumption of

normal voting procedure. The Assembly, however, in an overwhelming vote of 97 to 2 with 13 abstentions, overruled the
Albanian demand, both superpowers voting with the majority.
The United States, in a tactical retreat, permitted this one vote,
declaring that it was merely procedural and thus did not compromise the American position on Article 19. On February 18, the
General Assembly adjourned until September 1, 1965, with the
main problem—the issue of Article 19—as far from solution as
ever.

The Nineteenth General Assembly had thus managed to
avoid an open confrontation between the superpowers over the
application of Article 19. The Afro-Asian group had tried desper-
ately to find some middle ground and had succeeded in making
modest headway. The Soviet Union did offer to pledge a voluntary contribution, though it refused to name the amount and date
of payment under "American blackmail." And the United States
had to look on while the Soviet delegate cast his "vote" in the
consultation over the seating of Jordan and Mali on the Security
Council and had to permit a General Assembly vote to continue
the no-vote procedure.

As the Nineteenth General Assembly adjourned, a curious
situation prevailed. The superpowers continued to be at odds
with each other over the issue of Article 19. But the Afro-Asians
were becoming increasingly frustrated with the superpowers,
since no important UN business could be transacted on a no-vote
basis. Hence, by early 1965, the confrontation between the two
superpowers on the one hand and almost everyone else on the
other had become almost as important as the U.S.-Soviet confrontation itself. The financial crisis had become a mirror of a
significant political fact: The United States and the Soviet Union,
if they chose to, could still virtually paralyze the more than 100
other member states of the General Assembly. But finally, and
perhaps most important, almost the entire membership *including*
the superpowers made a common front against one member,
Albania, which—probably prompted by Communist China—
tried to precipitate a showdown that neither superpower wanted.
Hence, there emerged a partial community of interest between

the superpowers which made both of them rally to the defense of the United Nations itself.

What was basically at stake in the tug of war during the Nineteenth General Assembly was the principle of collective responsibility. The USSR opposed it, and the United States chose not to fight for it on its merits. While the USSR's opposition was understandable, the problem of the United States was far more complex. On the one hand, the United States had a clear commitment to the principle; its support of the UNEF and ONUC financing patterns and its approval of the World Court Advisory Opinion left little doubt on that score. On the other hand, from a tactical point of view, the United States feared that it would lose a showdown vote or, if it won, that the victory might be indecisive or even Pyrrhic. The Afro-Asians were most eager to avoid a confrontation and were deeply divided on the merits of the American position. Second, there was the nagging fear that the collective-responsibility principle might not always be congruent with the U.S. national interest in the future. Indeed, the right to pick and choose the peace-keeping operations one supported might one day be to the advantage of the United States. These conflicting considerations led to the ambivalence that characterized the U.S. position.

Finally, shortly before the opening of the Twentieth General Assembly, the United States gave up the fight over Article 19. On August 16, 1965, Ambassador Arthur J. Goldberg announced that "the United States regretfully accepted the simple and inescapable fact of life that a majority of the 114 member states was unready to apply Article 19." Thus, it now became unlikely that the United Nations would soon again venture into massive peace-keeping operations against the will of a superpower. It seemed, instead, that future operations would have to be based on a broader political consensus and be more modest in scale. It also seemed that the financial counterpart of collective responsibility, the assessment principle, would be superseded, at least temporarily, by that of voluntarism. The United Nations would require a period during which past gains would have to be consolidated before new advances could be made.

Conclusions

The financial crisis of the United Nations has aroused acute anxiety among many observers, who see it as the unmistakable symptom of an early death of the Organization. They point to the history of the League of Nations, maintaining that, in its case, financial atrophy was the first harbinger of doom, and claim that the same omens are now gathering over the United Nations: the penury of states and the Organization's mounting deficits.

On closer scrutiny, this analogy does not hold up. Many of the symptoms are similar, to be sure, but the root causes are quite different. The fiscal plight of the League had been the symptom of a struggle over its very existence. Many states had questioned the raison d'être of the League; others had tolerated it; certainly very few states wanted it to move beyond the concept of a "static conference machinery." In that sense, the League's chronic financial anemia had been the result of a struggle between nihilists and conservatives: those who would deny its existence altogether and those who would relegate it to the peripheries of their national policies. The former attitude had led to active hostility; the latter, to political neglect and indifference.

The UN's financial plight is not the expression of a struggle over the Organization's existence. All states, including the Soviet Union, have accepted its presence. The struggle has moved onto a higher plane. It is now being waged between the conservatives and the liberals: those who wish to maintain the United Nations as a "static conference machinery," and those who wish to endow it with increasing strength and executive authority. Viewed in this light, the financial crisis of the United Nations does not indicate that the Organization has fallen into political collapse, but rather that the membership has not yet been willing to ratify and sustain its rise to a higher plane of development.

If one examines the superpowers' attitude in detail, it is clear that the "liberal" and "conservative" labels must be used with caution in the areas of peace-keeping and financing. It is true that the United States has generally favored the creation of peace-keeping machinery as a collective responsibility of the membership, whereas the USSR has tended to reject the assessment principle for UN peace forces. But as we look at specific cases, it is clear that the Soviet Union has not always said "no" with equal vigor. In fact, until 1963 the Soviet Union paid for a considerable number of minor peace-keeping operations that were financed through the regular budget. It acquiesced in the establishment of UNEF and actually voted for the creation of the Congo Force and only later tried to destroy it. Finally, and under great pressure, it came close to offering a payment toward UNEF and ONUC costs, although ostensibly as an unspecified and general contribution to the United Nations. Hence, the Soviet attitude has varied and can be portrayed in terms of a spectrum ranging from acquiescence through passive resistance to active obstruction. Moreover, these attitudes often changed during one operation. The changing Soviet position toward the Congo Force is a case in point.

Similarly, the states favoring UN peace-keeping operations do not always say "yes" with the same degree of enthusiasm. Some states, like the United States, support the political resolutions authorizing the establishment of the peace forces, then vote for the financing resolutions and make payment as well. Others have second thoughts at the second stage and abstain or even vote against the financing resolutions. And some that vote "yes" in the first two stages finally refuse to make payment after all. The liberal position on peace-keeping forces also extends along a fluid continuum: enthusiastic support, moral support, and tacit consent. The more cautious form of liberalism and the permissive form of conservatism often meeting in voting terms, if not in principle, on the common ground of abstention.

Thus, both liberals and conservatives have varied their position over a broad spectrum. In fact, most states have responded to specific peace-keeping cases in terms of national interest rather than abstract principle. This is particularly true of the superpowers. From the U.S. point of view UNEF and ONUC sealed off a no man's land in the cold war from a possible East-West military confrontation and reduced the likelihood of unilateral intervention by the Soviet Union. The Soviet Union could reason that UNEF and ONUC prevented Soviet bridgeheads in the Middle East and Africa. Since, in the latter case, a bridgehead had already been established and had to be liquidated under UN pressure, Soviet opposition to ONUC may have taken a more active form. Thus, the financial crisis over UNEF and ONUC was really a political crisis over the proper role and control of these forces. The Soviet Union did not oppose UNEF and ONUC because it did not want to pay for them; it did not want to pay for them because it opposed them.

No one knows how the United States would react to a UN peace-keeping operation that conflicted with its national interests, because to date the United States has never been on the wrong end of a UN police action. In part, this fact is due to good luck. If Kasavubu had been killed in the Congo instead of Lumumba, the ONUC operation might have provided an interesting test of the American commitment to the principle of collective responsibility in the financing of peace-keeping operations. American voting supremacy in the United Nations, described in Part One, has also been important in preventing issues like the 1954 coup in Guatemala from being considered at any length by the United Nations. What the United States would do in a minority position against a UN operation is difficult to estimate, but, as we shall see in Part Three, the United States has not hesitated to attack UN operations contrary to its national interest in the far less sensitive economic and social areas of the Organization's work. The point here is not to indict the policies of the superpowers but to suggest that in peace-keeping matters it is misleading to associate the United States or the Soviet Union too closely with any philosophical position toward the United Nations in the abstract. Each case is decided in accordance with the national interest as it arises.

The truth of the above assertion was borne out in 1972. In May of that year, the House of Representatives passed a bill that contained a stern provision limiting the U.S. contribution to the UN regular budget to 25 percent of the total. The House saw fit to pass this bill in clear violation of the American treaty obligation to share the costs of the regular budget in accordance with assessments voted by the General Assembly. At the time of the House action, this assessment was set at 31.52 percent of the budget. While, on sober second thought, the Senate restored the cut in June 1972, it insisted that the desired level of 25 percent must be reached by the end of 1973. Accordingly, the U.S. delegation, in the fall of 1972, put the General Assembly on notice that it was determined to negotiate a reduction of the American assessment to a level not to exceed 25 percent.

A perusal of the debates in the House and Senate reveals the fact that a large number of American legislators had come to perceive the United Nations as, at best, a wasteful and inefficient body and, at worst, an organization that in the wake of the American defeat over the Chinese representation issue, had become inimical to the national interest. As one legislator crudely remarked: "I think that the finest thing that could happen to the United States of America would be to cut off every dime to the United Nations, go up there and take them by the nape of the neck and the seat of the pants and throw them out of this country."[8]

The irony of this episode lay, of course, in the fact that American legislators had been the first to chastise the Russians for their refusal to pay for peace-keeping costs in 1962 but that when the political situation had changed a decade later, they behaved in a manner somewhat reminiscent of the Russians.

In November 1972, a member of the U.S. Mission to the United Nations asserted that

The only time we get a spontaneous favorable comment from people we meet around the country is when we speak up in a tough and uncompromising way at the United Nations. That appears to be the mood of the nation, and that mood has to be reflected in our stand on the United States assessment.[9]

Accordingly, the U.S. delegation waged an all-out battle in the General Assembly's Finance Committee to have its assessment reduced to 25 percent. The Finance Committee, over bitter Soviet opposition, approved the American request by a vote of 61 to 30, with 32 abstentions. On December 13, 1972, the General Assembly endorsed this move and, in a vote of 81 to 27, with 22 abstentions, recommended the reduction of the U.S. assessment to 25 percent "as soon as practicable."

The impact of the American move on the United Nations' treasury was serious but not catastrophic since the admission of the two Germanys to the United Nations in 1973 more than made up the difference. China, too, in an unprecedented move, offered to raise her contribution to the regular budget from 3 percent to 7 percent over a period of several years.

By the mid-1970's, the financing of peace-keeping operations was determined exclusively by the Security Council. The Cyprus Force continued to subsist solely on the basis of voluntary contributions, but the assessment principle was applied once again to the two new peace forces in the Middle East. The Soviet Union made a contribution for the first time to UNEF II and to UNDOF in 1973 and 1974 respectively. China, however, expressed her ambivalence toward the United Nations' role in the Middle East by refusing to pay for the two forces. Though the United Nations was no longer as financially desperate as during the 1960's, a shortage of funds nevertheless continued to plague the Organization as virtually a chronic affliction.

The central truth that emerges from this case study is that no state, least of all a superpower, will adopt or easily acquiesce in paying for a policy that it considers inimical to its national interest. The key to superpower behavior in the United Nations is power and influence. Money is a symbol of that power. States will not oppose policies because they refuse to pay for them; they will refuse to pay for them because they oppose them. In this fundamental respect, the two superpowers remain very much alike.

SELECTED BIBLIOGRAPHY

Gross, Leo. "The International Court of Justice and Peace-Keeping Expenses of the UN." *International Organization* (Winter 1963).

Jackson, John H. "The Legal Framework for United Nations Financing: Peace-Keeping and Penury." *California Law Review* (March 1963).

Singer, J. David. *Financing International Organizations.* The Hague: Nijhoff, 1961.

Stegenga, James A. *The United Nations Force in Cyprus.* Columbus: Ohio State University Press, 1968.

Stoessinger, John G., et al. *Financing the United Nations System.* Washington, D.C.: Brookings, 1964.

————. "Financing the United Nations." *International Conciliation*, no. 535 (November 1961).

U.S., Congress, Senate, Committee on Foreign Relations, *Purchase of United Nations Bonds*, 87th Cong., 2d sess., 1962.

NOTES

1. UN General Assembly, *Official Records* (GAOR), Eleventh Session, Fifth Committee, 541st Meeting (December 3, 1956), par. 79.

2. GAOR, Fifteenth Session, Fifth Committee, 775th Meeting (October 26, 1960), par. 8.

3. UN Doc. A/C.5/843 (November 21, 1960), pp. 1, 8.

4. See GAOR, Fifteenth Session, Annexes, Agenda items 49/50 (A/C.5/860, March 27, 1961), and UN Doc. A/PV.977 (April 5, 1961), p. 11.

5. On October 30, the Assembly authorized the Secretariat to commit up to $10 million a month for the remainder of 1961. However, it left the mode of financing for "later deliberation."

6. These were: Australia, Canada, Central African Republic, Ceylon, Dahomey, Denmark, Finland, Gabon, Iceland, India, Ireland, Ivory Coast, Japan, Liberia, Malaya, Netherlands, New Zealand, Nigeria, Norway, Pakistan, Tunisia, Turkey, United Kingdom, United States.

7. General Assembly Res. 1731, XVI (December 20, 1961). The resolution was sponsored by the United States, Brazil, Cameroon, Canada, Denmark, Japan, United Kingdom, Liberia, Sweden, and Pakistan.

8. Representative James A. Haley (Democrat, Florida); Quoted in *Congressional Record*, No. 4690, May 18, 1972.

9. *New York Times*, 27 November 1972.

PART THREE

The Superpowers and
Development, Arms Control,
and Environment Operations

A United Nations Dilemma: Cuba and the Special Fund

7

"The assistance furnished by the Special Fund ... shall not be accompanied by any conditions of a political nature."

Principles governing assistance
furnished by the Special Fund

"The United States opposed this project when it was put up for approval in May 1961; we have reiterated our opposition on several occasions since; we are still opposed. Our policy toward Cuba involves opposition to any source of aid and comfort to the present regime. We pursue this policy in the United Nations and elsewhere by all means available to us."

Statement by Richard N. Gardner
U.S. Deputy Assistant Secretary of State
for International Organization Affairs,
Hearings on Special Fund,
February 18, 1963

By the mid-1970's, most of the energy of the United Nations was devoted to economic and social concerns. Almost 90 percent of the entire cost of the United Nations family was spent on economic and social projects. If measured by the sheer bulk of its activities, the Organization was gradually becoming a major vehicle for the world community's efforts to shape a new international economic order.

Economic development, however, has been a major source of strife between the world's rich and poor. The original hope of the framers of the Charter was that social projects could be insulated from the storms of political controversy and that decisions would be made on the basis of economic considerations alone. For the first fifteen years, the cold war did play a role in the superpowers' economic decisions in the United Nations family, but it never occupied the center of the stage. In 1960, finally, it intruded rather crassly and the United Nations has never been the same again. The watershed case of Cuba and the Special Fund marked the onset of the politicization process of the UN's economic and social activities, which began between East and West during the 1960's and continues between North and South in the 1970's. As a result, since 1960 there has been no such thing as a purely economic decision in the United Nations.

In particular, this case study will concentrate on the behavior of one superpower, the United States, in the area of economic development. The UN's specialized agencies and voluntary programs have been active in this field. The specialized agencies most directly involved have been the World Health Organization (WHO), the Food and Agriculture Organization (FAO), the International Labour Organization (ILO), and UNESCO. The two voluntary programs have been the Expanded Program for Technical Assistance (EPTA), launched in 1950, and the Special Fund, which began operations in 1959. In 1966 these two bodies were merged into the UN Development Program (UNDP). The specialized agencies have been financed through assessment; EPTA and the Special Fund have depended exclusively upon voluntary contributions from governments.

The two voluntary programs were largely the result of American initiative. The impetus for EPTA came out of Point Four of President Truman's inaugural speech of January 1949. Subsequently, the United States proposed to the UN Economic and Social Council that a concrete program be elaborated for enlarging technical-assistance activities. Since 1950, when EPTA began operations with $20 million provided by 54 nations, contributions have steadily increased. In 1955, 70 nations pledged over $27 million. And by 1964, pledges from 108 governments exceeded $50 million. The United States contributed 60 percent of the total at first, but by 1964 it had reduced its share to 40 percent.

The Special Fund was set up in 1959 for the purpose of financing preparatory and "preinvestment" projects which would make it possible for technical assistance and development to yield optimum results. In keeping with its mandate, the Fund has concentrated on relatively large projects. The sum total of government contributions has exceeded that for EPTA—$38.5 million in 1960 and $80 million in 1964. Again, the United States limited its contribution to 40 percent of the total. A dynamic force behind the drive for Special Fund resources was Mr. Paul G. Hoffman, the late managing director of the Fund who was an American citizen.

The attitude of the Soviet Union toward the UN development programs has been ambivalent. During the lifetime of Stalin, the USSR largely ignored the UN voluntary programs or attacked them as imperialist dominated. Certainly, it did not contribute to them, since the aid went to countries which were generally "on the wrong side" of the revolution. With the ascendancy of Khrushchev, however, the Soviet attitude became more flexible. Opportunity beckoned in the developing countries of Asia, Africa, and the Middle East. Anticolonial passions could perhaps be exploited for the Soviet cause. Moreover, it had become clear that EPTA was not going to fail, that its popularity would increase, and that more harm would come to the Soviet Union by remaining outside than by participating. Thus, the USSR in the mid-1950's rejoined most of the specialized agencies and began to make small contributions to EPTA amounting to somewhat less than 3 percent of the total. And when the Special Fund was established in 1959, the Soviet Union joined in its support with a similar contribution.

The evidence suggests that Soviet support of EPTA and the Special Fund was not motivated primarily by altruistic or humanitarian considerations. In the eyes of most recipient states, the two programs had become largely identified with the United

States. This trend was clearly not in the Soviet national interest. The new Soviet leadership in the mid-1950's saw the voluntary programs as possible forums for Communist propaganda. The possible gains to be made by participating justified the making of small contributions via the United Nations to countries in the non-Communist world.

In their deliberations on development projects, EPTA's Technical Assistance Board and the Special Fund's Governing Council considered all their programs in private and submitted a package of projects to be approved in a single vote. This procedure was adopted from the very beginning in order to minimize political considerations in the decision-making process. On a number of occasions, the Soviet delegate to the Special Fund objected to projects in anti-Communist countries like Formosa, South Korea, and South Vietnam, but never forced a separate vote on any one given project. Similarly, the United States, *inter alia*, regularly approved projects in Communist countries like Poland and Yugoslavia.

Indeed, until 1960, neither EPTA nor the Special Fund was deeply affected by cold-war politics. It was the Cuban case that changed all this and set two interesting precedents. It marked the first time that the cold war intruded blatantly into UN economic-development programs. And, second, it placed the United States in a new and unfamiliar role. For the first time in the history of the United Nations, the United States found itself in the position of the single dissenter trying to cast a "veto," as it were, on an issue affecting its national interest. For the first time, the usual roles of the two superpowers were reversed: The Soviet Union, in the majority, was eagerly advocating a project, while the United States, in the minority, was resisting it.

Cuba and the Special Fund

The origin of the Special Fund project came from Fidel Castro's request for aid at the time of his visit to the UN Fifteenth General Assembly in September 1960. The Cuban government saw the need for the diversification of agriculture in order to reduce its dependence upon its sugar crop. Accordingly, with the help of an FAO expert acting as the representative of the managing director of the Special Fund, it formulated a project proposal. Managing Director Paul Hoffman, acting upon the proposal, recommended to the Special Fund's Governing Council that twelve UN experts and some equipment be sent to the agricultural station at Santiago de las Vegas to study the fields of tropical animal husbandry, soil classification, conservation, and crop diversification.

The proposed project was to last five years. It called for an allocation from the Special Fund of $1,157,000, including a cash contribution from Cuba of $114,500. The Cuban government was to make available a counterpart contribution of personnel, services, land, and buildings in the equivalent of $1,878,000. The total Cuban contribution was thus to be $1,992,500; and the total cost to the Special Fund, $1,042,500. The FAO was designated as the executing agency of the project.

The project came up for formal approval before the Governing Council of the Special Fund in May 1961, a few weeks after the disastrous Bay of Pigs invasion. Needless to say, the American attitude toward Cuba was not conducive to approval of a project to aid Castro's island. Yet, when the Special Fund was created, it had been agreed that political considerations would play no part in the allocation of aid; projects were to be determined according to economic criteria. This stipulation had been carefully honored. The United States had agreed to projects in Communist countries; the Soviet Union had accepted aid projects to Taiwan and South Korea; and Egypt had acquiesced in one to Israel.

Nevertheless, American policy toward Cuba now was to oppose "any source of aid and comfort to the present regime."[1] The United States thus decided to oppose the project, but on economic rather than political grounds. When the project was brought before the Governing Council in May, U.S. representative Philip Klutznick stated the American objections. He noted that projects should be chosen according to certain criteria established by the managing director, among them: (1) the urgency of the recipient country's need; (2) the prospect that the project would lead to early results, have a wide impact on the country, and lead to new capital investment; (3) the certainty that the project would enjoy the full cooperation of the recipient government with trained personnel; and (4) the government's assumption of responsibility upon completion of the project. Mr. Klutznick then pointed out that "recent developments in Cuba [had] raised substantial question as to whether the above-mentioned criteria [could be] satisfied with respect to the project before us." He specified four developments which, in his view, would frustrate the objectives of the Cuban project and therefore led him to suggest its rejection. These developments were: (1) Cuba had failed to take advantage of existing mulilateral sources of technical assistance through the OAS; (2) the Cuban government had displaced or driven into exile qualified personnel at the same time that it had requested UN technicians to replace them; (3) the wholesale slaughter of livestock and misuse of other physical resources had raised doubts about the utility of any aid in livestock-raising techniques; (4) the existence of a bilateral technical-assistance agreement with the Soviet bloc which would bring 300 agricultural experts to Cuba had mitigated the urgency of the need for the UN project. Adding that political and economic conditions were interrelated and that the manner in which a country was governed had economic consequences, Mr. Klutznick concluded that the U.S. opposition was not based on political considerations:

Mr. Chairman, for the reasons I have stated, this project has not received the approval of my government. We have great respect for the judgment of the staff of the Special Fund. Under normal procedures, the Managing Director would examine any questions arising before entering into a plan of operations for any project. We are confident, therefore, that the project will not proceed until the staff has satisfied itself about the questions we have raised and is certain that the project can be completed successfully to the ultimate benefit of the Cuban people.[2]

Hence, the basic American argument in 1961 was that the Cuban government had so subordinated the economic and social welfare of the Cuban people to the narrow political aims of its leadership that the minimum standards of efficiency and effectiveness which must guide the implementation of cooperative development projects—whether in the UN system or without—could not possibly be met.[3]

The United States felt that its national interest could not permit the Cuban project and undertook a major diplomatic effort to block its recommendation in the Governing Council. Working against the United States was the general practice of the Council never to have a separate vote on any one project, but rather to vote on the whole package of proposals by the managing director. Moreover, many delegates on the Council felt that the economic arguments advanced by the United States against the Cuban project were thinly disguised political ones. Thus, when the United States tried to round up 7 votes, the necessary blocking third in the 18-member Council, it discovered that the other members were unwilling to aid in the precedent-breaking consideration of a single project. They were afraid lest this might lead the Soviet Union to force separate votes on aid to Taiwan, South Korea, and South Vietnam; or Egypt, on aid to Israel. There was general concern that approval of individual projects would turn the Special Fund into an East-West battleground.

In later testimony before the Senate subcommittee of the Committee on Foreign Relations in 1963, State Department officials explained U.S. policy. Since the United States could not obtain the necessary 7 votes to block the Cuban project, it decided not to press for a losing vote. Instead, it settled for going on record against the project, hoping that Paul Hoffman might be dissuaded from the project by other means. Hence, in May 1961, the Cuban project was approved, along with all the others.

The managing director now found himself in a dilemma. He was an international civil servant, but also a prominent American citizen. It was his duty to proceed with the project, once approved by the Governing Council, unless there were economic considerations to the contrary. He was under continual pressure from both Washington and Havana. The project hung fire for over a year and a half while Hoffman investigated whether there were any valid economic reasons for canceling it. He could find none. Also, as one observer put it:

Hoffman thought the political objections more emotional than rational. The proposed project was so minute and so long range that it could not possibly have any significant effect on Castro's tenure in office.

If the United States could not get rid of the dictator in the six to eight years before the project would come to fruition, diplomats pointed out to him, Washington probably would never be able to. Twelve men studying Cuban soil use could not remotely affect the outcome.[4]

On February 13, 1963, the United Nations announced that it would proceed with the agricultural project in Cuba. Hoffman made one concession, however: The five-year program would be reviewed after six months, and only five men would be sent to Cuba to study how the country might diversify its agriculture. If conditions proved propitious for the project and if the Cuban government did not renege on its responsibilities and sharing of the costs, then the other seven experts would be sent and the project would be put into full operation.

The reaction in the United States to Mr. Hoffman's decision was one of anger. The press was almost unanimous in its disapproval, and a Senate subcommittee of the Committee on Foreign Relations began an investigation of the Special Fund project. The senators wanted to know why the United States had not pressed for a reconsideration of the Cuban project at the January 1963 meeting of the Governing Council.

Mr. Richard N. Gardner, deputy assistant secretary of state for International Organization Affairs, explained that reconsideration to suspend the project required a two-thirds vote. Despite the shift of Latin-American opinion after the Punta del Este Conference of January 1962, and the more recent opposition to Cuba arising out of the missile crisis of the fall of 1962, a canvass had indicated that the necessary number of votes could not be obtained. Thus the United States had again decided not to bring the issue to a vote. Instead, it was the American hope that, owing to the economic and technical objections raised by Mr. Klutznick, the project would not be implemented. Moreover, it was feared that a public statement might create an uproar that would force Mr. Hoffman to authorize the full operation immediately.

Most of the senators, however, were of the opinion that the United States should have pressed for a vote, despite the possibility of losing. In addition, they suggested another reason for opposing the project—Cuba's delinquency in its payments to the United Nations. Although Cuba had pledged $55,000 to the Special Fund for the 1960–1963 period, it had made no actual payment. It had paid none of its UNEF and ONUC assesments nor its pledges to EPTA assistance—over $800,000 for the period 1961–1964. Finally, it was pointed out that Cuba was a year in arrears on its regular budget assessment.

Mr. Gardner replied that these points had been raised in January 1963 but that they had not impressed the necessary two-thirds of the Council's membership. He then forcefully stated the reason for not pressing for a vote that the United States was sure to lose:

If we had forced it to a vote it would have been the first time in history, in the history of the Special Fund, that a division was had on an individual project, and it would have meant that hereafter the Soviets would have forced a vote on all the projects in Taiwan, South Korea, in Vietnam, which they do not like, and we would have been, if I may put it this way, jeopardizing the 97 per cent of the Special Fund projects we do like for the sake of 3 per cent which we do not like.[5]

The Senate subcommittee hearings also brought out some interesting statistics about the Special Fund aid in general. The Communist bloc, including Yugoslavia, had paid $8 million into the Fund but had received in projects to Communist countries only $6 million. That is to say, the Communist bloc had paid 3 percent of the Fund's capital but received only 2.5 percent of the Fund's allocations. And the Communist bloc had been the recipient of 6 out of a total of 288 projects, that is, slightly more than 2 percent. Mr. Gardner's fear of jeopardizing the 97 percent of Special Fund projects that were backed by the United States was thus very understandable, even though his argument omitted the fact that the United States probably had the voting power on the Governing Council to push through most of the projects it desired by separate votes if it had to. Moreover, all but five countries aided by the Special Fund were also recipients of direct aid from the United States. Hence, a reduction of Special Fund aid to these countries as a result of Soviet pressure might merely have increased the necessity of more direct American aid. Indeed, Cuba was the only Communist country receiving Special Fund aid which the United States did not help in some way. Poland and Yugoslavia received both Special Fund and direct American assistance.

Thus, the first time a Special Fund project went directly against the American interest, the U.S. Congress decided to make an issue of it, although the project represented only .5 percent of total Special Fund aid. If the executive had followed suit and the American delegation on the Governing Council had pressed for a vote, the tradition of consensus governing that body's decision-making process would have been broken. The USSR would then probably have called for separate votes on other projects. While the United States probably could have won most of these votes, the cold war would nevertheless have been introduced into UN economic development.

The actual decision to acquicscc alienated congressional opinion and called into question the continuance of the large American contribution to the Fund and other UN aid operations by focusing on the single project which was not in the U.S. interest. The vehemence of the opposition brought the cold war into the Special Fund anyway, even though no separate vote was actually forced. The subcommittee hearings made it plain that a separate vote was not taken only because the United States would have lost. The United States had not merely registered its disapproval of an unpopular project, as the Soviet Union had done, but had pressed for its removal both behind the scenes and in public.

On balance, the Congress defended the short-range national interest of the United States: Its position was largely influenced by pressure from constituencies for satisfaction against Cuba. The executive was less impressed with the short-run gains against Cuba and more with the long-range losses to American interest if the United States had disrupted the nonpolitical voting tradition of the Special Fund.

Perhaps the most important element affecting this American dilemma was the tenor of the times. The timing of the project was unfortunate. As one correspondent put it: "A very large segment of American opinion screamed whenever the word Cuba was mentioned. Especially after the missile crisis, the very idea of aiding Castro with so much as a garden trowel was anathema to them and to Congress."[6]

An interesting postcript to the Cuban project is that six months after its inception, the Special Fund quietly put it on a regular five-year basis. This fact caused hardly a ripple in American congressional and public opinion.

Conclusions

The Cuban case shows that, in the United States, the executive and Congress may be deeply split in their perceptions of the American national interest in the United Nations. In both the Secretariat case discussed in Chapter 3 and the problem of UN finances examined in Chapter 6, congressional pressure tended toward a more short-range view of the national interest that was often in conflict with long-range American objectives in the United Nations. In the Cuban case, the split was profound. The view of the administration was best expressed in the following statement by Mr. Gardner:

The price of participating in any political institution is that you cannot get your way all the time. We cannot expect to get our way all the time in the United Nations. There will be entries on the debit as well as on the credit side of the ledger. The central question is whether credits exceed the debits—whether looking at the balance sheet as a whole the institution is making a net contribution to our national interest. The United States Government continues to believe that the answer to that question is overwhelmingly in the affirmative.[7]

As a result, the State Department preferred not to force the Cuban project to a vote. Many members of the Congress, however, under heavy pressure from their constituencies, found it difficult to justify "American money going via the United Nations to Cuba" and impossible to explain the complexities of the situation to the electorate.

When considered in the broader context of superpower interaction in the United Nations, the Cuban case puts in serious question the validity of the functionalist thesis: that the sphere of economic cooperation may be insulated from the storms of political controversy and that it may even be used as a stepping stone toward the building of political order. Indeed, the relationship of the two superpowers in the Special Fund suggests an inversion of the functionalist proposition. Certainly, Soviet participation in that body was inspired not by a desire for greater East-West accord but by the fear of Western gains in the uncommitted countries and the reluctance to concede leadership in technical-assistance activities to the United States.

The United States, in turn, has supported Special Fund programs, but only so long as most of these have been in accord with America's own national interest. The Cuban project demonstrated that, for the United States, too, it has proved impossible to separate economic from political considerations. When a development project was seen by the Congress as inimical to the American interest, the government was almost pressured into taking an even tougher line than the Soviet Union did in comparable situations.

Most important, perhaps, the Cuban case placed the United States in a minority position for the first time on an issue that the nation saw as clearly inimical to its national interest. And it showed that the United States, when placed in such a situation, faces severe congressional pressures that may compel it to fight the majority as fiercely and stubbornly as the Soviet Union. It suggests the possibility that the depth of the American commitment to the United Nations is yet to be tested. The Soviet Union has been a permanent minority since the beginning of the United Nations; on the other hand, the United States, at that time, still had relatively little experience with hostile majorities in the United Nations. In that sense, the Cuban case was a harbinger of things to come in a changing United Nations in which the United States would often be in opposition.

SELECTED BIBLIOGRAPHY

Asher, Robert E., et al. *The United Nations and the Promotion of the General Welfare.* Washington, D.C.: Brookings, 1957.

Gardner, Richard N., and Max F. Millikan, eds. *The Global Partnership.* New York: Praeger, 1968.

Jacobson, Harold K. *The USSR and the UN's Economic and Social Activities.* Notre Dame, Ind.: University of Notre Dame Press, 1963.

Laves, Walter H. C., and Charles A. Thompson. *UNESCO: Purpose, Progress, Prospects.* Bloomington: Indiana University Press, 1957.

Mitrany, David. *A Working Peace System.* Chicago: Quadrangle Books, 1966.

Myrdal, Gunnar. *An International Economy.* New York: Harper & Row, 1956.

Sewell, James Patrick. *Functionalism and World Politics.* Princeton, N.J.: Princeton University Press, 1966.

Sharp, Walter R. *The Economic and Social Council.* New York: Columbia University Press, 1969.

————. *Field Administration in the United Nations System.* New York: Praeger, 1961.

————. *International Technical Assistance.* Chicago: Public Administration Service, 1952.

NOTES

1. Statement of Richard N. Gardner to subcommittee of Senate Committee on Foreign Relations, in *Senate Committee on Foreign Relations, Hearings on the Special Fund,* February 18, 1963 (Washington, D.C.: Government Printing Office), p. 2.

2. Statement of Mr. Klutznick to the Governing Council of the Special Fund, in *Senate Committee on Foreign Relations, Hearings on the Special Fund,* February 10, 1963 (Washington, D.C.: Government Printing Office), pp. 25 ff.

3. Statement by Richard Gardner, op. cit.

4. W. Frye, "UN Approves Aid for Cuba—and Ducks," *Los Angeles Times,* 17 February 1963.

5. Mr. Gardner's testimony, op. cit., p. 37.

6. Frye, op. cit.

7. U.S., Department of State Press Release No. 99: *The United Nations in Crisis: Cuba and the Congo* (February 22, 1963), p. 6.

The Superpowers and Arms Control

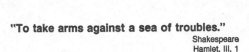

8

The United Nations presented a bleak landscape during the forties and fifties so far as arms control was concerned. Despite numerous initiatives taken by the superpowers and unremitting efforts by the first two Secretaries-General, no progress was made. The cold war dictated the need for a relentless arms race that almost culminated in nuclear catastrophe in 1962. The Cuban missile crisis compelled both the United States and the Soviet Union to look into the nuclear abyss for thirteen fearful days. The escape was narrow and the lesson awesome. Neither superpower was able to say to the other any longer: "Do as I say, or I shall kill you," but was compelled to say:

"Do as I say, or I shall kill us both." This common realization provided the catalyst for a change in policy. Both superpowers expressed an interest in signing a test ban treaty. This they did in Moscow in 1963. After this initial breakthrough, the United Nations provided the major forum for arms control negotiations. Under its aegis, three vitally important treaties were hammered out: the Outer Space Treaty of 1967, the Nuclear Non-proliferation Treaty of 1968, and the Sea-Bed Treaty of 1971. These provided the impetus for the historic Strategic Arms Limitation Treaty signed in Moscow in 1972.

This chapter will present an analysis of the political struggles that led to the signing of these five treaties. Needless to say, the superpowers were the main actors in the drama but by no means the only ones. The United Nations stood on the sidelines in Moscow in 1963 and again in 1972, but proved to be invaluable in the conclusion of the three treaties in between. Finally, it is important to remember that none of the five treaties to be analyzed succeeded in achieving disarmament, that is to say, in the actual destruction of existing weapons, but merely in arms control or "nonarmament," the prevention of the creation of additional weapons. While this was a more modest achievement, it was nevertheless a momentous one and one in which the United Nations managed to play a significant role.

The Limited Nuclear Test Ban Treaty of 1963

The goal of nuclear test cessation was always more modest than that of disarmament, since it implied no reduction of stockpiles nor any fundamental change in the arsenals of the negotiating powers. A nuclear test ban would accomplish two things: It would limit the further development of nuclear weapons already stocked in great quantities in the Soviet Union, the United States, Britain, and France; and it would halt further contamination of the world's atmosphere through radioactive fallout.

If disarmament has been the most important general problem before the General Assembly, the cessation of nuclear weapons testing was the most crucial specific issue related to disarmament. The pressures on the nuclear powers, especially by the atomic have-not nations, were enormous. In 1959, for example, the General Assembly passed by overwhelming majorities four resolutions urging a moratorium on nuclear tests. These resolutions were primarily a reflection of a world-wide concern with the damage to human health if tests were to continue.

Scientists have differed widely on the amount of damage that radioactive fallout inflicts on the human system. But all agree that there are at least four areas in which some harm is certain to result. For one thing, it has been established that exposure to radiation shortens the human life span. In the opinion of Dr. H. H. Muller, a leading American geneticist, the shortening of life span is "by far the most serious of the long-term effects on the exposed person himself."[1] The second danger derives from strontium 90, a radioactive substance produced by nuclear explosions but unknown in nature. This by-product of atomic tests causes cancer of the bone. Opinions differ on the extent of the damage, but there is wide agreement that each test results in bone cancer being incurred by a number of people. Most scientists also agree that children are more susceptible to the poison than adults.[2] Leukemia, a fatal disease of the white blood cells, has also been related to strontium 90.[3] Finally, the most far-reaching effects of fallout seem to be genetic mutations in future generations. Again, estimates vary, but there is wide agreement among geneticists that nuclear tests will be responsible for a considerable number of stillbirths, embryonic deaths, and defective mutations.[4]

As a result of constant prodding by the General Assembly, the Soviet Union, in May 1955, took the initiative in seeking a test ban. During the following year, the Soviet Union pressed the United States for the conclusion of a bilateral agreement. The Soviet position was that the question of a test ban could be separated from the general problem of disarmament and that controls to detect violations were unnecessary. As Premier Bulganin wrote to President Eisenhower in 1956:

It is a known fact that the discontinuation of such tests does not in itself require any international control agreements, for the present state of science and engineering makes it possible to detect any explosion of an atomic or hydrogen bomb, wherever it may be set off. In our opinion this situation makes it possible to separate the problem of ending tests of atomic and hydrogen weapons from the general problem of disarmament and to solve it independently even now, without tying an agreement on this subject to agreements on other disarmament problems.[5]

The Western powers agreed to discuss a test ban as a separate issue but flatly rejected the Soviet assertion that controls were unnecessary. In a counterproposal, the United States, Great Britain, and France suggested test cessation under an international control system. The Soviet Union declared itself willing to negotiate the vexatious matter of inspection. The next difficulty arose when the United States insisted on the need to continue testing until a cutoff agreement and a control plan had actually been negotiated. At this point, great pressure was exerted on the American government by a large majority in the General Assembly to agree to an informal test ban pending the conclusion of a formal treaty. Opinion among leading American scientists was deeply divided on this issue. On the one hand, Dr. Linus Pauling, an American Nobel Prize winner, represented a considerable body of opinion when he demanded that tests be halted immediately:

Each added amount of radiation causes damage to the health of human beings all over the world and causes damage to the pool of human germ plasm such as to lead to an increase in the number of seriously defective children that will be born in future generations. An international agreement to stop all testing of nuclear weapons now could serve as a first step towards a more general disarmament, and the effective abolition of nuclear weapons, averting the possibility of a nuclear war that would be a catastrophe to all humanity.[6]

The case for continuing tests was largely defended by scientists in the U.S. Atomic Energy Commission (AEC). In the opinion of Dr. Edward Teller, a leading scientist, testing had to continue because

further tests will put us into a position to fight our opponent's war machine while sparing the innocent bystanders. One development of the greatest importance is the progressive reduction of radioactive fallout. Clean weapons of this kind will reduce unnecessary casualties in a future war.[7]

Dr. Teller's colleague in the AEC, Dr. Willard F. Libby, also justified atomic tests on grounds of national defense:

It is not contended that there is no risk to human health. Are we willing to take this very small and rigidly controlled risk, or would we prefer to run the risk of annihilation which might result, if we surrendered the weapons which are so essential to our freedom and actual survival?[8]

While the United States was engaged in weighing the alternatives of a provisional test ban, the Soviet Union, in March 1958, announced a unilateral cessation of nuclear tests. Once again on the defensive, the United States proposed a meeting of technical experts to study the feasibility of a control system to detect violations of a test ban. This conference, attended by an equal number of scientists from East and West, took place in July 1958 and submitted a positive report, calling for three steps by which a detection system might be implemented.

1. A network of control posts around the globe. About 170 would be land-based. Of these, ten would be in the United States, fourteen in the USSR, and eight in Communist China. The remaining land-based posts would be distributed on the continents and on large and small oceanic islands. Ten additional posts would be on ships.
2. Creation of an "international control organ," which would run the global system, pick the staff, select the detection devices, study reports and generally see to it that no nation violated the test suspension agreement.
3. Use of weather reconnaissance aircraft to sample the air for radioactivity. They would rush to a suspicious area to see if a bomb had been set off or whether the tremor was due to other causes.[9]

The scientists' report, while welcomed by the negotiators, raised important new problems. What would be the composition of the "international control organ"? What would be the authority of the inspectors? Serious bargaining took place on all these questions at Geneva. The West suggested a veto-free control commission to be headed by a neutral administrator. The Soviet Union, however, insisted on a three-man directorate and the right of veto. The negotiators also argued over the number and role of the inspectors in the field. The West demanded international and mobile inspection teams with freedom of access to any area where an illegal atomic test was suspected. The Soviet Union emphasized the primacy of self-inspection but accepted the admission in principle of "foreign specialists" from the West. Another technical problem presented itself when the United States announced that it had underestimated the difficulty of detecting underground nuclear explosions. The U.S. position was that such explosions would be almost indistinguishable seismographically from natural shocks such as earthquakes. Hence, the American government demanded that the number of control stations be raised from 180 to 6,000.

More threatening than the technical problems of an atomic test ban was the sword of Damocles of the "nth nation." The main negotiators were three nuclear powers—the United States, the Soviet Union, and Britain. But France, of course, was already developing her own nuclear arsenal, and it was estimated that in the not-too-distant future several new nations would join the "nuclear club": Belgium, Canada, Communist China, Czechoslovakia, East Germany, India, Israel, Italy, Japan, Sweden, and Switzerland.[10] Would the new atomic powers agree to be bound by a treaty to which they were not parties? France, for example, insisted on the completion of a series of tests while the Big Three were engaged in negotiations in Geneva. Far more serious, even, was the problem of Communist China. The 1958 Geneva report of the technical experts recommended that 8 of the 180 control stations be placed on mainland China. If the "international control organ" were placed under UN authority, would it be reasonable to expect Communist China to admit UN control posts on her territory while she was not a member of the world organization? Even if the control organ were set up outside the UN framework, would Communist China consider herself bound by a treaty with nations that continued to refuse to recognize her as a legal government?

Despite the numerous difficulties, a remarkable lessening of differences occurred during 1959 and 1960, but in late 1961 the Soviet Union broke the informal moratorium and tested weapons of unprecedented explosive force. By the time of the Cuban missile crisis, a test ban agreement seemed more remote than ever. Yet the resolution of that crisis seemed to convince the Soviet leadership that more could be gained from a détente with the West than from a policy of intransigence. At any rate, in July 1963, Paul Henri Spaak of Belgium reported that Premier Khrushchev seemed genuinely interested in a test ban. A few days later, American and British negotiators, led by Averell Harriman and Lord Hailsham, respectively, arrived in Moscow to explore the seriousness of Soviet intentions. After five days of negotiations, tentative agreement was reached, and a copy of the draft treaty was publicized on July 24. All nuclear tests in the atmosphere, under water, and in space were to cease, but underground tests were to be permitted. On August 5, Soviet Foreign Minister Andrei Gromyko, U.S. Secretary of State Dean Rusk, and British Foreign Secretary Lord Home put their signatures to the document. After a protracted debate, the U.S. Senate, on September 24, ratified the Treaty by a vote of 80 to 19. A large majority of the world's nations quickly followed suit and deposited their instruments of ratification. A decade of arduous negotiations had finally produced concrete results.

On the negative side, France and Communist China made a common front against the Treaty. The former was bent on her own independent nuclear force, and the latter attacked the Treaty as a fraud and saw it as further proof of Soviet "softness on capitalism." Also, the test ban was only partial. Nevertheless, most observers agreed with President Kennedy's assessment of the Treaty as a step toward reason and away from war. In specific and immediate terms, it solved a major problem of public health by halting the further contamination of the atmosphere by radioactive fallout. More broadly, it was the first East-West agreement in the tensely guarded realm of military security.

Some 110 members of the United Nations have signed or acceded to the Treaty. France and the People's Republic of China, however, have not become parties. The Limited Nuclear Test Ban Treaty entered into force on October 10, 1963. While the Treaty did not end underground tests, it did reduce the danger of radioactive fallout and also acted as a brake on the unrestricted development of advanced nuclear weapons. The People's Republic of China exploded its first nuclear weapons in 1964, and she and France continued to conduct tests in the atmosphere, though less frequently than the Soviet Union and the United States had done in earlier years. The General Assembly continued to call for an end to all tests in all environments and to express the hope that there would be a universal and comprehensive ban on all testing. In May 1976, a major forward step was taken when the Soviet Union and the United States agreed on a treaty that limited the size of underground nuclear explosions set off for peaceful purposes and, for the first time, provided for on-site inspection of compliance.

The Outer Space Treaty of 1967

Ever since the first sputnik was launched into outer space in October 1957, there had been repeated attempts to ban nuclear weapons from space. Various proposals were put forward in the General Assembly by the Soviet Union and the United States. In 1959, the General Assembly established a Committee on the Peaceful Uses of Outer Space consisting of twenty-four nations and charged this body with the responsibility of furthering international cooperation in space. The resolution also asked the Secretary-General to maintain a registry of all objects launched into space, based on information supplied by the launching nation.

In 1962, Premier Khrushchev indicated an interest in concluding a treaty with the United States on joint assistance to astronauts and also expressed his willingness to consider a general treaty on outer space. These two proposals were submitted to the Committee on the Peaceful Uses of Outer Space in May 1962. In this forum the two superpowers disagreed over the question of liabilities for damages, but the Limited Nuclear Test Ban Treaty broke the deadlock. At the 1963 session of the General Assembly, the superpowers reached agreement in private talks to ban nuclear and other weapons of mass destruction from outer space. Taking this cue, the Assembly adopted a resolution banning nuclear weapons in space and welcomed the superpowers' new initiatives toward space cooperation. This resolution, which was approved by acclamation on December 13, 1963, became the precursor of the Outer Space Treaty of 1967.[11]

During this first phase, the Soviet Union and the United States essentially did their own negotiating. While they were prodded by the nonspace powers, it was not that prodding but the precedent of the Moscow test ban which provided the initial impetus toward agreement. The nonspace powers provided little more than a sounding board, and their relief at superpower agreement was so palpable that they were reluctant to slow down the momentum by bringing up too many considerations of their own.

Several knotty problems had to be overcome before a binding treaty could be agreed upon. In the first place, the likelihood of indiscriminate injury from the debris or misfire of space missions was sufficiently recognized to incorporate a specific provision making a state internationally liable for damages caused by objects launched from its territory or component parts thereof. During this debate, which took place in the Outer Space Committee, the United States generally took a more restrictive view of liability than the Soviet Union. It insisted, for example, that damage caused to persons or property within a launch facility or immediate recovery area not be included in the terms of an international convention, while the Soviet Union wished to hold states that had arranged for the launching, or from whose territory the launching was made, more generally liable. In this view, the Soviet Union was fully supported by the nonspace powers. The differences on this question were so great that a special Convention on International Liability for Damage Caused by Space Objects had to be added to the Outer Space Treaty. This Convention, embodying a large number of U.S.-Soviet compromises on technical and legal questions, was only adopted as late as September 1971, a full four years after the adoption of the Outer Space Treaty itself. Other differences concerned eligibility, adjudication, and the status of international organizations. The United States wanted to limit signatories to UN members, while the USSR argued for all-inclusive participation; the United

States was interested in giving the International Court of Justice a role in the adjudication of disputes, to which the Soviet Union objected; and finally, the United States wished to give international organizations the same status as states in the Treaty, while the Soviet Union, with an eye on NATO, wished to limit the Treaty to states. The nonspace powers agreed with the Soviet Union on the first point, were rather indifferent on the second, and took the American side on the last. The compromises ultimately hammered out leaned more heavily toward the Soviet than toward the American side.

By 1966, a draft treaty was ready. This document was approved on December 19, 1966, by the General Assembly. Only a single government objected: Tanzania, which felt that there had not been enough time to consider the Treaty before the vote. Once again, the role of the superpowers was dominant. Whenever they managed to agree, success was certain. During the negotiations, the Soviet Union had made some attempts to woo the Third World but had always kept its primary interests as one of the two space powers clearly in mind. The final result was a treaty that was essentially the product of Soviet-American compromise reached in a wider UN framework.

The Treaty on Principles Governing the Activities of States in the Exploration and Use of Outer Space, including the Moon and Other Celestial Bodies entered into force on October 10, 1967, with the ratification of the required number of states, including the Soviet Union, the United States, and the United Kingdom. Two of its provisions were especially important. First, the Treaty placed a categorical ban on "national appropriation" of outer space. This meant that no nation could claim sovereignty or in any other way assert unilateral control. But the Treaty was silent on who *did* have the right to appropriate. It failed to designate the United Nations or any other international body as the proper custodian of space in the name and interest of mankind. Second, the Treaty put into formal language the obligation to ban nuclear weapons from outer space and essentially demilitarized space and the celestial bodies. Verification was to proceed by reciprocal inspection, but responsibility was to rest with national governments, not an international body. Thus, in essence, the effectiveness of the Treaty was to depend on the willingness of the two space powers to accept inspection on a basis of reciprocity.

The year of the Outer Space Treaty, 1967, was also a year of two space tragedies and one near tragedy. In January, three American astronauts died in their spacecraft when a fire broke out during a test countdown; in April, a Soviet cosmonaut was killed; and in September, a U.S. spacecraft developed communications difficulties and had to change its scheduled course. These events put pressure on the space powers to compromise on two corollaries to the Outer Space Treaty: First, a convention dealing with assistance to, and return of, astronauts and cosmonauts was approved by the General Assembly in December 1967 and entered into force in December 1968. Second, the stubborn problem of liability had to be faced. Here a compromise was more difficult to attain, and only in November 1971 did the General Assembly adopt a Convention on International Liability for Damage Caused by Space Objects.

In overall perspective, the Outer Space Treaty and its two corollaries were essentially the business of the two space powers. The UN General Assembly provided a diplomatic convenience and gave the nonspace powers the opportunity to prod the Russians and Americans into action. Substantively, the nonspace powers played only a marginal role. Perhaps they even slowed down the process of reaching the numerous compromises that went into the Treaty in its final form. But the United Nations succeeded in defining the demilitarization of outer space as everybody's business and, by so doing, injected a multilateral note into space exploration at the very beginning of its operation. It might have been far more tempting for Americans and Russians alike to think of colonizing the celestial bodies had it not been for the existence of the United Nations. Even the People's Republic of China, which did not accede to the Treaty, took no initiatives to violate its provisions after it sent its first space satellite into orbit. Thus, in this very limited but potentially vital area, the United Nations did serve as a kind of collective conscience for the leading space powers and succeeded in protecting the interests of mankind as a whole.

The Nuclear Non-proliferation Treaty

The struggle over the Nuclear Non-proliferation Treaty went through two distinct phases. Between 1961 and 1965, the nonnuclear nations of the world steadily urged the superpowers to take the initiative in negotiating a non-proliferation treaty. The Soviet Union and the United States showed interest but found themselves unable to agree on an acceptable draft. In 1965, however, the pattern changed. An open partnership gradually developed between the two superpowers, which, for the next four years, attempted to "sell" a non-proliferation treaty to the nonnuclear nations. On June 12, 1968, they succeeded when the General Assembly commended a draft treaty on the non-proliferation of nuclear weapons by a vote of 95 in favor and 4 against, with 21 abstentions.[12] The two phases of this three-cornered struggle are well worth examining.

The origins of the Treaty are found in an Irish draft resolution, submitted on November 17, 1961, that called upon all states, particularly those possessing nuclear weapons, to secure an international agreement under which nuclear states would agree not to relinquish control of nuclear weapons or to transmit information necessary for their manufacture and nonnuclear states would agree not to manufacture or otherwise acquire control of them. This proposal was adopted unanimously by the General Assembly on December 4, 1961.[13] Sweden suggested that, in addition, the Secretary-General inquire under what conditions nonnuclear states might be willing to bind themselves not to seek to acquire or themselves manufacture nuclear weapons in the future. The Soviet Union, having in mind West Germany, considered the Swedish proposal weak but nevertheless supported it. The United States opposed it on the grounds that it might jeopardize the right of collective self-defense. The major American concern of course was NATO. The majority of the General Assembly approved of the Swedish proposal, hoping that it would facilitate agreement between the superpowers to suspend nuclear tests and to agree on other measures of arms control. The proposal was adopted by a vote of 58 in favor and 10 against, with 23 abstentions.[14] That same year, the Assembly also endorsed the creation of a new negotiating forum for disarmament—the Eighteen-Nation Committee on Disarmament (ENDC)—comprising not only the then nuclear powers and some of their respective allies in NATO and the Warsaw Pact but also eight nonaligned nonnuclear powers that were to represent every region of the world. This Committee, meeting in Geneva, henceforth became the main forum for the deliberations over the Nonproliferation Treaty.[15]

Sixty-two governments responded to the Secretary-General's inquiry. Reciprocity was mentioned most frequently as the condition under which governments would adhere to the Treaty. The Soviet Union showed particular concern about the adherence of West Germany.

Little progress was made in 1962, because the attention of the superpowers was absorbed by the Cuban missile crisis. In 1963, the Soviet Union attacked an American plan for the establishment of a NATO multilateral nuclear force (MLF) as contrary to the principle of non-proliferation. The United States saw no incompatibility between the proposed MLF and a non-proliferation treaty. These mutually exclusive positions remained the main obstacles to progress in 1964 and early 1965. Despite persistent prodding by the nonnuclear and nonaligned nations, both in the ENDC and in the United Nations, the Soviet Union and the United States refused to cooperate. The main difference between them remained the question of access to nuclear weapons through military alliances.

In mid-1965, the picture changed. First, the superpowers were beginning to enjoy the fruits of détente after they had agreed to a limited test ban treaty in 1963. Second, in 1964, they had both been jolted by the first nuclear explosion on mainland China. Third, by 1965, it had become clear that at least twelve other nations were on the threshold of becoming nuclear powers: Japan, India, West Germany, Sweden, Italy, Canada, Israel, and over a little longer period, Brazil, Switzerland, Spain, Yugoslavia, and the United Arab Republic. Fourth, the MLF project was abandoned by the United States, which removed the main source of Soviet opposition. Fifth, both superpowers wished to maintain open channels in spite of, or perhaps because of, the Vietnam

War. And finally, both the United States and the Soviet Union were eager to show themselves receptive to the prodding of the nonnuclear and nonaligned countries. Thus, on June 15, 1965, the UN Disarmament Commission recommended by a vote of 83 to 1 that the ENDC "accord special priority" to a non-proliferation treaty. One month later, the ENDC reconvened in Geneva to hammer out the broad outlines of a treaty.

During the summer of 1965, the eight nonaligned members of the ENDC still held the initiative. They proposed five basic principles to guide the negotiations:

1. The treaty should be void of any loopholes for the direct or indirect proliferation of nuclear weapons in any form.
2. It should embody an acceptable balance of obligations of nuclear and nonnuclear powers.
3. It should be a step toward disarmament, particularly nuclear disarmament.
4. It should include acceptable and workable provisions to ensure its effectiveness.
5. It should not adversely affect the right of states to join in establishing nuclear-free zones.

On November 23, these principles were adopted by the General Assembly, in a vote of 93 to 0, with 5 abstentions.[16] Both the United States and the Soviet Union voted for the resolution.

The year 1966 was one of transition. Both superpowers began to work in earnest on a formula for a treaty. But they were deterred from assuming joint initiative by one stubborn problem, that of inspection. The Soviet Union favored the International Atomic Energy Agency (IAEA) as the main inspection organ for the treaty; whereas the United States, under pressure from the Western European countries, preferred the European Atomic Energy Community (Euratom) as the inspection organ for its European allies. The Soviet Union accused the United States of trying to package two conflicting objectives: non-proliferation outside NATO and proliferation within NATO.

The United States was caught between its desire for a treaty and the demands of its allies in Western Europe for a nuclear voice. Gradually, the former assumed greater importance than the latter. The Soviet Union, for its part, felt a new urgency since China had joined the nuclear club. Both superpowers, with an eye on the lengthening list of nuclear-threshold powers, agreed that a non-proliferation treaty would have a stabilizing effect and that further delays might spur the nonnuclear countries to raise the price of their adherence.

In 1967, the superpowers assumed the initiative. In view of the stubborn disagreement surrounding the inspection provisions of the Treaty, they agreed to disagree. On August 24, 1967, after intensive secret negotiations, they submitted separate but identical drafts in the ENDC, leaving blank the article that was to embody the inspection provision.

As the United States and the Soviet Union began to make a common front in late 1967, it was now the turn of the nonnuclear states to express reservations. As the discussions on the draft treaty began in the ENDC, all its members save Canada, Czechoslovakia, and Poland expressed reservations. The main issue that worried the nonnuclear powers was their security. India stated that she would sign only if she obtained guaranteed protection from both the United States and the Soviet Union. Most of the other members of the ENDC shared this view.

While presenting a common front vis-à-vis the nonnuclear states, the superpowers managed to settle on a compromise with regard to the thorny problem of safeguards. It was agreed that the IAEA verification procedures would ultimately apply to all nonnuclear states but that an inspection role would be maintained for Euratom during a transitional period.

On March 14, 1968, the ENDC submitted a full report of its deliberations to the General Assembly. This report contained the text of a complete draft treaty jointly submitted by the United States and the Soviet Union as cochairmen of the ENDC. The draft included provisions for safeguards under Article 3.

The last stage of the struggle for General Assembly endorsement of the draft treaty was marked by a U.S.-Soviet partnership all the way. The two superpowers now lobbied hard for adoption of their joint product. Most of the reservations of the nonnuclear states continued to revolve around the problem of their own security. Many felt that the balance between the responsibilities of nuclear and nonnuclear states was not equitable because it was tilted against the latter. Many specific reservations were proposed by African, Asian, and Latin-American countries, all of which, in one form or another, expressed their displeasure with what they perceived as a double standard. These objections were met in part when the superpowers agreed to provide security assurances to the nonnuclear powers through a formal Security Council resolution.

Finally, on June 12, 1968, the General Assembly endorsed the treaty to halt the spread of nuclear weapons. The vote was 95 in favor, 4 against, 21 abstentions, and 4 not voting.[17] On June 19, 1968, the three nuclear powers on the Security Council gave their formal pledge to assist any nonnuclear country that was threatened by nuclear aggression. A resolution in the Council welcoming these pledges of assistance was passed by a vote of 10 in favor and 0 against, with 5 abstentions.[18] With this vote, the UN phase of the Non-proliferation Treaty came to an end.

The evolution of the U.S.-Soviet partnership during the late 1960's was a reflection of each power's perceived national interest. Once again, the Soviet Union's interest as an atomic power dictated that the dispersion of atomic weapons be stopped. On the other hand, the USSR wished to appeal to the new nations, which perceived certain features of the Treaty as an effort by the nuclear powers to impose a double standard. The United States, as the other leading atomic power, shared the USSR's interest in stopping proliferation. This common concern once again injected a high degree of harmony into U.S. relations with the Soviet Union. On the other hand, the United States had many difficulties with its Western European allies, some of which felt rather left out of the decision-making process. In fact, the United States faced at least as much friction over the Treaty within the ranks of NATO as it did in its negotiations with its superpower adversary.

The nonnuclear nations, which in the early phases of the negotiations had spurred the superpowers to greater cooperation, wound up at the end with the uneasy feeling that something might have been put over on them. One happy though probably fortuitous by-product of this entire evolution was the gradual resuscitation of the International Atomic Energy Agency. First created by the superpowers, then by-passed and virtually ignored, the Agency was given a new lease on life when the superpowers managed to invest it with a significant role in the inspection procedures that were to govern the Non-proliferation Treaty. Thus, while the Agency was originally conceived in order to produce more atomic plowshares, its major purpose might yet become the blunting of the atomic sword.

The Treaty was opened for signature on July 1, 1968, but the Soviet-led invasion of Czechoslovakia delayed the ratification process on the American side. The Soviet Union in turn refused to ratify until West Germany had done so. These obstacles were overcome, and the Treaty entered into force on March 5, 1970. By that time more than ninety countries had signed and more than half of these had ratified. France and Communist China once again were conspicuous by their absence, but neither of these two nuclear powers chose to violate any of the terms of the Treaty. The members of the nuclear club had taken a major step toward sanity and away from war.

The terms of the Treaty provided for a Review Conference after five years. This conference took place in Geneva in May 1975. It convened under the shadow of a nuclear explosion for "peaceful purposes" that had been conducted by India in May 1974. The Review Conference itself was rather uneventful. Of the ninety-six signatories, only fifty-seven attended. Most participants agreed that the NPT could not prevent proliferation, but it would make proliferation somewhat more difficult. The need for stricter safeguards against nuclear explosions for purposes of war was widely seen as highly desirable, especially in view of the fact that many states were considering the nuclear option as an alternative to serious energy shortages at home. By the mid-1970's, the number of nuclear "threshold powers" had reached approximately a dozen. Hence, the danger of nuclear war by design or accident continued to loom large despite the NPT, but without it the nuclear peril would no doubt be graver still.

The Sea-Bed Treaty

In 1967, Ambassador Arvid Pardo from the seabound state of Malta proposed to the United Nations that it declare the deep bed of the sea, beyond the limits of national jurisdiction, to be "the common heritage of mankind." This initiative led to four years of strenuous debate in the United Nations and finally produced the Sea-Bed Treaty of 1971, which barred the emplacement of weapons of mass destruction on the ocean floor or its subsoil. Once again, the political struggle was a three-cornered one: The United States, the Soviet Union, and the nonaligned nations were the main architects of the Treaty. The main areas of friction among them were three: first, the types of arms to be banned; second, the geographical extent of the Treaty's jurisdiction; and third, the problem of verification.

The USSR, in its draft of March 18, 1969, proposed the complete demilitarization of the sea-bed.[19] The United States, in its draft of May 22, 1969, merely advocated the denuclearization, rather than the total demilitarization, of the sea-bed and the ocean floor.[20] The American negotiators pointed to the military uses of the ocean floor as strictly defensive in nature and therefore essential to the security of the United States. They also maintained that, since conventional weapons could not threaten the territories of states from the sea-bed, there was no need to include them in the Treaty.[21]

The majority of the nonaligned countries favored the principle of complete demilitarization. They pointed out that the sea-bed must be used for the benefit of all states and, consequently, that any type of military activity, whether conventional or nuclear, would endanger the peaceful exploitation of the marine environment.

On October 7, 1969, the USSR changed its position and embraced the U.S. stand. On the same date, the United States and the Soviet Union tabled a joint draft on the Prohibition of the Emplacement of Nuclear Weapons and Other Weapons of Mass Destruction on the Sea-Bed and the Ocean Floor and in the Subsoil thereof. The draft was submitted to the Conference of the Committee on Disarmament (CCD), which was in fact an enlarged ENDC. This unexpected Soviet move left the nonaligned countries supporting a policy of total demilitarization against the alliance of the superpowers, which now favored only denuclearization. The superpowers, not wishing to alienate the nonaligned countries, tried to make the draft more acceptable by including in the preamble a paragraph that, they felt, would partially meet their demands. The preamble stated that the Treaty was a stepping stone toward excluding the sea-bed from the arms race and, at the same time, a step toward a treaty on general and complete disarmament. Negotiations to these ends were to continue by the parties.[22] Nevertheless, the nonaligned nations were most dissatisfied. Numerous criticisms were made. Mexico felt that, since the Treaty was restricted to a nuclear ban and the majority of the countries concerned did not possess nuclear weapons in any case, the best alternative would be for the few nuclear powers to make unilateral commitments to a nuclear ban until the time when a wider and more complete ban on armaments could be enacted.[23] Sweden suggested the inclusion in the text of a determination to continue negotiations leading to a comprehensive armaments ban on the sea-bed and ocean floor.[24] India supported the Swedish formula. Most countries were willing to accept a nuclear ban first if there were firm commitments to continue negotiations toward preventing an arms race on the sea-bed. As a result of the criticisms from the nonaligned nations, the two superpowers compromised and inserted in the final version of the Treaty a separate article worded after the Swedish proposal.

Thus, on the matter of the range of weapons to be prohibited on the sea-bed, the alliance between the superpowers prevailed. The impact on the nonaligned nations was limited to a superpower commitment to continue negotiations, which appeared as Article 5 of the Treaty.

The question of the Treaty's geographical jurisdiction led to considerable controversy. The Soviet Union argued for a broadly constructed ban that would prohibit all military use outside a twelve-mile coastal limit.[25] The United States, on the other hand, favored a ban on all weapons of mass destruction beyond a three-mile coastal limit.

The majority of the nonaligned countries supported the Soviet draft. India, the United Arab Republic, and Brazil all wanted a twelve-mile limit. Most of the other smaller coastal countries, fearful of limiting their underwater defense facilities, followed suit. In October 1969, the Soviet Union revised its position and now proposed a ban on weapons of mass destruction outside a twelve-mile limit. The United States accepted this compromise, and the two superpowers then submitted their joint draft resolution regarding the Prohibition of the Emplacement of Nuclear Weapons and Other Weapons of Mass Destruction on the Sea-Bed and the Ocean Floor and in the Subsoil thereof. Significantly enough, the Soviet Union reversed itself by accepting denuclearization over general demilitarization in return for a twelve-mile coastal limit. Once again, the two superpowers formed a united front against the nonaligned nations.

A Canadian proposal to establish a 250-mile "security zone," in which coastal states could set up defense establishments, was rejected by both the United States and the Soviet Union.[26] Hence, the final version of the Treaty ignored the claims of coastal states—most of them nonaligned—for a right to have a security zone adjacent to the twelve-mile coastal band.

The Soviet Union and the United States advanced similar proposals on the question of verification. The Soviet Union introduced the idea of free access based on reciprocity,[27] while the American text provided for free observation of the activities of other states on the sea-bed without interfering with such activities or otherwise infringing upon rights recognized under international law, including the freedoms of the high seas. In the event that such observation would not prove satisfactory, the United States proposed that the "Parties undertake to consult and cooperate in endeavouring to resolve the question."[28]

Both proposals were subjected to severe criticism on the part of the nonaligned countries. Although the majority of the nonaligned nations favored the less restrictive approach of free access, they felt that this concept, if based on reciprocity, implied that only those powers with undersea technological know-how would be able to participate in the verification procedures. They also pointed out that the interests of the technologically less advanced states would be left unprotected and at the mercy of those nations that were more developed. A number of proposals were submitted in which the idea of international cooperation was advanced through the good offices of either the UN Secretary-General or the UN Security Council. The superpowers finally agreed that complaints could be taken to the Security Council in accordance with the provisions of the Charter.

In the final text of the Treaty the demands of the coastal states were partially met in an additional paragraph of Article 3, which reads:

Verification activities pursuant to this Treaty shall not interfere with activities of other States Parties and shall be conducted with due regard for rights recognized under international law including the freedoms of the high seas and the rights of coastal States with respect to the exploration and exploitation of their continental shelves.[29]

Thus, in the area of verification procedures several compromises were reached. The article was enlarged; provisions for verification were clarified to a certain extent; and the essence of the many proposals suggested by the nonaligned countries was drafted into the final version. However, in the most basic matters the superpowers had their way.

The overall bargaining process which led to the Sea-Bed Treaty of 1971 resembled that of the Non-proliferation Treaty. At first, the two superpowers disagreed; then the Soviet Union reversed itself to make a common front with the United States. This left the nonaligned countries alone in their fight and reduced their bargaining position considerably. The Treaty finally settled on the least common denominator: the banning of nuclear weapons on the ocean floor or its subsoil, with both superpowers free to inspect for violations. Sixty-two nations signed the Treaty on February 11, 1971. Once again France and Communist China were not among the signatories, but once again they did not violate any of the terms of the Treaty. On balance, the Treaty was a major accomplishment: It guaranteed that five-sevenths of the earth's surface would be free of nuclear weapons.

The Strategic Arms Limitation Treaties of 1972 and 1975

On May 26, 1972, President Richard M. Nixon and Soviet Party Chairman Leonid Brezhnev signed in Moscow two historic arms control documents that represented the culmination of almost three years of arduous Strategic Arms Limitations Talks (SALT) in Helsinki and in Vienna.

The first document was an Anti-Ballistic Missiles Treaty of unlimited duration that placed limits on the growth of Soviet and American strategic nuclear arsenals. The Treaty established a ceiling of 200 launchers for each side's defensive missile system and committed both sides not to build nationwide antimissile defenses. Each country was limited to two ABM sites: one for the national capital and the other to protect one field of ICBM's. Each such site would consist of 100 ABM's.

The United States already had a protected ICBM field in North Dakota and thus, under the terms of the Treaty, could add an ABM site around Washington. The Soviet Union already had an ABM site for the defense of Moscow and thus was permitted to add an ABM site to protect an ICBM field. At the time of the agreement, the Soviet Union had a total of 2,328 missiles: 1,618 ICBM's and 710 on nuclear submarines, compared with 1,710 for the United States: 1,054 ICBM's and 656 on submarines.

The second concrete arms control achievement of the Moscow Summit was an Interim Agreement limiting ICBM's to those under construction or deployed at the time of the signing of the Agreement. This meant the retention of 1,618 ICBM's for the Soviet Union, including 300 large SS-9's and 1,054 for the United States, including 1,000 Minutemen and 54 Titans. The Agreement also froze the construction of submarine-launched ballistic missiles on all nuclear submarines at existing levels: 656 for the United States and 710 for the Soviet Union. However, each side could build additional submarine missiles of an equal number of older land-based ICBM's or older submarine missile launchers were dismantled. The Agreement was to be in force for five years, and both sides pledged themselves to follow-up negotiations in order to achieve a full-fledged treaty.

Both arms control instruments signed at Moscow placed no limitations on the qualitative improvement of offensive or defensive missiles, nor were ceilings imposed on the number of warheads that could be carried by offensive missiles or on strategic bombers permitted each side. Modernization of missiles, including the emplacement of new missiles in new silos, was permitted. Both sides pledged "not to interfere with the national technical means of verification of the other," and each side retained the right to withdraw from either agreement if it felt that its supreme national interest was in jeopardy.

The two agreements managed to freeze a rough balance into the nuclear arsenals of the two superpowers. There remained "missile gaps," of course, in specific weapons. The United States, for example, retained the lead in the technology of "multiple independently targeted reentry vehicles" (MIRV's), while the Soviet Union possessed a larger quantity of missile launchers. Nevertheless, the overall effect was one of achieving a rough equilibrium.

The process of achieving this equilibrium went through eight stages, lasting almost three years. SALT 1 was held in Helsinki in late 1969 and was exploratory, without any formal proposals submitted by either side. SALT 2, held in Vienna from April to August 1970, got down to specific proposals. The two superpowers agreed in principle on the terms of a defensive missile treaty that would have limited each side to 100 missiles each around Moscow and Washington. But several months later, the American delegation, fearful of Congress, backed away and advanced a new proposal that would have given the United States a 4-to-1 advantage. This was angrily rejected by the USSR, and it took a few more months before the original two-site, 200-missile compromise was reaffirmed. SALT 3, held in late 1970, broke up in disagreement over offensive arms. SALT 4 took place in Vienna from March to May 1971, and during this period President Nixon and Chairman Brezhnev began to engage in top-secret correspondence. The result was a Soviet initiative proposing an ICBM freeze as well as an ABM treaty. SALT 5, held from July to September 1971 in Helsinki, saw further progress on the proposed ICBM freeze. SALT 6, in late 1971 and early 1972, produced the outlines of the ABM treaty; and SALT 7, the last round before the Moscow Summit, led to the inclusion of submarine-based missiles in the accord. The final accords were thus the result of protracted and painstaking bargaining and negotiations.

Several conclusions are worthy of note in connection with the two Moscow agreements. First, it must be remembered that Soviet-American relations had improved significantly by the early 1970's, partly as a result of the common determination to resolve long-standing differences in Europe and partly as a result of the Soviet fear of China. At any rate, the political climate had thawed considerably since the days of the cold war. Second, the SALT agreements did not depend primarily on verification to be effective. Each side knew that if it cheated and surprised the other with a devastating nuclear attack, the other side, though mortally wounded, could still inflict a retaliatory blow that would be unacceptable to the offender. Hence, the agreements were based primarily not on mutual trust but on the mutual capacity to absorb a first strike. Third, there was no doubt that even if the two agreements did not qualify as disarmament, they nevertheless signified a momentous breakthrough in superpower relations and a large step toward a saner world.

In November 1974, another modest advance was made. At their first meeting, in Vladivostok, President Gerald Ford and Soviet Party Chairman Leonid Brezhnev agreed to an overall ceiling of about twenty-four hundred nuclear missiles and bombers on each side—about half of these could be missiles with multiple nuclear warheads (MIRV's). The advance was modest since these ceilings were high and, furthermore, were only quantitative. No restrictions were set on the development of qualitative improvements such as missile flight tests to increase accuracy or the development of land-mobile and air-mobile intercontinental ballistic missiles (ICBM's). Nor was the development of cruise missiles launched from submarines restricted under the terms of the accord.

Secretary Kissinger expressed the hope that SALT II would "put a cap on the arms race between 1975 and 1985." This "cap," however, did not signify the reduction of existing stockpiles, but merely a quantitative limitation on the development of further weapons. In that sense, SALT II was a "nonarmament" treaty, not a genuine breakthrough in real disarmament.

Despite these recent gains, the arms race remains a very real and very expensive fact of life in the 1970's. Internationally, the money devoted each year to military expenditures is more than the total income of all the peoples of Africa, South America, and Southeast Asia. It is nearly three times what all the world's governments spend on health, nearly twice what they spend on education, and nearly thirty times what the industrialized countries give in aid to the developing countries. These massive military expenditures have continued to rise over the years despite the arms control agreements. Arms control has managed to slow down the mad momentum toward nuclear obliteration, but not to arrest it.

While the SALT agreements did not involve the United Nations, it is nevertheless difficult to conceive of them without the three preceding treaties in which the United Nations had played a part: Outer Space, Non-proliferation, and Sea-Bed. In that sense, the United Nations helped to prepare the ground and thus deserves some of the credit.

Conclusions

It would be naïve to regard the United Nations as the prime mover in the arms control treaties of the sixties and seventies. The catharsis of the Cuban missile crisis ushered in a détente between America and Russia, and the Limited Nuclear Test Ban Treaty of 1963 was the first concrete bilateral manifestation of that détente. Even the three treaties that followed—Outer Space, Non-proliferation, and Sea-Bed—would have been unthinkable without close superpower collaboration. The UN's contribution must be seen in more subtle and less tangible terms. The negotiating process that culminated in the signing of these treaties signified the first occasion in UN history on which the two superpowers discovered truly identical interests as leading space and nuclear powers. This discovery introduced a new constellation of forces into the United Nations. At first, the nonaligned nations, impatient with cold-war rhetoric and deadlock, urged the superpowers to cooperate; but when they did—perhaps even too much in Third World eyes—the nonaligned began to fear that something might have been put over on them. Thus, the traditional East-West tensions were superseded by new tensions between the nuclear-space powers and the earthbound have-not nations. As the Soviet Union and the United States gradually decontaminated themselves of shopworn ideological slogans and began to conduct their negotiations in a more businesslike and pragmatic manner, new rifts appeared between the "Establishment" on the one hand and the "wretched of the earth," on the other. The United Nations brought this transition into focus and provided the arena for a new multilateral dialogue. The debate in the United Nations underlined the fact that space and sea-bed were not superpower monopolies but the business of mankind as a whole. Even the People's Republic of China, which refused to sign any of the UN Treaties, did not see fit to violate their terms.

The United Nations also played a significant role in yet another area of potential horror: environmental warfare. Cloud-seeding had been used by the United States in Vietnam during the 1960's, and the technology to make nature itself into an ally in warfare was being rapidly developed in both the United States and the Soviet Union. In 1974, by an overwhelming vote, the General Assembly recommended a ban against any uses of the environment for hostile purposes. This resolution provided the impetus for a superpower agreement that was reached in 1975. When one considers the dreadful potential of artificially triggered earthquakes, tidal waves, and hurricanes, mankind may have been spared "winds of war" even more terrible than nuclear conflict. Once again, the United Nations had helped in preventing matters from becoming even worse than they already were.

The initial multilateralization of space and of the ocean floors was perhaps the UN's greatest contribution. By injecting itself into the negotiating process right from the beginning, the United Nations, and in particular its smaller nations, probably preempted superpower nuclear fortification of the sea-bed and superpower colonization of the celestial bodies. By so doing, the

UN placed mankind's claim to *terra nova* at the very beginning of exploratory activities, before it was too late and the point of no return was reached. For an organization that, during the first quarter century of its existence, tended to play the role of crisis manager at the edge of disaster, this new farsightedness was encouraging indeed. It portended the beginning of a larger vision that the planet's fate was one and that it would survive the challenge of atomic power as a planet or not at all.

SELECTED BIBLIOGRAPHY

Edwards, David V. *Arms Control in International Politics.* New York: Holt, Rinehart, & Winston, 1968.

Epstein, William. *The Last Chance.* New York: The Free Press, 1976.

Friedmann, Wolfgang. *The Future of the Oceans.* New York: Braziller, 1971.

Kolkowicz, Roman, et al. *The Soviet Union and Arms Control: A Superpower Dilemma.* Baltimore: Johns Hopkins Press, 1970.

Spanier, John W., and Joseph L. Nogee. *The Politics of Disarmament: A Study in Soviet-American Gamesmanship.* New York: Praeger, 1962.

Stoessinger, John G. "Atoms for Peace: The International Atomic Energy Agency." In *Organizing Peace in the Nuclear Age,* edited by Arthur N. Holcombe, pp. 117–233. New York: New York University Press, 1959.

Waltz, Kenneth N. *Man, the State, and War: A Theoretical Analysis.* New York: Columbia University Press, 1959.

Young, Oran R. *The Politics of Force: Bargaining During International Crises.* Princeton, N.J.: Princeton University Press, 1969.

NOTES

1. "Race Poisoning by Radiation," *Saturday Review,* 9 June 1956.
2. "The Biological Effects of Bomb Tests," *New Statesman and Nation,* 8 June 1957.
3. *The New Scientist,* 16 May 1957.
4. Philip Noel-Baker, *The Arms Race* (New York: Oceana Publications, 1958), p. 255.
5. Ibid., p. 263.
6. *New York Times,* 14 January 1958.

7. Cited by Noel-Baker, op. cit., p. 261.
8. *New York Times*, 8 June 1957.
9. *New York Herald Tribune*, 1 September 1958.
10. Noel-Baker, op. cit., p. 298.
11. General Assembly Resolution 1962 (December 13, 1963).
12. General Assembly Resolution 2373 (June 12, 1968).
13. General Assembly Resolution 1665 (December 4, 1961).
14. General Assembly Resolution 1664 (December 4, 1961).
15. The ENDC is composed of eighteen nations: the United States, Canada, Britain, France, and Italy for the West; the Soviet Union, Poland, Czechoslovakia, Bulgaria, and Rumania for the East; and eight nonaligned countries: Brazil, Burma, Ethiopia, India, Mexico, Nigeria, Sweden, and the United Arab Republic.
16. General Assembly Resolution 2028 (November 23, 1965).
17. General Assembly Resolution 2373 (June 12, 1968). Voting against were Albania, Cuba, Tanzania, and Zambia. Not voting were Cambodia, the Dominican Republic, Gambia, and Haiti. Abstentions were Algeria, Argentina, Brazil, Burma, Burundi, Central African Republic, Congo (Brazzaville), France, Gabon, Guinea, India, Malawi, Mali, Mauritania, Niger, Portugal, Rwanda, Saudi Arabia, Sierra Leone, Spain, and Uganda.
18. Security Council Resolution 255 (June 19, 1968). Those abstaining were Algeria, Brazil, France, India, and Pakistan.
19. ENDC/240.
20. ENDC/249.
21. ENDC/PV.397.
22. CCD/269.
23. A/C.1/995,p.3.
24. CCD/271.
25. ENDC/240.
26. ENDC/PV.424.
27. ENDC/240.
28. ENDC/249.
29. CCD/269/Rev.3.

"Only One Earth": The United Nations Conference on the Human Environment

9

"The Planet will survive the ecological crisis as a whole or not at all."

U Thant
UN Secretary-General, 1970

The Problem

In June 1972, about 1,200 delegates from 114 nations met for two weeks in Stockholm, Sweden, in order to produce an international action plan to halt the deterioration of the environment and to conserve the earth's dwindling resources. The UN Conference on the Human Environment had been four years in the making and was initiated by a 1968 resolution of the General Assembly, originally proposed by the government of Sweden. It was to be man's first global attack on the deepening environmental crisis, and it was mounted under the aegis of the United Nations.

Man has always lived in two worlds: the "biosphere," the world of living things from which he draws his physical existence, and the "technosphere," the world of tools and artifacts, of social and political institutions that he has forged for himself. For centuries, the planet's fields and forests, its reserves of fertile soil and minerals, its oceans and rivers could carry without strain the entire freight of man's technological inventions and desires. In the last few decades, however, and with explosively increasing force in the last few years, the balance between the planet's biosphere and the technosphere has been critically affected. Man no longer lives almost overwhelmed by the scale of his environment. It is the environment that is beginning to be overwhelmed by man. At stake is nothing less than the quality of life on this planet.

From its inception, the United Nations has been concerned about the quality of life for the peoples of the world, and its involvement with environmental issues dates back to the 1949 International Technical Conference on Conservation. The Stockholm Conference of 1972 was convened under UN auspices because the United Nations alone had the world-wide system through which an essentially cooperative and international response to the global challenge could be launched. It also provided a forum in which industrialized and developing countries could most easily meet to discuss and devise joint policies for development that would enhance, rather than injure, the shared biosphere. And finally, the United Nations, as a continuing body, could set in motion a whole range of actions without which fragmentation and disunity would continue to mark man's approach to his global environment.

Under the leadership of Maurice F. Strong, the secretary-general of the Conference, and under the slogan "Only One Earth," the delegates converged upon Stockholm in order to address themselves to the multiple aspects of a single theme: How can man control the technosphere in order to save planet earth? The challenge was well expressed by Dr. Margaret Mead, one of the speakers at the Conference:

What is required is a revolution in thought fully comparable to the Copernican Revolution by which, four centuries ago, men were compelled to revise their whole sense of the earth's place in the cosmos. Today we are challenged to recognize as great a change in our concept of man's place in the biosphere. Our survival in a world that continues to be worth inhabiting depends upon our translating this new perception into relevant principles and concrete action.[1]

The Actors

The constellation of political forces that dominated the Conference was unique. First, there was no Soviet-American interaction because the Soviet Union decided not to participate. Second, the Conference provided the stage for a remarkable performance by the People's Republic of China. Third, the East-West struggle as a whole was superseded, if not entirely eclipsed, by a tug of war between the rich the the poor nations.

The Soviet Union decided to boycott the Conference because East Germany—not a member of the United Nations—was denied full participation. The Soviet boycott resulted in the absence of Bulgaria, Czechoslovakia, Hungary, Poland, and Cuba as well. Rumania and Yugoslavia, however, decided to attend. There had been hope, until virtually the last minute, that the USSR might be persuaded to attend, but efforts toward that end finally proved futile.

While the Soviet decision not to attend did not seriously delay Conference operations or hold up its proceedings, some delegates expressed considerable dismay at the circumstances leading to the Soviet boycott. Many felt that East Germany should have been invited to attend as a full participant despite its nonmember status. This, in turn, would have assured the presence of the Soviet Union. On the other hand, it was the majority's view that the Conference, which was after all a subsidiary organ of the UN General Assembly, could not arrogate to itself the right to recommend fundamental changes in UN membership policy.

Most delegates at the Conference believed that the Soviet boycott stemmed from a matter of principle rather than from a lack of interest in the environmental problem. Hence, there was considerable sentiment during the Conference not to adopt policies that would antagonize the Soviet Union or prejudice its future association. One concrete manifestation of this sentiment was the decision to leave vacant those posts originally earmarked for the USSR and the Eastern European states on the Conference Bureau and not to redistribute them to other participating states. In view of the fact that the two superpowers had just concluded an agreement at the Moscow Summit to cooperate on environmental protection and research, there was hope that the active participation of the Soviet Union could be enlisted in the not-too-distant future.

The thirty-five-member U.S. delegation adopted a low-profile approach to the Conference. The delegation was headed by Russell E. Train, chairman of the White House Council on Environmental Quality, and Christian A. Herter, Jr., who served as special assistant to the secretary of state for environmental affairs. There were two important reasons for the cautious approach adopted by the United States. First, the delegation reflected a division within the United States between the forces that pushed for continued technological growth and those that warned against the rising dangers of environmental abuse. Thus, representatives from the petroleum industry as well as environmental scientists found themselves on the delegation. Second, the United States was fearful of massive criticism that might be leveled in Stockholm against its bombing and defoliation policies in Vietnam. These twin considerations prompted the United States to remain somewhat in the background. Hence, when the Conference opened, one superpower was absent, and the other attempted to avoid the spotlight.

Even though the People's Republic of China had been admitted to the United Nations in October 1971 and had attended the Twenty-sixth Session of the General Assembly, her real debut was made in Stockholm. In fact, the Chinese delegation even occupied the center of the stage some of the time. China consistently cast her lot with the have-not nations of the world and refused to be associated with either of the superpowers, both of which she accused of wanton pollution of the environment. China even went so far as to claim that the advanced countries owed "reparation payments" to the have-not nations for having polluted their environments in addition to their own. It was clear from virtually every statement that the Chinese delegation at

Stockholm was making a determined bid for the leadership of the Third World.

The poor countries attending the Conference outnumbered the rich by a ratio of about 2 to 1. Many of the smaller nations, especially from Africa and other parts of the Third World, looked at pollution as a "rich man's disease" and regarded the entire movement to protect the environment as a luxury. They worried more about eating today than about choking tomorrow and hence tended to emphasize the continuing need for modernization and economic development.

The alignment of actors at Stockholm thus prevented the usual East-West tensions from materializing in their traditional form. The Soviet Union was absent, and the United States preferred to play a subdued role. The stage was set in such a manner that the tensions between the rich and the poor overshadowed the more typical manifestations of the East-West struggle. The tug of war between them in fact reflected the most basic issue with which the 114 nations represented at the Conference had to deal.

There were times, however, when, upon closer scrutiny, the arguments between the rich and the poor over environment versus development seemed more semantic than real. Many African states, for example, acknowledged that they had problems with water pollution that frequently led to disease. In their view, the solution to this problem lay in development and modernization; while in the view of the richer nations, the answers were to be found in environmental protection. When, however, the debate came down to practical recommendations to be made in order to deal with a specific instance of water pollution, the technical measures that were advocated by both developed and developing nations frequently exhibited a remarkable degree of convergence.

The Political Alignments

A unique set of political alignments became manifest at the Stockholm Conference and, even more sharply, at the Environment Forum that met at the same time as the Conference. At one end of the spectrum were the advocates of a "zero-growth" world, one in which the current progressive deterioration of the environment, degrading the quality of the world's air, land, and water, would be virtually brought to a halt. It would be a world in which population would be stabilized and the consumption of raw materials held to a level not substantially greater than the production of such materials. Energy use would be compatible with the planet's long-term reserves of nuclear and fossil fuels. Those who supported this view—largely groups and individual spokesmen from the modern industrial nations of the West— believed that social chaos and major wars would erupt over access to the world's depleting resources unless the developed countries decided to arrest their heedless growth.

At the other extreme were those—primarily the developing countries—who saw no need in the foreseeable future to alter their emphasis on technological advancement. They contended that a zero-growth world would merely compound the problem, leading in effect to the destruction of the world's economies that must expand in order to prosper. In other words, a zero-growth world would merely freeze the status quo in favor of the rich countries.

In this tug of war between environmentalists and developmentalists, Secretary-General Maurice F. Strong took a middle course. "No growth is not a viable policy for any society today," he said. "Indeed, people must have access to more, not fewer opportunities to express their creative drives. But these can only be provided within a total system in which man's activities are in dynamic harmony with the natural order." "To achieve this," he added,

we must rethink our concept of the basic purposes of growth. Surely we must see it in terms of enriching the lives and enlarging the opportunities of all mankind. And if this is so, it follows that it is the more wealthy societies—the privileged minority of mankind—which will have to make the most profound, even revolutionary, changes in attitudes and values.[2]

Mr. Strong's carefully charted middle course between the advocates of development and the defenders of the environment attempted to avoid a confrontation between the have and the have-not nations at the Conference. Nevertheless, the debate was often sharp and intense. A number of African nations, for example, raised the question of reparations for colonialism and racism, which, they maintained, had squandered African human and natural resources. They conceded, however, that such reparations need not be paid in cash but could take the form of trade concessions or additional assistance to finance pollution control activities.

China took up the theme of reparations with a vengeance and injected the Vietnam War into the discussion. The United States was guilty, in the Chinese view, of "the massive killing of innocent old people, women, and children," as well as of "the unprecedented and serious destruction of the human environment." Turning to the role of the superpowers more generally, China asserted that the United States and the Soviet Union did not hesitate to spend huge sums of money on the arms race but were unwilling to spend a minimum sum as compensation to smaller states for the destruction of their environment through pollution. While the Vietnam theme was echoed, to the consternation of the American delegation, by Sweden's Prime Minister Olof Palme, the Chinese case lost a great deal of its potential effectiveness because of China's ambivalence on the subject of her own status as a growing nuclear power. She tried to justify her own decision to continue nuclear tests in the face of massive Third World opposition by pointing to the "superpower monopoly" of atomic weapons. The emphasis that the Chinese delegation placed on its own "non first use" policy did not prove sufficient to win the support of those delegations from the Third World whose support China was seeking. In the end, China's twin goals at Stockholm—to seize the leadership of the Third World but simultaneously to protect her status as a growing nuclear power—effectively canceled each other out.

The United States had hoped that the Vietnam issue would not surface, but when it did, the response was sharp. When the Swedish prime minister made reference to the "outrage" of American bombings of Vietnam that, he said, amounted to ecological warfare, Mr. Russell Train responded with a scathing rejoinder to Mr. Palme's "gratuitous politicizing" of the Conference. In addition, the Swedish ambassador in Washington was called in to receive an American protest. The circle was completed when the Swedish Foreign Office, in turn, protested against American hypersensitivity to Palme's remarks. In the words of one observer of the Conference, the United States was "utterly unable or unwilling to grasp how deeply Vietnam had damaged the American image abroad."[3]

Perhaps the sharpest cleavage which marked the Conference was that between the developed and the developing countries over the issue of development versus environment. Mr. Strong had feared that only the rich countries would pay attention to the need for environmental protection, while the poor would consider it a luxury. Hence, months before the Conference began, the secretary-general had made it a point to visit nearly every participating nation and to hold several regional seminars in order to emphasize his conviction that pollution was everybody's problem. While to many of the developing countries the entire concept of environmental protection still seemed somewhat of an abstraction, they nevertheless pledged their support. But they demanded a dual price for their environmental cooperation. This they termed "additionality" and "indemnity." The logic of additionality and indemnity was based on the fear of the poor countries that high environmental standards in the advanced countries would hurt their export trade. As poor countries industrialized, it would cost them more to add antipollution equipment. Brazil, for example, asked to be compensated for building environmental protection devices into its new automobile plants. This additionality proviso was based on the assumption, generally shared by the poor nations, that "the polluter must pay." Moreover, if the poor nations' export trade suffered because their products did not meet the environmental standards of a developed country, that country should pay an indemnity in the form of special trade concessions or financial assistance.

The United States strongly opposed both of these initiatives on the ground that they were wrong in principle and would be a "disincentive to environmental responsibility." As one member of the American delegation put it: "Imagine how Congress would vote if Peru claimed damages for a drop in her lead exports to the United States because we had banned leaded gasoline."[4] Not only did the United States take a hard line on this question, but the delegation was under strict instructions not to acquiesce in any moves that would divert any financial contributions intended for environmental protection to developmental assistance. It took Robert S. McNamara, president of the World Bank, to inject a conciliatory note into the discussion. He observed that three-quarters of the human race was living at levels of deprivation which simply could not be reconciled with any rational definition of human decency. While criticizing the developing nations for not moving decisively enough to reduce the severe social and economic inequities among their own peoples, he took the rich countries severely to task for "not moving decisively enough to reduce the gross imbalance between their own opulence and the penury of the less-privileged nations."[5]

Since most of the developing countries shared a common perspective on the environmental problem, they made a deep impact on the Conference. By and large, they defined the issue of environment in development terms and sought to convert this conception into a major Conference priority. They pointed out again and again that the most urgent environmental reality of the developing countries was development and a substantial improvement in the living conditions for the vast majority of mankind. They were virtually unanimous in their rejection of all proposals for environmental protection that would impede or obstruct their own growth processes.

This position aroused considerable emotion, since the Conference had convened under the shadow of an explosive report prepared by the Club of Rome under the title *Limits to Growth*, which strongly advocated zero growth in order to save the planet from self-destruction. The developing countries attacked the report as an effort by the Western countries to freeze the status quo in their favor. Finally, the secretary-general's moderate view prevailed, and strenuous efforts were made by developed and developing countries alike to work out differences over environmental priorities in many specific cases. On the whole, these compromises were translated into meaningful accomplishments.

Yet another element injected a soothing influence into the tense relations between the rich and the poor at the Conference.

There was increasing evidence that there was under way a global "shift of comparative advantages" that would benefit the developing countries. Initiatives were being taken to relocate polluting industries from saturated regions to areas that could—in ecological terms—"afford" them. One by-product of such shifts would, of course, be the developmental and economic benefits that would accrue to the poor countries. To many of these, pollution still was no serious threat, but rather seemed to be a status symbol of modernization. In addition, there were increasing indications of shifts from synthetics to natural products that would help to restore the ecological balance. Hence, in the view of many ecologists attending the Conference, the somber prophecies made by the Club of Rome did not seem warranted by the facts.

Accomplishments

The Conference had set for itself four specific goals: first, the formulation and adoption of a Declaration on the Human Environment; second, a comprehensive list of recommendations for international initiatives, including an action plan for the implementation of these recommendations; third, the establishment of a voluntary fund for the financing of environmental programs and research; and fourth, the establishment of institutional machinery for the coordination of environmental activities within the UN system. In addition, it was decided to recommend the observance of World Environment Day on June 5 each year. The political struggle over the attainment of these goals is deserving of analysis.

The Declaration on the Human Environment had been the subject of protracted negotiations for many months before the Conference convened. Informal working groups had managed to hammer out delicately balanced compromises between have and have-not nations, trying whenever possible to soften the tensions between environmentalists and developmentalists. Principle II, for example, states that: "the environmental policies of all states should enhance and not adversely affect the present or future development potential of developing countries, nor should they hamper the attainment of better living conditions for all. . . ." It seemed as if adoption of the draft at Stockholm would be an easy matter. This was not to be the case, however. China, which had not been a member of the United Nations in the drafting stages, stated that she had been denied representation and insisted upon the establishment of a new working group at Stockholm to review the draft in its entirety. During these new negotiations, China made her determined bid to appeal to the have-not nations and tried to tilt the Declaration in their favor. Her position on nuclear testing, however, greatly reduced her credibility in the Third World. Principle 26 of the Declaration totally rejected the Chinese position by stating that:

man and his environment must be spared the effects of nuclear weapons and all other means of mass destruction. States must strive to reach prompt agreement, in the relevant international organs, on the elimination and complete destruction of such weapons.

In the end, the Declaration was adopted with only minor changes from the original draft.

It is quite conceivable that the Declaration on the Human Environment, as adopted at Stockholm, may be one of the most significant documents in UN history, comparable perhaps to the Universal Declaration of Human Rights. It has far-reaching political implications. In recent history, states have tended to use the environment as an instrument of war. The use of defoliation, fire storms, or rainmaking in the forest areas of Vietnam is only one example of what may be described as "environmental warfare." Policies of apartheid, or racial discrimination, have been condemned as inimical to an environment of quality that permits a life of dignity and well-being. Needless to say, there is nothing that is binding on any state in the Declaration, but like its predecessor of 1948, it will probably be invoked frequently as an instrument of moral sanction.

The second concrete achievement of the Conference was the Action Plan. This Plan consisted of 109 specific recommendations that were adopted by the Conference and that were to become the basis of international action. At its core was an "Earthwatch" Program of systematic assessment and monitoring of global conditions as a basis for national measures to curb environmental abuses. One typical Earthwatch recommendation called for a global early warning system designed to monitor changes in the world's climate and levels of air pollution. A large number of stations dispersed throughout the world and coordinated by the relevant UN specialized agencies would provide vital information that, it was hoped, would stimulate national action. In addition to Earthwatch, a large number of stations dispersed throughout the world and coordinated by the relevant UN specialized agencies would provide vital information that, it was hoped, would stimulate national action. In addition to Earthwatch, a large number of recommendations had to do with "environmental management." One such recommendation called upon all nations to minimize the release of toxic metals and chemicals into the environment. Another called for action to save threatened species, such as the whale, from complete extinction. A third aspect of the Action Plan dealt with education, organizational arrangements, and financial assistance. These were discussed most heatedly at the Conference because their adoption depended upon tangible commitments that had to be made by national governments.

In the debates over the Action Plan, the tensions between the rich and the poor surfaced continuously. In one of its supporting measures, for example, the Conference decided to establish a World Housing Fund, a financial institution that would assist in the environmental improvement of human settlements. Even though the recommendation was adopted, the division between developed and developing countries remained till the end. Speaking on behalf of the latter, Mrs. Indira Gandhi asked: "How can we speak to those who live in villages and slums about keeping the oceans and air clean when their own lives are contaminated at the source?"[6] Most of the Third World delegates agreed and stated that their need was not expertise but resources. The Conference, in their view, should offer solutions, not diagnoses. One objective of the Conference was to help in giving homes to the homeless of humanity. Most of the developed countries regarded the World Housing Fund proposal as a thinly disguised attempt by the poor to "soak the rich" and to convert environmental diagnosis into developmental assistance. Significantly enough, the minority of states voting against the Housing Fund included most of the world's developed nations: Australia, Canada, Denmark, West Germany, France, Ireland, Italy, Japan, Liechtenstein, Luxembourg, Monaco, Sweden, Switzerland, the United Kingdom, and the United States.

Conspicuous by its absence from the Action Plan was any program to deal with the world's population problem. While some of the developed nations favored recommendations aimed at population control, the Third World nations were virtually unanimous in their opposition. In this view they were supported by China, which asserted that population per se was not a cause of environmental degradation, but rather the cause was the exploitation that had been inflicted by the West upon its former colonies. Western effort to check population growth in the Third World was just a new form of racial imperialism aimed at freezing the status quo in favor of the white minorities. These arguments were so effective that the entire population problem was dealt with only tangentially at Stockholm. The United States was too ambivalent on the matter to adopt a strong position one way or another.

The money for environmental activities was to come from an Environment Fund to which governments were to contribute on a voluntary basis. The United States suggested a figure of $100 million for a five-year period and pledged to contribute 40 percent of the total, insisting however, that no funds must be diverted from environmental activities such as monitoring, data assessment, research, public education, and training into outright development assistance. The developing countries strongly supported the Fund but again asserted their priority of development. China, torn between her desire to woo the Third World and her dissatisfaction over the Conference's rejection of her atomic weapons policy, voted "absent" on the question of the Environment Fund. One of Secretary-General Strong's aides approached the Chinese delegate and said: "With all the Chinese wisdom and experience, perhaps you could clarify what you want"; to which the Chinese delegate replied: "Yes, China has wisdom but we are inexperienced in these matters."[7]

Finally, a resolution on new machinery was adopted by the Conference without a vote. It was recommended that a representative group of fifty-four of the world's nations, elected every three years by the General Assembly on the basis of equitable geographical distribution, would meet regularly as a Governing Council for Environmental Programs. This body would provide general policy guidance and serve as the central organ for international cooperation on the environment. In addition, the day-to-day work of the United Nations in this sphere would be performed by a small environmental secretariat that would serve as a focal point of coordination within the UN system and ensure effective management. Its executive director would be elected by the General Assembly or nominated by the UN Secretary-General.

On June 16, 1972, the closing day of the Conference, Mr. Strong emphasized the need for cooperation beyond Stockholm. Otherwise, he warned, the Conference would only have been "a brief flash, a meteor burning its way through the blackness of space." What had to be done, first of all, was to secure the approval of the General Assembly. This was by no means a mere formality. The Soviet Union, the most prominent absentee, would have to clarify its stand. The triangular politics among China, the Soviet Union, and the United States were changing the international constellation profoundly. Japan and Western Europe were growing in economic strength, and much of the Third World continued to live in desperate plight. As the Twenty-seventh Session of the General Assembly opened in September 1972, a new item dealing with the human environment figured prominently on the agenda.

Beyond Stockholm

The most dramatic decision taken by the General Assembly in the wake of the Stockholm Conference had to do with the geographical location of the new secretariat that was to coordinate the UN Environmental Program. Most Western diplomats, who expected the secretariat to be placed in Geneva or in New York after a routine debate, were startled by the unified and forceful efforts made by Asian, African, and Latin-American countries to establish the secretariat in a developing nation, namely in Nairobi, the capital of Kenya.

Most of the Western states, particularly the United States, the United Kingdom, and Sweden, defended the view that the establishment of the environment secretariat should be determined primarily by factors of efficiency, effectiveness, and cost. When judged by these standards, Geneva or New York seemed to be logical choices.

The developing countries, in an intense and emotional debate, held that the site of the environmental headquarters was essentially a "political" decision. One of the most remarkable features of the debate was the extraordinary display of bloc solidarity and discipline in evidence among the developing states. Even when a UN Secretariat estimate revealed that the annual cost of the environment secretariat in Nairobi would be $2.3 million, whereas the cost in Geneva would come to only $1.4 million, this did not change a single vote. The delegate of Kenya stated that if, in fact, it cost a little more to build a UN agency in a developing state, the United Nations would "in effect pay a little rent for the omissions of the past."[8] China supported the pro-Nairobi group, but the Soviet Union, torn between its superpower status and its efforts to woo the poor nations, found itself among the abstainers.

Thus, the developing nations, in their drive for status and prestige as well as funds, established a new principle: the observance of geographical representation in the establishment of new UN bodies. In a more fundamental sense, the Nairobi decision symbolized the growing rift between rich and poor and the somewhat anachronistic nature of the traditional ideological divisions between East and West. It underlined once again with growing force the emergence of a new power constellation and the United Nations.

The Soviet position was of considerable interest during the 1972 General Assembly because that nation had not participated in the Stockholm Conference. To begin with, the Soviet Union asserted that the capitalist system was inherently predatory toward nature, while the socialist countries practiced conservation. Beyond that, Soviet policy pronouncements were marked by extreme caution. After restating its regret at the absence of East Germany from the deliberations, the Soviet Union displayed great ambivalence on most substantive issues. It leaned toward the Western position by opposing a special Housing Fund and voted against a resolution advanced by the developing nations enlarging the membership of the proposed Governing Council from fifty-four to fifty-eight states. On balance, the Soviet Union supported the poor nations with its rhetoric but, in most instances, backed the rich nations with its votes. Over and over again, the Soviet delegate reiterated the vital importance of national sovereignty and, in particular, took exception to a statement made by Secretary-General Maurice F. Strong to the effect that the task of environmental protection dictated a "new and more effective means of enabling nations to exercise sovereignty collectively where they can no longer exercise it effectively alone."[9] On balance, the Soviet view was conservative and tentative, with a pronounced tilt toward the have nations of the world.

The tug of war between the rich and the poor was even more pronounced in New York than it had been in Stockholm. While the Declaration on the Human Environment and the Action Plan were approved without much difficulty, the arguments over the institutional and financial implications of these proposals were often hard and bitter. An Assembly decision to go beyond the Environment Fund and to appeal to the World Bank for further financial assistance for housing, as well as the decision to locate the new secretariat in Kenya, demonstrated the thrust and urgency of the developmental rather than the strictly environmental priorities of the poor nations that made up the majority of mankind. On balance, the environmental debate, more than any other issue, symbolized the transition of the United Nations from the cold-war era into a multipolar world.

Environmental breakdown does not respect national or ideological boundaries. It threatens capitalists and communists, the rich and the poor alike. The environmental challenge may yet prove to be the great leveler of international relations. It might even become a catalyst toward a saner world order, since it may compel nations to cooperate on basic problems common to all. Perhaps the greatest achievement at Stockholm and beyond lay in the fact that more than 100 nations found it possible to face a crisis before it had reached the point of no return and to take action on a global basis to arrest it. Most delegates sensed that the planet would survive the ecological crisis as a whole or not at all. Hence, they turned to the United Nations as a logical means of action. This decision also infused new life and hope into the world organization itself. Having languished for years with the realization that it could not free the planet of most of its wars and political crises, the United Nations could now draw strength from the hope that it might make a major contribution toward making life on this planet worth living at all.

SELECTED BIBLIOGRAPHY

Commission to Study the Organization of Peace. *The United Nations and the Human Environment.* Twenty-second Report. New York, 1972.

Commoner, Barry. *The Closing Circle.* New York: Knopf, 1971.

Ehrlich, Paul R., and A. H. Ehrlich. *Population, Resources, Environment: Issues in Human Ecology.* 2nd ed. San Francisco: Freeman, 1972.

Falk, Richard A. *This Endangered Planet.* New York: Random House, 1972.

Kormondy, E. J. *Concepts of Ecology.* Englewood Cliffs, N.J.: Prentice-Hall, 1969.

Meadows, Donella H., et al. *The Limits to Growth.* New York: Universe Books, 1972.

Shepard, Paul, and Daniel McKinley, eds. *The Subversive Science: Essays Toward an Ecology of Man.* Boston: Houghton Mifflin, 1969.

Ward, Barbara, and René Dubos. *Only One Earth: The Care and Maintenance of a Small Planet.* New York: Norton, 1972.

NOTES

1. United Nations Press Release HE/143, June 19, 1972.
2. Ibid.
3. Edward P. Morgan, "Stockholm: The Clean (But Impossible) Dream," *Foreign Policy* (Fall 1972), p. 150.

4. Ibid., p. 152.
5. Ibid., p. 153.
6. Ibid.
7. Ibid., p. 154.
8. *New York Times*, 11 November 1972.
9. Statement made by Maurice F. Strong before the Second Committee of the General Assembly, October 19, 1972.

PART FOUR

Conclusions

The United Nations and the Superpowers

The conflict between the superpowers has dominated international politics since World War II and, naturally, has cast its shadow over the United Nations. The split between the United States and the Soviet Union quickly destroyed many of the basic assumptions on which the United Nations had been founded. For example, the assumption that the UN's peace-keeping strength could be based on the unity of the Great Powers collapsed almost immediately. Since that time the United Nations has passed through a succession of dark nights of the soul: the Soviet walkouts, the Korean police action, the American attack on the Secretariat, the simultaneous crises in Hungary and Suez, the ten-year membership stalemate, the Congo crisis, the Soviet troika attack, coupled with the tragic death of Secretary-General Hammarskjöld, the dispute over payments for peace-keeping operations, and the long struggle over Chinese representation. At each crisis there have been prophets of doom claiming that the United Nations was living on borrowed time and predicting that *this* time the Organization, like the League before it, would finally go under. Yet the United Nations has weathered each crisis and has even appeared to grow more resilient with the years.

If the United Nations has not been living on borrowed time, even its advocates must admit that it has been living on borrowed money. The issues at stake in the peace-keeping crisis were not resolved with finality despite the American decision to drop the fight over the application of Article 19. For this reason, the outcome of the 1964–1965 crisis over the payment of assessments for peace-keeping operations was one of the most important watersheds in the Organization's history. It determined how much of its past was to be consolidated for use in the future. Some leading contemporary analysts were far from hopeful. In March 1965, Professor Hans Morgenthau found that "the Security Council [was] powerless, the General Assembly [was] powerless, and the Secretary-General [was] powerless. The United Nations has ceased to be an effective international organization."[1] In short, while Professor Morgenthau might admit that before the financing crisis the United Nations had appeared to grow stronger over the years, in 1965 he suggested that this growth had not only been halted but cut back severely.

The year 1965 was crucial in the life of the United Nations in the sense that it witnessed the first American defeat on an issue that was crucial to that superpower. Even though no formal vote was ever taken, the United States admitted defeat on the Article 19 controversy. After 1965, it became increasingly difficult for the United States to build winning coalitions in the General Assembly and even in the Security Council. The logical result of this process was the American defeat in 1971 on the issue of Chinese representation.

While there is little doubt about the decline of American power and influence in the United Nations of the mid-1970's, it would be wrong to assert that there has been a corresponding rise in Soviet influence. If any group of nations has gained, it has been the Third World. But as a number of contradictory resolutions passed by the Thirtieth General Assembly in 1975 demonstrated, even the Third World has not been a cohesive entity. As the UN's concerns have tended to shift from an East-West to a North-South axis, the new nations' priorities have virtually dominated the Organization. China, very much aware of this evolving trend, has wooed the Third World nations while steering clear of the two superpowers. The Soviet Union has tended to compete with China for their favor. And the United States has been cast into the role of the opposition, at times warning that the United Nations might become an empty shell.

Despite this new cold war between the world's rich and poor, the superpowers have continued to exert enormous influence. From the perspective of the preceding nine chapters, it seems that in order to survive for the past three decades, the United Nations has had to learn one vital lesson: how to deal with the superpowers. The interaction between the United States and the Soviet Union has been central to the UN's development. Since 1971, China has become a major actor in the UN arena. This book has examined these interactions in the constitutional, peace-keeping, development, arms control, and environment fields of UN activity. In each of these areas the relationship between the United Nations and the superpowers has revealed certain basic themes. First, the superpowers' national interest has been the major determinant of their policies toward the United Nations; when the United Nations serves that interest, the Organization is allowed to go forward; when it does not, its evolution is hindered. Second, the United Nations has dealt with these clashing national interests in a pragmatic and flexible manner. Third, through this flexible policy, the United Nations has emerged from a harrowing series of crises as a resilient force in international politics. The extent of that progress in each of the fields noted above will now be evaluated.

Constitutional Evolution

The major theme that emerges from the analysis in Part One is the controlling role that the superpowers' national interest has played in the evolution of the United Nations. We have noted the decisive impact of superpower policies on three major UN organs: the Security Council, the General Assembly, and the Secretariat. In analyzing the use of the veto in the Security Council, we have seen that among the most effective Soviet vetoes have been the ones employed in direct defense of the USSR's national interest in confrontations with the West. The United States, for its part, developed an equally effective though less conspicuous hidden veto with which to guard its vital interests. The struggle over membership policy in the General Assembly showed the United States first defending a policy of exclusion, which resulted in its retention of an automatic majority. The USSR pressed for package deals that would have improved its relative voting position. After 1955, both superpowers saw their interests better served by opening wide the gates of admission in order to cultivate the newly emergent nations. The case study on the Secretariat demonstrated that each superpower was prepared to attack that Office when it saw danger to its national interest, although the American attack was led by the Congress, not the executive.

On the whole, the three case studies support the contention that, during the first two decades of the UN's life, the United States was more successful in the pursuit of its national interest than was the Soviet Union. After 1965, however, this ceased to be the case. Our examination of the USSR's absolute weapon, its 110 vetoes, revealed that only 28 of these had conclusively prevented further action. Twenty-five had been circumvented by compensatory UN action, often under American pressure; and 57, including the 43 membership vetoes, had been superseded through direct negotiations. After 1965, however, it became increasingly difficult to circumvent Soviet vetoes. In fact, all but one of the Soviet vetoes cast since then have been final.

On the American side, the hidden veto remained an effective weapon until 1965. In 1966, its edge was somewhat blunted by the enlargement of the Security Council. In 1970, the United

States cast its first veto; and shortly after casting its second in 1972, the announcement was made that henceforth the veto would be used much more freely to block "bad" resolutions. By the mid-1970's, the voting behavior of the superpowers on the Security Council had become increasingly alike. In fact, by then, the United States was casting vetoes more frequently than the Soviet Union. China's first vetoes suggested that she, too, had placed Machiavelli above Mao Tse-tung and that consensus in the Council of the 1970's would never be an easy matter.

In the Assembly, the United States had commanded easy majorities during the first twenty years. Thereafter, the job of building winning coalitions became more difficult, and the superpowers began to neutralize each other. In 1967, for example, in the wake of the Arab-Israeli War, neither superpower was able to muster a two-thirds majority for its respective position. And in 1971, the United States lost its showdown vote over Chinese representation. Thereafter, the Third World countries increasingly came to dominate the General Assembly as the United States went into opposition.

A similar trend may be observed in the evolution of the Office of the Secretary-General. The United States had its way with Trygve Lie and the Secretariat during the 1950's, while the Soviet troika attack on Dag Hammarskjöld failed in 1960. During the tenure of U Thant, however, care was taken not to antagonize *either* superpower, and the same concern was evident in the administration of Kurt Waldheim, even though the fourth Secretary-General was a far greater activist than his predecessor.

The second major theme evident in Part One is the extraordinary flexibility demonstrated by the UN's principal organs. In response to various challenges, the United Nations has shifted power pragmatically to the organ most free to cope with the particular crisis. In this manner, the locus of power has moved from the Security Council to the General Assembly and the Secretary-General and back again to the Security Council. The Organization has responded to political problems in a political manner, relying heavily on the arts of improvisation and compromise. In this sense, the United Nations contrasts sharply with the League of Nations, which was unable to muster any countervailing forces when confronted by threats from the future Axis powers and the Soviet Union. Three of the major UN organs have exercised important international responsibilities, and in a crisis some precedent would exist for their use. Or else, the United Nations, by applying its "flexible-response" doctrine, might devise an entirely new solution. In short, like any living institution, the United Nations has remained resilient.

Upon reflection, one can see that these two themes—national interest and the UN's evolution through flexibility—are interconnected. The UN's evolution has been forced in part by the pressure of the superpowers' striving to achieve their national interests. For example, the U.S.-Soviet struggle was primarily responsible for shifting the locus of power within the UN system. In 1950, the United States, eager to circumvent the Soviet veto, persuaded the General Assembly to pass the Uniting for Peace Resolution, which broadened that organ's mandate in peace and security matters. The United States saw its interest better served in an Assembly that its allies controlled than in a veto-bound Security Council. In 1956, again as a result of American initiative and, significantly, after the first increase in membership, the locus of power moved from the Assembly to the Office of the Secretary-General. The large influx of new members in the Assembly that had been actively sought by the Soviet Union had cost the United States its automatic majority. Hence, the United States encouraged the passage of broadly conceived resolutions that invested the Secretary-General with increasing policy-making responsibilities. The subsequent Soviet attack on the Office in 1960 was an attempt to eliminate that increased responsibility. Beginning in 1961, after the troika's failure was evident, the Soviet Union exercised more restraint in its use of the veto. By so doing, the USSR could retain some authority over an operation in the Council rather than lose it to the Assembly or to the Secretary-General. Thus, the Security Council was resuscitated as a major UN power center. As the Third World countries gradually took control of the General Assembly during the 1970's, the United States, and to some extent even the Soviet Union, sought refuge in the Council and constantly reiterated its primary responsibilities for the peace.

Hence, the first three case studies suggest that the superpowers' quest for national interest through the United Nations and the development of the international organization itself may not necessarily be contradictory. On the most practical level, if the United Nations did not serve *some* national interest of the superpowers, it would be ignored by them. To be relevant in world politics, the United Nations must be used; to be used, it must serve. Part of the price of relevance, therefore, is service. On a deeper level, however, we have also seen that if the superpowers are going to use the United Nations to promote their national interests, they must first give it sufficient power and authority to act. Once given, this power cannot always be so easily withdrawn. For example, in order to use the General Assembly in peace-keeping operations, the United States broadened its mandate through the Uniting for Peace Resolution. Today this procedure is theoretically available to any group that can muster the requisite majority. The participation of the Secretary-General in the Suez crisis, a role that the Soviet Union did not actively oppose, made it natural in the Congo crisis to turn once again to the Secretary-General, whom the USSR later opposed violently. In short, some residue of authority seems to remain with the United Nations even after the superpowers' immediate goals are met. Hence, one can picture the United Nations as a midget caught between two giants—being used and abused by each in turn—but all the while stealing strength from each. And since the superpowers frequently attempt to use the United Nations against each other, it appears that part of the UN's growth in resilience has actually taken place *because* of superpower conflict as well as in spite of it.

In the United Nations of the 1970's, the midget's balancing process is even more delicate. The bipolar world is over. The entrance of China, the rise of Japan, the growing power of the Third World, and the unification process of Western Europe have placed the United Nations in the midst of a multipolar world. In a world of such increased complexity, there may arise more frequently constellations that will permit the United Nations to act. But it will take discerning eyes to perceive such favorable constellations and political courage to inject the United

Nations into them in time for meaningful and decisive action. This is especially true in a world in which the temptation to turn the United Nations into a vehicle for the interests of a single group—the Third World—is strong indeed. In such a climate, it may not be easy to remember that the United Nations was not meant to be an advocate of any one particular cause, but rather a referee and mediator among many.

Peace-Keeping Operations

In Part Two we examined the superpowers' role in the establishment, political control, and financial support of several major UN peace-keeping operations. One striking similarity between UNEF I and ONUC was the environment in which each crisis developed. In each case, a local dispute escalated into a conflict between nationalism and colonialism that, in turn, led to a major confrontation between the superpowers. With each phase, the conflict became wider and more dangerous. The speed of the escalation process was in part a result of a pattern of mutual exploitation among the various actors involved. The new nations sought support by raising the specter of colonialism, which brought in the Soviet Union in an attempt to exploit the situation by using these appeals for help as a pretext for intervention. Since the United States could not stand idly by, superpower involvement became inevitable. But at the outset of both crises, the United States and the USSR both saw their interests better served through UN action than through direct conflict.

The superpowers' national interests played a vital role in both peace-keeping operations. In the case of UNEF, the United States sought to extricate its allies, Britain and France, from their embarrassing positions and to remove any pretext for Soviet intervention in the Middle East. Unilateral American action would have aroused the misgivings of the Afro-Asian nations and provided an excuse for a similar Soviet move. Hence, the United States favored a UN buffer force as an instrument of neutralization. The Soviet national interest was not as clear-cut. On the one hand, the embarrassment to America's two traditional allies and the subsequent reverberations in NATO were a singular coup. So was the expulsion of much of Anglo-French influence from the Middle East. Moreover, the action helped to bolster the Soviet image as champion of the underdeveloped world. On the other hand, however, the United Nations effectively negated any Soviet excuse for intervention; and, besides, the General Assembly was conducting the Operation under the auspices of the Uniting for Peace procedure, in violation of the Soviet view of the Charter. Thus, the USSR abstained from the initial vote authorizing UNEF, looking the other way while the Uniting for Peace procedure was invoked against the two Western powers, and it limited its objections to nonpayment of assessments. Although the two superpowers had very different motives, they both permitted the establishment of UNEF, which, in turn, helped maintain a truce on the Israeli-Egyptian border for over a decade.

The superpowers' national interests also led them to favor the creation of ONUC, thus launching that Operation in an atmosphere of consensus. The USSR voted for the establishment of ONUC, since it was eager to speed the withdrawal of the "colonialist" Belgian forces and to enable the Lumumba government to establish control. Once again, the United States wanted to interpose the United Nations between East and West and to prevent the Congo from becoming another cold-war battleground. Both superpowers recognized that the African states massively favored UN, rather than superpower, intervention, which was another reason for standing clear. Thus, the United States and the USSR, though their basic objectives in the Congo clashed, permitted the Security Council to act.

When the Congolese government broke down and the Soviet favorite was overcome by a more pro-Western candidate, the superpower consensus dissolved. The Security Council was stymied by the veto, and the General Assembly carried on ONUC against the active opposition of the Soviet Union. But when seceded Katanga continued its rebellion, a partial consensus was restored in the Council. The superpowers, again for very different reasons, approved two of the strongest resolutions in the Council's history in order to end the secession.

The financial crisis over UNEF and ONUC was a reflection of the political crisis and hence also deeply influenced by the superpowers' national interests. In the case of UNEF, the Soviet interest dictated only mild criticism of the Operation and therefore nonpayment of assessments. But in the later stages of ONUC, the USSR felt its national interest directly jeopardized; hence, an attack on the Secretary-General and an attempt to act unilaterally in the Congo, as well as complete refusal to pay for ONUC, followed. From the Soviet point of view, UNEF and ONUC prevented Soviet bridgeheads in the Middle East and Africa. In the latter case, since a bridgehead had already been established and was liquidated at least in part under UN pressure, Soviet opposition assumed a more violent form. In neither case was the USSR willing to pay for an operation that did not favor its national interest.

It may be legitimate at this point to raise a hypothetical question: Would the United States pay for an operation that did not favor its national interest? If Lumumba instead of Kasavubu had been victorious in the Congo, would the United States have continued to support ONUC? Or suppose the Afro-Asian majority backed by China recommended the creation of a UN peace force to "establish order" in South Africa. Had such an operation been initiated by circumventing an American veto in the Security Council and overcoming vigorous American opposition in the General Assembly, one wonders if the United States would still pay one-quarter of the expenses. In short, if the national interest so dictates, the United States might some day find itself opposing a UN peace-keeping action, while the USSR or China urged the United Nations forward.

Perhaps the toughest problem for the United Nations in the realm of peace and security is how to deal with the opposition of the superpowers. It seems, in this connection, that the distinction between active and passive opposition may be crucial. If opposition remains limited to nonpayment, as was the Soviet opposition to UNEF, the other superpower may risk overriding it, provided the money can be found to pay the share of the recalcitrant power. But if more active obstruction is overridden, then the obstructionist power may consider the United Nations too inimical to its national interest and abandon it altogether. In short, it seems that the launching of an operation in the face of either active or passive opposition is to ask for a financial crisis. No

Great Power, least of all a superpower, will adopt or easily acquiesce in paying for a policy that it considers inimical to its national interest, and those overriding the opposition may have to face the responsibility of assuming additional financial burdens.

An interesting point emerges from a comparison of UNEF with ONUC; although the superpowers' interests in both the Congo and the Middle East were not compatible, the United Nations managed to launch peace-keeping forces. At the outset of an operation, therefore, it would seem that basically antithetical interests need not necessarily preclude concrete UN action. However, as an operation evolves, it may become difficult to maintain the consensus and to collect payment.

The delicate task of acquiring and sustaining superpower support for peace-keeping operations falls to the United Nations itself and, particularly, to the Secretary-General. The key to the UN's success in the peace-keeping field—as in the realm of constitutional development discussed in Part One—has been flexibility. UNEF, as we have seen, needed the support and tacit consent, respectively, of the United States and the USSR in order to be launched. But since one purpose of the Operation was to insulate the Middle East from a superpower conflict, it was necessary to exclude both superpowers from direct participation in the Operation. Hence, UNEF meant a curious inversion of the UN Charter. The original belief of the founding fathers at San Francisco had been that concerted action by the Great Powers in any potential conflict would be necessary to preserve the peace. Now it seemed that concerted action would have to be taken to exclude the Great Powers from any potential conflict if the peace was to be preserved. Though the superpowers would have to give their blessings to the Operation, they would at the same time have to be kept at arm's length.

In ONUC, too, superpower consensus launched the Operation, but exclusion of the superpowers became necessary in order to sustain the peace-keeping force. One of the most difficult periods in that complex operation came when the Soviet Union began to introduce personnel and matériel into the Congo. The UN's flexibility in establishing ONUC without the physical participation of the superpowers seemed even more impressive when one observed the sensitive diplomatic maneuvers employed by the Secretary-General in readjusting ONUC's basis of support as the attitudes of the superpowers and of other nations changed during the course of the Operation. From start to finish, ONUC was an outstanding example of UN flexible diplomacy.

Yet, upon reflection, can one account for the success of UNEF and, especially, ONUC solely on the grounds of the UN's flexibility? The United Nations did receive a certain amount of "delegated" strength from the superpowers to deal with the crisis, and the Organization used that strength flexibly and intelligently. But certain facts suggest that, once this mandate was granted, the UN Operation developed additional strength of its own. This fact emerges with greatest clarity in the case of ONUC, where the attempts to limit the UN's actions were formidable. Of the five permanent members of the Security Council, the Soviet Union was violently opposed for considerable periods and refused to pay anything at all while the Operation was in progress; China was indifferent and unable to support the Operation financially owing to lack of resources; Britain disapproved of parts of the Operation sufficiently to withhold weapons from ONUC forces; France's political opposition was strong, and it refused to pay its assessment; and in the United States, influential elements in the Congress and the executive were increasingly ambivalent about UN policy toward Katanga and concerned with the high cost of the entire Operation. Thus, at various times ONUC had almost all the Big Five, in addition to other, smaller powers, ranged against it. Where did the strength to continue come from?

Once again, it is important to distinguish between the kinds of opposition a UN operation may face. Passive or semiactive opposition by minor or even major powers can be endured. But in case of violent superpower opposition a UN operation needs an equally strong countervailing force in order to survive. Now, when, with the rise of Kasavubu, the Soviet Union violently opposed ONUC, the United States had an equally strong interest in seeing it continued. Hence, a countervailing force was generated which helped sustain the Operation. More broadly, in assessing the politics of survival for a given UN peace-keeping action, it is important to consider not only who is opposed, but how strongly opposed and what countervailing forces are created. As a political rule of thumb the United Nations might ask the questions: Who is mad? and how mad? Who is glad? and how glad?

On balance, it would seem therefore that once a UN peace-keeping operation is launched by superpower consensus, it can acquire a certain amount of independent strength and momentum. In the cases of UNEF and ONUC, at least part of this momentum was supplied by the strong backing of the newly emergent nations in the General Assembly. The United Nations has not only stolen strength from the two giants but on occasion has gained enough additional strength to maneuver somewhat independently.

The Secretary-General has played a crucial role in this development. Political sense, timing and flexibility have been his major weapons. A UN peace-keeping action may have enemies, but not too many enemies at the same time. The superpowers must approve initially but must not participate physically. As the operation develops, its original consensus may change, and the Secretary-General must weigh carefully the often-conflicting demands of the superpowers, the participating states, other UN members, and his obligations as an international civil servant and defender of the UN Charter. Moreover, the Secretary-General must find some way to pay for the operations.

In the financial crisis over the UNEF and ONUC assessments, the moderate amounts of money at issue were soon obscured by the larger political and constitutional implications. Many states, including the two superpowers, revealed their basic positions on the United Nations in the course of the negotiations. In fact, the 1964–1965 financing crisis clearly illustrated the three major themes we have noted in the course of this book: the dominance of national interest, the flexibility of the UN system, and its resilience.

While the financial crisis was plainly the result of the clashing superpower national interests over UNEF and ONUC, the stalemate in the Nineteenth Assembly nevertheless revealed that both superpowers did find value in the UN system as a whole. For example, the Soviet Union hinted that it might make some payment on its debt in an effort to reach a compromise that would allow the United Nations to function normally again. And the United States, which insisted that the Soviets could not vote until they paid, did relent and permitted consultations and one procedural vote. Even the Afro-Asians permitted a year of deadlock and inaction in economic and social affairs rather than precipitate a showdown. In sum, almost everyone, including the superpowers, made compromises in an effort to keep the United Nations in being. This was best seen in the united front which all states, led by the United States and the USSR, took against the Albanian attempt to force a showdown. Thus, while the superpowers did not agree on the UN's exact nature, they indicated by their behavior that they did want *some* kind of United Nations.

Control of the Assembly had now moved into the hands of the Afro-Asian nations. It is interesting to note in this regard that, throughout the 1964–1965 debate on financing, the United States did not seek a vote on the merits of the USSR's constitutional case and, in fact, went to great lengths to provide ways in which the Soviet Union could pay its debt but keep open the constitutional question about the Assembly's powers of assessment. Once again, the superpowers, despite their opposing positions, realized that they had certain interests in common. This partial community of interests has been underlined since 1965 by the tacit agreement of the superpowers to conduct most of their peace-keeping business through the forum of the Security Council. To some extent, Moscow's view of yesterday has become Washington's view today. Certainly, American and Soviet views on peace-keeping have increasingly emphasized the need for political consensus.

Since the deaths of UNEF I and ONUC, UN peace-keeping has been the responsibility of the Security Council. Between 1964 and 1973, the solitary major peace-keeping operation under the Council's direction was UNFICYP, the United Nations Force in Cyprus. Acting by consensus, the Council has extended UNFICYP's mandate regularly at least once every six months. With the entry of the People's Republic of China in 1971, there was some apprehension lest China might veto the extension of the Cyprus Force. China, however, decided to abstain and thus the consensus of the Council on the Cyprus question has continued undisturbed. The creation of UNEF II and UNDOF, in 1973 and 1974 respectively, signified a modest gain for peace-keeping in the United Nations. It was, of course, the climate of super-power détente that had made these two new experiments possible at all. Yet they demonstrated that the difficulties posed by a Security Council with a vastly more complex constituency were not insurmountable. In addition, the principle of collective re-sponsibility received a welcome boost when the Soviet Union set a new precedent by making financial contributions. Thus, by the mid-1970's, three major peace forces were on active duty under United Nations aegis.

In the final analysis, one must see the constitutional and political dilemmas of UN peace-keeping as symptoms of consolidation that mark the growth of all political institutions. From their origins in the mid-nineteenth century, international organizations have grown in fits and starts. The United Nations, like its predecessors, will have periods of rapid growth and periods of consolidation. The prophets of doom tend to overlook this time dimension. They pronounce the United Nations dead at a fixed point in time but ignore the *overall* trend, which is clearly in the direction of a dynamic and evolutionary concept of the process of internationa organization.

Development, Arms Control, and Environment Operations

The primacy of the national interest is as clear in development, arms control, and environment operations as it is in the realm of peace-keeping. Neither superpower has a preconceived attitude toward these operations as a whole, but determines its position in each case in accordance with the national interest as it perceives it at the time.

The interest of the Cuban Special Fund case lies in its prophetic quality. It placed the United States in a minority position for the first time on an issue that the Congress considered vital to the American interest. It showed as early as 1961 that the United States, when placed in such a position, would face severe congressional pressures that would compel it to fight the majority regardless of previous commitments or policy pronouncements. And most important, it showed that, if that fight were unsuccessful, the U.S. attitude toward the United Nations might undergo an "agonizing reappraisal." In that sense, the Cuban case foreshadowed the American response to its defeat over the Chinese representation issue ten years later and adumbrated the decline of American interest in the Organization.

The Soviet-American relationship on matters of arms control has gone through three distinct phases: open conflict, partial cooperation, and full cooperation. In all three phases, the United Nations provided a forum and a diplomatic convenience, but at no time did it function as a prime mover.

During the bleak years of the cold war, the United Nations provided one of the meeting grounds in which the superpowers wrestled with the arms race. Numerous proposals were made by each side only to be rejected by the other. All came to grief on the rock of suspicion and the absence of even a minimum of mutual trust. Mankind's narrow escape from the nuclear abyss in the wake of the Cuban missile crisis brought the Soviet Union and the United States together for the first time in a determined effort to break the impasse. The result was the Limited Nuclear Test Ban Treaty signed in Moscow in 1963. The United Nations played no role in the negotiations, although, after 1963, the General Assembly continued to urge an end to *all* tests, including those that were permissible under the Treaty.

The thrusts into outer space during the 1960's created another partial community of interest between the two superpowers: They had now become space powers. Each was eager to prevent the other from colonizing the celestial bodies, and the United Nations provided a convenient multilateral forum toward that end. The earthbound nations prodded the Russians and Americans to agree, but the Outer Space Treaty, signed in 1967 under UN auspices, was more the result of direct superpower negotiations than the product of genuine multilateral diplomacy. The Treaty, however, did prohibit national appropriation and, by so doing, protected the interest of mankind as a whole at the very beginning of space exploration. In that sense, the United Nations performed a most useful service: It acted before, rather than after, the unilateral appropriation of celestial bodies might be considered a matter of vital interest by a space power or a potential space power.

The struggle over the Nuclear Non-proliferation Treaty saw the transition from partial to full cooperation between the superpowers. Between 1961 and 1965, the nonnuclear states, fearful of an atomic holocaust by design or accident, urged the two leading nuclear powers to outlaw the dispersion of atomic weapons. The superpowers, still eager to woo their respective clients with atomic bribes, were reluctant to comply. By 1965, however, the fearful spectacle of twelve nations on the threshold of nuclear power, as well as the nuclear explosion in China, made the superpowers more receptive. By 1967, they had made a united front, and in the end they had to lobby hard to make their joint product palatable to a majority of nonnuclear states which had developed the uneasy feeling that something had been put over on them. By the time the Nuclear Non-proliferation Treaty was signed in 1968, the Soviet Union and the United States were widely regarded as "Establishment powers" by the nonnuclear states, and a new division between haves and have-nots had begun to supersede the traditional cold-war divisions between East and West.

A similar pattern prevailed during the negotiations over the Sea-Bed Treaty. Once again, the struggle turned out to be a three-cornered one: The Soviet Union and the United States, after smoothing over the differences between them, realized their special community of interest as high-technology powers and made an alliance against the smaller and poorer states. The latter played only a marginal role in affecting the final product. Once again, however, the Sea-Bed Treaty of 1971 preempted the emplacement of nuclear weapons on five-sevenths of the earth's surface. And once again, by accomplishing this feat earlier rather than later, the United Nations may have placed itself in the position of crisis preventer rather than the more familiar role of crisis manager or even receiver in bankruptcy. The Strategic Arms Limitation Treaties of 1972 and 1975 were admittedly strictly bilateral affairs. Yet, the United Nations had played a part by keeping channels of communication open during the years of the cold war, and the three UN treaties preceding SALT I and II no doubt served as stepping stones and confidence builders toward that historic accord in Moscow.

The problem of the human environment made manifest the latent changes in the United Nations of the 1970's. The old bipolar world was clearly over. China had burst upon the scene and attempted to define her new role in the world community. In so doing, she quickly discovered the primacy of the national interest. She made an effective appeal to the Third World by casting her lot with the poor and wretched of the earth, but when pressed to cease her nuclear tests, she refused to do so and thus promptly lost most of the support among the smaller states that she had gained before. Russians and Americans discovered the simple fact that pollution respected neither ideological differences nor national frontiers. The most basic divisions that came to the fore at Stockholm were not those between the superpowers but those between the haves and the have-nots over priorities of development and environment. As the superpowers decontaminated themselves to some extent of shopworn cold-war slogans, new fissures in the planet's fabric became more painfully visible: the widening gap between the rich and the poor and the terrible inequities in how the world's resources and wealth were distributed.

If the most fundamental challenge to the United Nations of the 1940's was perhaps to help prevent another world war, the great challenge to the United Nations of the 1970's may be the preservation of the possibility of a decent life on spaceship earth. The United Nations has begun to rise to this momentous challenge. The 1970's witnessed an integrated approach to some of the most critical problems threatening the world's survival. A series of global conferences were organized under UN auspices to address the main challenges to an endangered Planet Earth. The first of these was the World Conference on the Human Environment, held in Stockholm in 1972. The year 1974 saw a whole bevy of global conferences: the Sixth Special Session of the General Assembly on raw materials and development; a Conference on the Law of the Sea held in Caracas; a World Population Conference held in Bucharest; and a World Food Conference held in Rome. All these conferences emphasized the need to respond to planetary challenges with planetary intiatives. What became painfully clear during the debates in Stockholm, New York, Caracas, Bucharest, and Rome was that interdependence was no longer a slogan or an abstraction, but a gut reality. Planetary crisis demanded planetary management.

The Sixth Special Session of the General Assembly on raw materials and development met in New York in April 1974 in order to search for a more just and viable basis for international economic cooperation. The session was convened by Algeria and became a forum for Third World initiatives on behalf of the poor developing nations. A package of proposals was adopted including a Declaration and Program of Action on the Establishment of a New International Economic Order. The poor countries demanded the establishment of a special emergency fund and rejected as insufficient an American proposal for a $4 billion assistance program for the most seriously affected. The oil-rich Arab nations pressed the point that the industrialized countries should shoulder the main burden of aiding the world's poor. The Western nations rejected this point of view, and the session ended with few concrete achievements. The plight of the poor was clear to all, but no consensus was reached on how to share the responsibility of helping them.

The United Nations Conference on the Law of the Sea was held in Caracas in the summer of 1974 after six years of preparation. A follow-up conference was held in Geneva in 1975 and another in New York in 1976. The major problem areas before the conferences were: the establishment of the limits of national jurisdiction over territorial waters presently ranging from three to two hundred miles; fisheries questions; preservation of the marine environment; the establishment of international machinery to regulate activities on the high seas such as the dumping of waste into the oceans; the passage through international straits; the exploitation of the mineral resources of the sea-bed; and the conduct of scientific research. Negotiations were arduous and difficult, but the conferences represented tentative first steps in the direction of a new international regime governing the world's oceans. All the participating nations agreed that the need for new laws was urgent and that the process of forging them should be continuous.

The World Population Conference, which was held in Bucharest in August 1974, placed the problem of population in the front ranks of the world's agenda. Since population was related to the issues of economic development, diplomacy, human rights, and institutional change, it was analytically impossible to insulate it from the crosscurrents of international politics. Despite wide divergencies among the participating countries, a consensus was reached on a World Population Plan of Action that looked toward a target of reducing world fertility from 38 per 1,000 to 30 per 1,000 by 1985. In addition, there was general agreement on certain key principles of population planning and individual human rights. For example, all countries agreed to respect and ensure the right of persons to determine, in a free, informed, and responsible manner, the number and spacing of their children and to encourage the participation of women in educational, social, economic, and political life on an equal basis with men. On the whole, the Bucharest Conference symbolized the evolution of the international population movement from a preoccupation of scholars and students to a global need and a major political force. As in the Conferences on the Law of the Sea, the delegates realized that only a beginning had been made and that the problem required the continuous and vigilant attention of the United Nations and its Member States.

In November 1974, most of the world's nations gathered in Rome on the occasion of the first World Food Conference in history. The conference was sponsored by one of the United Nation's specialized agencies, the Food and Agriculture Organization. The delegates met under the specter of famine in Africa and the Indian subcontinent and amid reports that the world's food reserves had reached dangerously low levels. Flood, drought, and fertilizer shortages had created grain shortages that were estimated at 20 million tons. The United States, Canada, and Australia agreed to make emergency food supplies available on a short-term basis. The most concrete long-term achievement of the Rome Conference was the establishment of a World Food Council that was to serve as an umbrella organization to funnel food and money to needy nations. Donor nations, consisting of the "old rich" of the industrialized West and the "new rich" of the oil-producing areas, agreed to provide both food and money to ensure that 10 million tons of food would be shipped annually to the needy nations. The Conference also accepted a proposal by Secretary of State Kissinger for a system of nationally held but internationally coordinated grain banks for emergency needs in natural disasters. All things considered, the Rome meeting signified the beginning of a global survival pact between the rich and the poor nations of the world.

The global conferences held under the UN's aegis in the mid-1970's were an impressive beginning. They were primarily diagnostic in nature and tried to focus attention on the most dangerous illnesses of Planet Earth. In some cases, as in Bucharest and in Rome, there were attempts to prescribe a cure even though the sovereign states gathered there insisted on the right of final decision. What emerged with clarity and force, however, was the new insight that the real divisions in the world of the 1970's were no longer between capitalists and Communists, or white and non-white, young and old, or even rich and poor, but between those who could see only the interests of a limited group and those who could see the interests of mankind as a whole. The mid-1970's saw the beginnings, through the United Nations, of a world environment policy, a world energy policy, a world food policy, and a world population policy, to bring man and nature into balance.

The Superpowers
and the Future of the United Nations

"The crisis of our loyalty to the United Nations," the late Ambassador Adlai E. Stevenson said, "is still ahead of us." These were prophetic words. When the United States enjoyed an automatic voting majority within the United Nations, it was not hesitant to identify UN majorities with its national interest, because the two were usually synonymous. It was even willing to undermine the safeguards given to the Great Powers at San Francisco by circumventing the veto power with the Uniting for Peace Resolution and relying on majority diplomacy. For some time, the belief that UN majorities and the American national interest were congruent seemed justified. During that period, the United States frequently used its voting power to obtain decisions against the Soviet national interest and enforce them in the name of the United Nations.

Today the General Assembly has a majority of developing countries and is dominated in particular by the Afro-Asian-Arab group. While the United States has been remarkably successful in avoiding many major setbacks, the close correlation between UN decisions and the American national interest has, of course, been disrupted. The case of the Special Fund was prophetic in this respect. An economically unimportant agricultural project became a cause célèbre within the American government, and only the total lack of UN support for the American position prevented the destruction of the consensus principle of the Fund. And in the Chinese representation case ten years later, the United States suffered its first major public defeat in the General Assembly. The question arises: What would happen if the United States faced a Special Fund situation in the peace-keeping field? How would the United States react to a UN peace-keeping force mounted to suppress a more successful Bay of Pigs operation? If the Afro-Asian-Arab majority, backed by the Soviet Union or by China, passed it over American objections, would the United States pay for it?

The seating of China in the Albanian, rather than in the American, manner in 1971 generated an anti-UN mood in the U.S. Congress and particularly its House of Representatives. One concrete manifestation of this mood was the recommendation made by the House to reduce the American contribution to the United Nations from 31 to 25 percent without concern for the legal treaty obligation of the United States. Only the intervention of the Senate saved the United States from taking an action that would have been in clear violation of the Charter.

This episode points up a problem that is peculiar to American relations with the United Nations: the importance of the congressional view of the national interest and the fact that it does not always agree with that of the executive. The congressional view has been an important determinant of American policy in several key cases: the attack on the Secretariat in 1952, the long exclusion of Communist China, the attack on the Special Fund, the pressure to apply sanctions against members defaulting on their peace-keeping assessments, and the drive to reduce the American contribution to the UN budget. In each case, the Congress fought for what it believed to be the national interest. Its position close to the American public and its reponsibility to the electorate have made it understandably sensitive to the more immediate U.S. interests. But it is an open question whether America's *ultimate* interest was better served by continuing to exclude Communist China from the family of nations or by taking her in. Was it necessary to attack the UN Secretariat so vehemently in order to eliminate possible security risks? And was it desirable to recommend action that would have taken the UN one step closer to bankruptcy? It seems that the Congress is playing a major role in the crisis of American loyalty to the United Nations and that it will favor a position that has in view the immediate benefits to the American national interest.

As Third World dominance of the United Nations become increasingly apparent during the 1970's, American opposition became more and more outspoken. The Twenty-ninth General Assembly in 1974 served as a catalyst in this respect. Ambassador Scali's statement about the "tyranny of the majority" and Secretary Kissinger's warning that the United Nations might become "an empty shell" demonstrated that the Executive now shared the view of the Congress and that the general American attitude toward the United Nations had become increasingly ambivalent since the World Organization no longer clearly reflected the interests of the United States. The General Assembly's passage in 1975 of a resolution equating Zionism with racism further alienated many Americans from the United Nations and cast the United States even more clearly than before into a role of opposition. A Gallup poll taken in late 1975 revealed that only one American out of three believed that the United Nations "was doing a good job," but three out of four Americans still wanted the United States to remain in the World Organization.[2]

Our analysis of American behavior in the United Nations in three major fields reveals that the United States does not have a single, undifferentiated philosophical approach toward the international organization. From the nine case studies it is clear that the United States reacts to specific situations in a pragmatic manner. It does not tailor its national interests to fit a general philosophy toward the United Nations but adjusts its "philosophy" to its national interests. When the national interest dictates a larger role for the United Nations, the United States favors expanding the roles of the General Assembly and the Secretary-General, urges major peace-keeping operations, and sustains costly economic and social programs. On the other hand, when the American interest dictates a more conservative role for the United Nations, the United States has employed the hidden veto, attacked the Secretariat, prolonged the membership stalemate, fought for the exclusion of China, attacked the consensus principle of the Special Fund, and advocated a policy of financial retrenchment.

Like the U.S. position, the Soviet Union's attitude toward the United Nations is more easily understood in terms of the national interest rather than as an abstract philosophical position. When the United Nations endangered the Soviet national interest, the USSR attacked the attempts to circumvent its vetoes, opposed an increased role for the General Assembly and the Secretariat, and attacked the peace-keeping Operation in the Congo. But on certain occasions, the Soviet national interest dictated a larger role for the United Nations, as in 1956 in Suez against Britain and France, in 1967 against Israel, in the Congo to help Lumumba against Belgium, and in the Special Fund on behalf of Cuba. The fact that, until recently, the United States was associated with expanding the role of the United Nations more often than was the USSR tells more about the relative voting strengths of the two superpowers than about their philosophies toward the Organization.

If we turn from a consideration of the superpowers to the future of the United Nations itself, it becomes clear that, for the time being, the Organization is condemned to live between two giants in international politics and to be used or abused by each according to the service it renders the national interest. In addition, it must maneuver in the context of a changing global constellation: the rise of China and Japan, the tug of war between the rich and the poor, and the process of unification in Western Europe. Each power—large, medium, or small—essentially perceives the United Nations as an instrument for the pursuit of its national interest. Yet, if the United Nations is to remain relevant in the world politics, it must remain in this position and serve enough of the member states' interests for them to choose to deal with it rather than to ignore or crush it. Serving many masters with frequently divergent interests is no easy task. In this dilemma the practice of flexible diplomacy, evolved into a fine art by the UN Secretary-General, has stood the Organization in good stead.

The United Nations has demonstrated this flexible diplomacy in at least four major ways. First, it has reinterpreted the Charter on a number of occasions, even inverting it by excluding the superpowers from actual participation in peace-keeping operations. Second, it has shifted the locus of power within the Organization among the Security Council, the General Assembly, and the Secretariat in order to function more effectively. Third, it has financed its operations by a wide variety of means: assessment, voluntary contributions, or the splitting of costs between benefiting parties. Finally, the Secretary-General has tried to guide the course of operations in such a manner that a minimum of political consensus would be maintained and not too many enemies would be made at the same time.

The dominant role of the national interest in the superpowers' policies in the United Nations has not been, and need not become, an insurmountable obstacle to the growth of the Organization. Needless to say, if the superpowers had never been in conflict, many, though not all, of the UN's problems would be eased, and the work and development of the international organization would perhaps be further advanced. The superpower struggle has not been a blessing for the United Nations, but it has not made a meaningful life impossible. Nor will the new power constellation emerging in the United Nations change this fact in any fundamental way. Provided the United Nations remains flexible, it should be able to provide some service to states both large and small. And provided the United Nations continues to serve, it can continue to grow. The fact of the matter is that if the superpowers want to use the United Nations in their national interest, either against each other or in any other matter, they must first give the Organization sufficient strength to act. This strength, once given, cannot always be entirely recalled. And at times, as we have seen, the United Nations has supplemented this delegated strength with a momentum of its own.

Thus, in 1946, the outbreak of the superpower struggle dashed many hopes that the United Nations would participate meaningfully in international politics. Yet today, by a unique and pragmatic course, the United Nations has carved out for itself a significant role to play between the superpowers. It has had to learn to live between the giants and, ultimately, to capitalize on that position. In this sense, the United Nations has moved forward *because* of the superpower struggle as well as in spite of it.

It has often been said that between the two great chess players—the Soviet Union and the United States—the United Nations is a pawn. There is truth in this assertion. But perhaps the past three decades have shown another truth: that if the United Nations was a pawn, it was also permitted by the superpowers slowly to advance across the board. It will not reach the eighth rank in our time, but it does have certain earmarks of a queen.

The first generational cycle of the United Nations has now run its course. It was marked by the dominance of the two superpowers in the United Nations and, in particular, by the preeminent position of the United States. In the United Nations of the 1970's, the power equation is more complex. Today neither superpower controls the United Nations. Instead, the world's poor have challenged the world's rich and have attempted to use the United Nations as their instrument. And today the United States complains about the "mathematical majority" led by the Third World in very much the same way that the Soviet Union had complained about the "mathematical majorities" led by the United States a decade or two ago. Once again, national interest is paramount to all and provides the key to a nation's view of the United Nations.

This new power balance will not doom the United Nations to paralysis. So long as the Organization serves, it will be used. It cannot, however, always be expected to engage in rescue operations at the edge of disaster.Member states will have to learn not to regard the United Nations as a receiver in bankruptcy and then, in addition, blame it for being bankrupt. They will have to learn to use it preventively, and with foresight, before a crisis has arisen and the point of no return has been reached. They will have to learn not to dump problems on the United Nations only when they have become insoluble. In short, they will have to make a political commitment to use wisely and well the instrument that they have themselves created.

Political institutions pass through periods of growth and periods of consolidation. The United Nations is no exception, and in an overall assessment, it is vital to bear in mind this time dimension. In this fundamental sense, it is not true that the United Nations has fallen so low as many fear; it has merely not yet been permitted to rise as high as many had hoped.

SELECTED BIBLIOGRAPHY

Boyd, Andrew. *United Nations: Piety, Myth, and Truth.* London: Penguin Books, 1962.

Claude, Inis L., Jr. *Swords into Plowshares.* 4th ed. New York: Random House, 1971.

Cox, Arthur M. *Prospects for Peacekeeping.* Washington, D. C.: Brookings, 1967.

Gardner, Richard N. *In Pursuit of World Order.* New York: Praeger, 1964.

Gordenker, Leon, ed. *The United Nations in International Politics.* Princeton, N.J.: Princeton University Press, 1971.

Kay, David A. *The New Nations in the United Nations.* 1960–1967. New York: Columbia University Press, 1970.

Riggs, Robert. *US/UN: Foreign Policy and International Organization.* New York: Appleton, 1971.

Russell, Ruth B. *The United Nations and United States Security Policy.* Washington, D.C.: Brookings, 1968.

Stoessinger, John G. *The Might of Nations: World Politics in Our Time,* 5th ed. New York: Random House, 1975.

Young, Oran. *The Intermediaries.* Princeton, N.J.: Princeton University Press, 1967.

NOTES

1. *New York Times Magazine,* 14 March 1965, p. 37.
2. *New York Times,* 28 December 1975.

Index

Acheson, Dean, 87
Addis Ababa, 47
Adoula, Cyrille, 114–17
African nations: in Conference on
    the Human Environment, 194,
    196; in UN, 30, 32, 33, 34, 43;
    see also Third World
Aiken, George D., 130–32
Albania, 8, 28, 137–38, 224; and
    Chinese representation in UN,
    43–45
Algeria, 229
Angola, 18, 35
Anti-ballistic missiles (ABM's), 183
Anti-Ballistic Missiles Treaty (1972),
    183–85
Aqaba, Gulf of, 92, 93
Arab-Israeli War, 91–97, 102; UN
    force in, 82, 98–104; vetoes on,
    9, 14
Arab League, 91
Arab nationalism, 83, 89, 90, 91,
    102–03
Arabs, 32, 34, 229
Arafat, Yasir, 31
Argentina, 16
Australia, 129
Austria, 28, 101, 102

Bangladesh, 14, 47
Belgium, 126, 167; in Congo crisis,
    107–11, 115–17
Berlin Blockade, 7, 8, 13
Biosphere and technosphere, 191
Bond issue, 128–33
Bouteflika, Abdelaziz, 31

Brazil, 122, 174, 181, 197
Brezhnev, Leonid, 183, 184, 185
Bulganin, Nikolai A., 85, 164–65
Bulgaria, 28, 192
Bunche, Ralph, 73
Burma, 129
Burns, E. L. M., 98
Burundi, 16

Cambodia, 28, 32, 42
Canada, 129, 167, 174; and nuclear
    arms control, 176, 181, 187;
    peace-keeping forces, 98, 101,
    102, 122; in Suez crisis, 86–87
Castro, Fidel, 152
Ceylon, 10, 16, 28, 42, 68, 129; in
    Congo crisis, 110, 112, 113
China, Nationalist, 4, 13, 16, 127;
    excluded from UN, 45; in Sec-
    retariat, 51; in UN, 36, 38–39,
    41–44, 85
China, People's Republic of, 14, 58,
    101, 144, 204; in Arab-Israeli
    War, 92, 94; in Conference on
    the Human Environment, 192,
    193–94, 196, 199–200, 202, 228;
    invasion of India, 9, 42, 43, 116;
    and nuclear arms control, 49,
    167, 168, 169, 172, 176, 178, 182,
    196; nuclear weapons, 169, 174;
    in Security Council, 20, 47–49,
    215; Soviet Union's ideological
    break with, 41, 47; in UN, 46–
    53, 213, 222, 224, 232; UN mem-
    bership, votes on, 35–45; U.S.
    airmen interned in, 67

Claude, Inis L., 38
Cleveland, Harlan, 130
Club of Rome, 198, 199
Collective responsibility, 139
Colombia, 17, 98, 122
Committee on the Peaceful Uses of Outer Space, 169, 170
Communists: loyalty investigation of Secretariat employees, 59–65; U.S. investigation of 58–59
Conference of the Committee on Disarmament, 179–80
Conference on the Human Environment, 190–203; 228; Action Plan, 200–02, 205; Declaration on the Human Environment, 199–200, 205; poor and developing nations in, 194–98, 201–02
Conference on the Law of the Sea, 228, 229
Congo, Democratic Republic of, 112–14
Congo, UN operation in (ONUC), 13, 21, 67–71, 73, 82, 109–11, 113–19, 136, 218–24; financial crisis, 124–28, 130, 134–35, 142, 219–21, 223; Soviet vetoes on, 7, 8, 68; UN Civilian Operation, 117
Congo crisis, 67–68, 106–19
Convention on International Liability for Damage Caused by Space Objects, 170, 172
Cooper, John Sherman, 14
Cordier, Andrew W., 68, 73, 111–12
Corfu Channel dispute, 8
Cuba, 73, 150, 192; missile crisis, 156, 159, 162, 168, 174, 186; and Special Fund, 152–60, 225–26
Cyprus, 10; peace-keeping operation, 82, 134–35, 144, 224–25; UN force in (UNFICYP), 47–48, 224
Czechoslovakia, 98, 167, 176, 192; Soviet invasion of, 178; Soviet veto on, 7, 8, 12

Declaration on the Human Environment, 199–200, 205
Denmark, 98, 122
Drummond, Sir Eric, 56
Dulles, John Foster, 39, 84, 86

Earthwatch Program, 200–01
Eban, Abba, 93, 100
Ecuador, 16
Eden, Sir Anthony, 84, 87
Egypt, 48, 135; and Arab-Israeli War, 91–93, 95–97; and Suez crisis, 6, 9, 83–91; and UNEF, 99, 100
Eighteen-Nation Committee on Disarmament (ENDC), 176–77, 180
Eisenhower, Dwight D., 69, 85, 86, 164
Eisenhower Doctrine, 91
Elisabethville, 115, 117
Environment: China's position on, 49–50, 196, 228; conferences on, 228–31; developing nations concerned with, 194–98, 201–02, 204–05; pollution versus development, 193–95, 197; UN action after Stockholm Conference, 203–06, 228–31; Use in warfare banned, 187, 200
Environment Forum, 194
Environment Fund, 202
Ethiopia, 110, 129
European Atomic Energy Community (Euratom), 175
Expanded Program for Technical Assistance (EPTA), 150–52

Fedorenko, N. T., 111
Fifth Committee of the General Assembly, 111; in financial crisis, 124–26, 128, 129
Finland, 17, 28; peace-keeping forces, 98, 101, 122

Food and Agriculture Organization
(FAO), 150, 153
Ford, Gerald, 185
France, 4, 16, 17, 119, 218, 222; in
Arab-Israeli War, 92, 93, 94, 99;
in financial crisis, 123, 126, 127,
134, 137; and nuclear arms
control, 165, 167, 168, 169, 178,
182; in Suez crisis, 9, 83–91;
vetoes, 13, 14, 18, 31, 85

Gandhi, Indira, 201
Gardner, Richard N., 156–57, 159
Gaza Strip, 91, 93, 95
General Assembly, 26–27; in Arab-
Israeli War, 93–94; and Chinese
representation, 36–45; in Congo
crisis, 112–14; and environ-
mental program, 203–04, 228,
229; in financial crisis, 123, 125–
29, 131, 134–39, 143; and nuclear
arms control, 164, 165; and
Nuclear Non-Proliferation
Treaty, 173–77; and Outer
Space Treaty, 169–70, 172; Secu-
rity Council revived by, 21–22;
in Suez crisis, 85–87; U.S.
dominance in, 27–30
Germany, East, 144, 167, 192
Germany, West, 144, 173, 174, 178
Ghana, 101, 110, 113, 126, 129
Gizenga, Antoine, 114–15
Goa, Indian invasion of, 6, 9, 12
Golan Heights, 82, 95, 96, 97, 102
Goldberg, Arthur J., 139
Governing Council for Environmental Programs, 203
Great Britain, 4, 8, 16, 17, 123, 171,
218; in Arab-Israeli War, 92, 93,
94, 99; and Chinese representation, 36, 38; in Congo crisis,
115–17, 119, 222; and nuclear
arms control, 165, 167; in Suez
crisis, 9, 83–91; vetoes, 13–14,
18, 31, 85

Greece, 8, 48
Gromyko, Andrei, 168
Guatemala, 8, 142
Guinea, 110, 112–13

Hailsham, Lord, 168
Hammarskjöld, Dag, 21, 55, 67–68,
212, 215; in Congo crisis, 68–71,
106, 109, 110, 115; in financial
crisis, 122–25; Khrushchev's
attack on, 69–71; in Suez crisis,
6, 9, 67, 87; and UNEF, 98, 99
Harriman, W. Averell, 168
Herbert, E. S., 61
Herter, Christian A., Jr., 193
Hickenlooper, Bourke B., 130–32
Hiss, Alger, 58
Hoffman, Paul G., 151, 153, 155–56
Home, Lord, 168
Hungary, 28, 192; rebellion, Soviet
veto on, 7–8, 12
Hussein, King, 93

Idi Amin, 33–34
India, 36, 42–43, 113, 167, 174;
Chinese invasion of, 9, 42, 43,
116; Goa invaded by, 6, 9, 12;
and nuclear arms control, 176,
180, 181; nuclear explosion, 178;
peace-keeping forces, 98, 100,
110, 116, 122; Soviet vetoes on
behalf of, 9–10, 47
India-Pakistan War, 10, 47
Indonesia, 10, 42, 113, 135; peace-
keeping forces, 98, 101, 122;
Soviet vetoes on, 10
Intercontinental ballistic missiles
(ICBM's), 183, 184, 185
International Atomic Energy Agency
(IAEA), 175, 176, 178
International Labor Organization
(ILO), 150
International Technical Conference
on Conservation, 191–92

Iran, 85
Iraq, 7, 9, 15, 93, 96
Ireland, Republic of, 10, 28, 129, 173; peace-keeping forces, 101, 102, 110
Israel, 31, 32, 48, 167, 174; in Suez crisis, 6, 9, 84, 86, 87, 89–91; and UNEF, 100, 123; U.S. vetoes on behalf of, 17, 18; Zionism condemned by UN vote, 32–34, 233
Italy, 10, 15, 16, 28, 167, 174

Japan, 10, 167, 174
Jerusalem, 93, 94, 95
Johnson, Lyndon B., 92
Jordan, 10, 16, 28, 137, 138; in Arab-Israeli War, 91, 93, 95, 96

Kasavubu, Joseph, 68, 107, 108, 109, 111, 113, 114, 118, 142, 220, 222
Kashmir, 9, 82
Katanga, 107, 108, 110, 115–17, 219, 222
Kennedy, John F., 72, 129, 168
Kenya, 101; environmental secretariat in, 204
Khrushchev, Nikita, 15, 56, 151, 168, 169; attack on Secretariat, troika proposal, 69–71; in Congo crisis, 109
Kissinger, Henry, 34, 35, 44, 185, 231, 233; in Middle East peacekeeping, 97, 101, 102, 104
Kitona Agreement, 116
Klutznick, Philip M., 129, 130, 153–54, 156
Korea, North and South, 10, 18, 29, 34
Korean War (police action), 19, 29, 32, 39, 58, 59, 82; Soviet vetoes on, 6, 12
Kosygin, Aleksei, 93
Kuwait, 7, 9

Laos, 28, 82
League of Nations, 56, 140, 215
Lebanon, 9, 82; foreign troops in, 67
Léopoldville, 107, 108, 111
Libby, Willard F., 166
Liberia, 126
Libya, 28
Lie, Trygve, 7, 13, 19, 71, 215; and Chinese representation, 36–38, 58; and U.S. attack on Secretariat, 57–66
Limited Nuclear Test Ban Treaty (1963), 163–69, 186, 226
Limits to Growth, 198, 199
Lodge, Henry Cabot, 65, 110
Lon Nol, 32
Lumumba, Patrice, 68, 70–71, 107–14, 118, 142, 219, 220

McCarran, Pat, 63
McCarthy, Joseph, 58, 59
McNamara, Robert S., 198
Malaysia, 10
Mali, 110, 113, 137, 138
Mauritania, 42
Mead, Margaret, 191–92
Mexico, 126, 180
Middle East, 17, 48, 81–104
Mitchell, W. D., 61
Mobutu, Joseph, 111
Mollet, Guy, 84
Mongolia, 42
Morgenthau, Hans, 212
Morocco, 110, 113
Moynihan, Daniel P., 18, 33–34
Muller, H. H., 164
Multiple independently targeted reentry vehicles (MIRV's), 184, 185

Nasser, Gamal Abdel, 83–84, 90–93, 95, 100, 102
NATO: multilateral nuclear force (MLF), 174; and nuclear arms

control, 173, 174, 175, 177; and
    Suez crisis, 87–89, 218
Nehru, Jawaharlal, 70
Nepal, 16, 28, 101
Netherlands, 129, 135
New Guinea, West, 135
New Zealand, 98
Nicaragua, 17
Nixon, Richard M., 44, 97, 183, 184
Nkrumah, Kwame, 70
Norodom Sihanouk, Prince, 32
Norway, 98, 122
Nuclear arms control, 162–88, 226–
    28
Nuclear Non-proliferation Treaty
    (1968), 49, 173–78, 227

ONUC, see UN Congo Force
Outer Space Treaty (1967), 49, 169–
    72, 226–27

Padelford, Norman J., 15
Pakistan, 9, 98, 125, 126; civil war,
    52; India-Pakistan War, 10, 47
Palestine, 82
Palestine Liberation Organization,
    31, 32, 102; terrorism, 17, 48, 50
Palme, Olof, 196, 197
Panama, 101
Panama Canal, 17, 48–49
Pardo, Arvid, 179
Pauling, Linus, 165
Peace-keeping operations, 217, 218–
    25; in Cyprus, 82, 134–35, 144,
    224–25; in Middle East, 48, 82,
    91, 98–104
Pearson, Lester, 86, 98
Peru, 101, 102
Poland, 16, 112, 158, 176, 192; peace-
    keeping forces, 101, 102
Population control, 202
Portugal, 10, 28

Quaison-Sackey, Alex, 137

RB-47 plane incident, 7, 8
Rhodesia, Southern, 47, 50; vetoes
    on, 14, 16, 18
Rogers, William P., 17
Roschin, A. A., 129
Rumania, 28, 98, 192
Rusk, Dean, 130, 168

Sadat, Anwar, 95–96
SALT, see Strategic Arms Limita-
    tion Talks
Saudi Arabia, 45, 96, 135
Scali, John A., 17, 32, 233
Sea-Bed Treaty (1971), 49, 179–82,
    227
Secretary-General, Office of, 55–57,
    215, 216, 221–23; increasing
    power of, 21; loyalty investiga-
    tion of U.S. employees, 59–65;
    Soviet attack on, 66–75; U.S.
    attack on, 57–66, 74–75
Security Council: in Arab-Israeli
    War, 93, 95, 97; Chinese Peo-
    ple's Republic in, 20, 47–49; in
    Congo crisis, 109, 110, 114, 115;
    enlargement, 16; General
    Assembly in revival of, 21–22;
    and Nuclear Non-proliferation
    Treaty, 177; and peace-keeping
    forces, 101–02, 224; and Sea-Bed
    Treaty, 182; in Suez crisis, 85;
    U.S. domination of, 14–15; veto
    in, 3–23, 214–15
Senegal, 101, 125
Sharm El-Sheik, 91, 93
Sierra Leone, 16, 17
Siilasvuo, Ensio, 101
Sinai, 82, 91, 95, 96, 97
Smith, Ian, 16
South Africa, 14, 47, 50, 126; sus-
    pended from UN, 32; veto on
    expulsion, 18, 31

Southwest Africa, 14
Soviet Union: in Arab-Israeli War, 92–97; attack on Secretariat, 66–75; China's ideological break with, 41, 47; and Chinese representation in UN, 36–45, 47–51; Conference on the Human Environment boycotted, 192–93; in Congo crisis, 68, 109–14, 116–19; Czechoslovakia invaded by, 178; and economic development programs, 151–52; and environmental program, 204–05; in financial crisis, 123–24, 126–27, 129, 134–44; hostility to Lie, 58, 66; and nuclear arms control, 164–88; and Special Fund for Cuba, 152, 153, 155, 157, 158; in Suez crisis, 85–91; Troika proposal, 69–75; in UN, summary of influence, 213–16, 218–27, 234; and UNEF, 99–100, 104; and U.S. vetoes, 15–17, 19; vetoes by, 3–4, 6–14, 21–25, 28, 47, 68, 214
Spaak, Paul Henri, 168
Spain, 17, 28, 174; Soviet vetoes on, 10–11
Spanish Sahara, 34
Special Fund, 150–52, 232; and Cuba, 152–60, 225–26
Stevenson, Adlai, 72, 130, 231
Strategic Arms Limitation Talks (SALT), 183–86
Strategic Arms Limitation Treaties (1972 and 1974), 183–85, 227–28
Strong, Maurice F., 191, 195, 197, 203, 205
Suez crisis, 6, 9, 67, 83–91, 102
Superpowers, 211–13; and Chinese representation, 36–45; in Congo crisis, 106–14; in financial crisis, 122–44; and nuclear arms control, 162–88; in Security Council, 4–6; in Suez crisis, 83–91; and UNEF, 98–102; and UN

membership, 27–32, 35–36; and UN's future, 231–37; veto used, 3–23; see also China, People's Republic of; France; Great Britain; Soviet Union; United States
Sweden, 15, 167; and nuclear arms control, 173, 174, 180; peacekeeping forces, 98, 101, 110, 122
Switzerland, 167, 174
Syria, 9, 17, 48, 102; in Arab-Israeli War, 91, 93, 96, 97

Tanzania, 171
Teller, Edward, 165
Thailand, 8
Thant, U, 73, 91, 215; in Congo crisis, 115, 116; in financial crisis, 128, 135; and UNEF, 100–01
Third World, 13, 19; China's ideological leadership, 47, 49, 50, 196, 213; in UN, 27, 29–31, 33–35, 215, 216, 218, 224, 229, 232, 233
Thomas, Albert, 56
Thorn, Gaston, 33
Train, Russell E., 193, 196–97
Troika proposal, 21, 69–75
Truman, Harry S., 150
Tshombe, Moise, 107, 108, 110, 115–17
Tunisia, 15, 16, 68, 91, 110, 112, 125, 126
Turkey, 48

U-2 plane episode, 16
United Arab Republic, 113, 174, 181
United Nations: budget, 51; competitive exclusion from, 27–30; constitutional evolution, 214–18; developing nations in; economic and social projects, 149–51; environmental activities, 203–06; 228–31; financial

crisis, 121–44, 219–21, 223; membership policy, 28–36; superpowers and future of, 231–37; *see also* General Assembly; Security Council

UN Congo Force (ONUC), 68, 69, 82, 109–11, 113–19, 136, 218–24; financial crisis, 124–28, 130, 134–35, 142, 219–21, 223

UN Congo Fund, 117

UN Development Program (UNDP), 150

UN Disarmament Commission, 175

UN Disengagement Observer Force (UNDOF) 102, 104, 144, 225

UN Educational, Scientific, and Cultural Organization (UNESCO), 32, 150

UN Emergency Force (UNEF), 14, 67, 218–25; financial crisis, 122–24, 127, 128, 130, 134–35, 142, 144, 219–21, 223; in Middle East, 48, 82, 91, 98–104

UN Force in Cyprus (UNFICYP), 47–48, 224

UN Temporary Executive Authority (UNTEA), 135

United States: in Arab-Israeli War, 92, 94–97; attack on Secretariat, 57–66; and Chinese representation, 36–45; in Conference on the Human Environment, 193, 196–98, 202; in Congo crisis, 68, 108–09, 111–14, 116–19, 222; Congress and UN bond issue, 129–33; in economic programs, 149–52; and finances of UN, 51, 123–27, 130, 134–43; hidden veto, 4, 14–15, 16, 22, 28; and nuclear arms control, 164–88; and Special Fund for Cuba,

150, 152–60; in Suez crisis, 84–91; in UN, summary of influence, 212–15, 218–22, 224, 226–27, 232–34; and UNEF, 99, 101, 104; veto, 3–4, 14–19, 22, 31, 48, 214–15

Uniting for Peace Resolution, 21, 22, 29, 85, 88, 216, 217, 219, 232

Veldekens, P., 61

Veto in Security Council, 3–25

Vietnam, North and South, 8, 10, 18, 29

Vietnam War, 16, 174–75, 187, 193, 196–97

Waldheim, Kurt, 51, 102, 215

Working Group in financial crisis, 127–28, 134

World Court, 28, 133–34, 139

World Food Conference, 228–31

World Health Organization (WHO), 150

World Housing Fund, 201–02

World Population Conference, 228, 230

Yemen, 82, 135

Yugoslavia, 85, 157, 158, 174, 192; peace-keeping forces, 98, 100, 122

Zambia, 16, 17

Zero growth, 195, 198

Zevallos, Gonzalo Briceño, 102

Zionism, 32–34, 233

Zorin, Valerian, 72

About the Author

Born in Austria, John G. Stoessinger, at age eleven, escaped to Czechoslavakia during the Nazi occupation. Three years later, he fled via Siberia to China, where he lived for seven years. In Shanghai, he served the International Refugee Organization.

Dr. Stoessinger came to the United States in 1947. He received his B.A. degree from Grinnell College in 1950 and attended Harvard University, where he earned his Ph.D. degree in 1954. He entered the teaching field immediately and has taught at Harvard, Wellesley, M.I.T., Columbia, and Princeton. In 1969 he led the International Seminar on International Relations at Harvard University, and in 1970 he received an Honorary Degree of Doctor of Laws from Grinnell College, Iowa. From 1967 to 1974, he served as Acting Director of the Political Affairs Division at the United Nations. He is now Professor of Political Science at the City University of New York.

Dr. Stoessinger is the author of *The Might of Nations: World Politics in Our Time* (1962), which was awarded the Bancroft Prize by Columbia University as the best book in international relations published in 1962. A second edition was published in 1965, a third in 1969, a fourth in 1973, and a fifth in 1975. He is also the author of *The Refugee and the World Community* (1956), *Financing the United Nations System* (1964) for the Brookings Institution, *Power and Order* (1964), *Nations in Darkness: China, Russia and America* (1971), and *Why Nations Go to War* (1974). He served as Book Editor of *Foreign Affairs* for five years and is a member of the Council on Foreign Relations.

Dr. Stoessinger's latest book, *Henry Kissinger: The Anguish of Power*, was published in 1976.

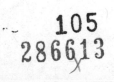